D1600788

RINGSIDE
SEAT
AT
THE
CIRCUS

By the same author

And Every Day You Take Another Bite

The National Football Lottery

RINGSIDE SEAT AT THE CIRCUS

by Larry Merchant

HOLT, RINEHART AND WINSTON · NEW YORK

Library of Congress Cataloging in Publication Data

Merchant, Larry.
  Ringside seat at the circus.

  1. Sports stories. 2. Sports—United States—Mis-
cellanea. I. Title.
GV707.M46 796.0973 76–3959
ISBN 0–03–015631–9

Designer: Robert Aulicino
Printed in the United States of America
10/9/8/7/6/5/4/3/2/1

CONTENTS

FOREWORD

Sportswriting, like everything but the cockroach, has undergone significant changes in the last generation. The determined romanticism of a ᴍore innocent age has yielded to higher standards of journalism.

This has not been a wholly unmixed blessing. The best of the old-timers, who saw their roles primarily as drama critics and bards, were facile essayists. Some of them may not have recognized an unscheduled news story if it had a letter of introduction, but with their quills they could tell you who got the game-winning hit while they tickled you. They told a mean fairy tale.

Many of us, meanwhile, with our degrees in journalism and our electric typewriters, have merely traded one set of clichés for another, substituted pointless or insincere quotes for our own perceptions, and remained patsies for a new breed of promoter and athlete-entrepreneur. Treacle still sticks to a few of us.

But we are climbing out of the ooze. We are more willing to confront the social issues and deal with the psychological forces that inhabit our sanctuary. By using the tools of the trade—two feet, two eyes, two ears, two fingers —we find that truth usually is more interesting than fiction. All the time remembering that we are still spotted between the theater section and the funny papers.

In the mid-fifties I was part of a broad-based movement that sprang up in New York, Philadelphia, Boston, Pittsburgh, Miami, North Carolina, Texas, no doubt elsewhere. We hurried along changes that began after World War II when Dick Young of the *New York Daily News* and Milt Gross of the *New York Post* descended from the Olympian view of the press box to the dugouts and dressing rooms, much as Ernie Pyle had gone into foxholes. John Lardner's incredibly rich column in *Newsweek*, A. J. Liebling's tapestries on boxing in the *New Yorker*, Red Smith's urbane wit, Jimmy Cannon's personalized style showed us other possibilities. So did John Updike and Norman Mailer later, as Ernest Hemingway had earlier, when they trained their novelists' antennae on the sporting life. These weren't fans who wrote sports, as most sportswriters seemed to be; they were reporters and writers who wrote sports.

We funneled that mainstream in different directions. We were irreverent, announcing ourselves by debunking heroes and myths that didn't stand up to scrutiny. We were humanistic, measuring athletes as people as well as performers. We felt we had ringside seats at the circus, not pews in church.

We were apprenticing, it turned out, for the exotic new acts of the sixties. We laughed with the miserable Mets and the unsinkable Cassius Clay. We defended Muhammad Ali and were not offended by Joe Namath, emotion-charged symbols of change in a society polarized by war. We tried to maintain our equilibrium in the whirlwinds that buffeted athletes, from the black movement to the women's movement, from political jeans to political hair, from militant unionism to militant lawsuits, from sex pills to mind-bending pills, from Tinker to Evers to Chance.

The columns in this collection, some of which have been abbreviated, represent about 5 percent of my output at the *New York Post* from 1966 to 1975. I have culled those columns that are most clearly my signature.

LARRY MERCHANT

September 1975

I.
Baseball, Gentlemen, Baseball

It was a Sunday in Cincinnati, the last day of the season, and a pennant hung in the balance. Some young whippersnappers—Casey Stengel was one of the few old whippersnappers—were babbling in the press box about the football scores coming in on the Western Union ticker. "Baseball, gentlemen, baseball," admonished Jimmy Cannon.

Baseball it is. Baseball is the best of all team sports to write about because its history and statistics provide meaningful references, because its geometry and tempo enable us to isolate events, because day-to-day exposure across a long season opens up even the most constipated personalities, and because humor and humanity are implicit in its rhythms.

Strike one! The first sportwide strike of regular season games took place in the spring of 1972, when the start of the baseball season was delayed for a week. It seems appropriate to lead off with this column because the war between labor and management is one of the new things sportswriters must deal with. The general response to the strike was hysterical—prophecies of disenchantment and decline, etc. (Attendance records have been set almost every year since then.) This was an attempt to go back to basics.

THE OPENERS

The crowds were small, but the baseball season opened yesterday, on schedule, in all the important places.

At Washington Square Park, where on many spring afternoons a wisp of a cheery nun plays pitcher-umpire-commissioner in a softball game with students, there were two games under way on different sides of a brick out-house.

A mother underhanded a rubber ball to her four-year-old prospect, while another toddler played the outfield with a professional stance ten feet behind her. The son swung and missed three times, announced "Strike three!" and calmly put the bat down and exchanged positions with his friend. The friend swung and missed twice, then hit a line drive at the pitcher. He swung and missed three more times, announcing, "Strike three, strike four, strike five." He was very agitated when informed that he had struck out.

A bearded father was playing with two six-year-olds. The father took a turn at bat and hit the hard ball too zealously. It thudded into his son's stomach and knocked the wind out of him. The boy went down to one knee, fought back tears while the father bent over him apologetically, got up with a grimace and fearlessly resumed his chore on the mound.

In a playground on Catherine Street a dozen kids were playing stickball. One of them fungoed, then laid the stick on the ground. To get a lick, the kid who caught the ball had to hit the stick with his throw so the batter couldn't catch the carom before it bounced. A kid threw the ball from way out in the outfield, hit the stick on the fly and trotted in to the cheers of the others as it spun off crazily.

In a playground on Hudson and Saint Lukes, a group of kids ten to sixteen years of age huddled around home plate and then fanned into the field, finding their positions haphazardly but logically. The biggest kid fungoed for what seemed an interminable length of time, until he decided to go out in the field and was replaced by the next biggest kid. When a small kid had difficulty catching flies, the others stood by patiently while the batter hit five or six to him until he caught one.

On Carmine Street there was a stoopball baseball game, and in an empty lot nearby there was a sign on an apartment house wall: "Home Run 118 ft."

Came a letter in the morning mail, coincidentally, from a crazy baseball fan and champion wiffle ball player, Elliott Ames:

"Love as a cure for the world's ills is overadvertised. It's baseball we need more of—where strategy is not brutality, violence is not the key to victory and for as long as you can succeed, time is on your side.

"In fact it's the only game where front-runners and early speed can't hide behind the hands of the scoreboard clock. In baseball there's always time—time for quality to win out. It's the only game where the brawniest bully on the block isn't always the captain and tallest guy isn't automatically the star.

"Roger Angell of the *New Yorker* once said that 'since baseball time is measured in outs, all you have to do is succeed utterly; keep hitting, keep the rally alive, and you have defeated time. You remain forever young.'"

The point of all this is that baseball is bigger than any opening day in the major leagues.

The people who own the teams and the players who play the game for money are not what baseball is about. Whether either or neither side is right in the pension rhubarb, baseball will go on. Whether the official opener was yesterday or tomorrow is irrelevant. The game goes on because the kids play it for as long as there is a snatch of daylight in the spring and summer. The game goes on because adults remain enchanted by it, some of them musing philosophically over exactly what it is that enchants them.

It's pointless to get dyspepsia over the baseball strike. Just look around. The season has begun.

The warm-up for the strike began three years earlier at what might be called sport's first labor congress.

COMES THE REVOLUTION

Nobody said, "Give me a pension or give me death." Nobody said, "I have but one life to give for the Players Association." Jim Bunning, Steve Hamilton and Willie McCovey could not be mistaken for Trotsky, Lenin and Stalin, or Debs, Lewis and Quill. But the mood and muscle of a successful revolution were there.

They were in a room at the Biltmore Hotel, where in a time of innocence young lovers met under a clock. This was not a time of innocence. Some 125 major league ballplayers, from the Art Shamskys to the Al Kalines, were demonstrating that they don't spend their winters hunting rabbits and milking cows and throwing baseballs at the sides of barns anymore.

The workers' revolution had come to a room in the Biltmore crowded with right-thinking athlete-businessmen, bourgeois in the $20,000 to $100,000 class, dressed smartly in insurance or stockbroker grays or modly in rock or decorator cuts, covering the political spectrum from Nixonite Jim Bunning, who made it to the White House for the inauguration, to McCarthyite Jim Bouton, who dedicated his last winning game as a Yankee to Senator Eugene McCarthy.

The issue was one that the average union man would have difficulty relating to—not because he can't conceive of a $20,000 salary, even to play a game, but because he couldn't conceive of working for the kind of people ball-players work for. Not in the third third of the twentieth century.

The players are unhappy because the owners are try-ing to renege on the pension plan. The players have a very generous pension which can be viewed as a sort of deferred payment arrangement for their short, high-income but high-tax careers. The pension is financed largely by televi-sion revenues. The owners now propose to change from a percentage that yielded $4.1 million last year to a flat sum of $5 million or so, rather than a percentage of newer, richer television contracts.

Marvin Miller, the attorney for the Players Associa-tion, a labor leader who used to lead steelworkers, called yesterday's meeting as a show of union solidarity. It was an impressive show. One look around the room—Billy Wil-liams, Jim Kaat, Maury Wills, Tim McCarver, Bob Gibson, et al.—got the message across. The message was that with-out these ballplayers the owners own only the balls and the bases but not the product they are selling: major league baseball.

"They might put a label of major league baseball on it," said Bill White, "but it wouldn't be major league base-ball without us. They might put a major league uniform on Charlie Brown, but that wouldn't make him a major leaguer."

"Without these players," said Tom Tresh, getting to the nitty-gritty, "NBC might cancel its contract with base-ball."

Television revenue is what this is all about. Miller presumes quite logically that the owners want to change from a percentage to a flat sum because they are looking ahead to dramatic escalations. So it came down to a matter of principle as well as principal, and the players passed a unanimous resolution in support of an enlarged striking zone.

"I was amazed by the response," said Bunning. "I had no idea they were this strong in back of us. No more than two or three players in the room have signed their contracts. It's a revelation."

Said Steve Hamilton, "We're supposed to be All-American boys, but the owners forced us into this. They said in the past, 'Don't rock the boat, son. I'll take care of you.' But for how much and how long? We don't want this kind of paternalism. We're not looking for privileges; we want our rights."

The owners reply to the players with their own bluff, to the effect that they have many marginal players under contract. Marginal players have to be less firm, but fans do not pay to see marginal players. The owners eventually will have to capitulate simply because they have more at stake than the best-paid players.

The owners did capitulate, but a year later they went to the wall, the federal court wall, in defense of the reserve clause. It was my professional debut in court and it provided an opportunity to visit with an old friend who enlivened and defined the proceedings.

TRAITOR

Twenty-nine years ago Bill Veeck wrote a letter to Commissioner Kenesaw Mountain Landis suggesting that the reserve clause was immoral and illegal and therefore should be abolished. A supernumerary responded. "I can remember it word for word," said Veeck. " 'Some very knowledgeable fellow once said that a little knowledge is a dangerous thing, and you just proved him a wizard.' "

Sensing a class traitor in its midst, Baseball spent the next twenty years watching Bill Veeck very closely, rejecting or ignoring his constructive ideas, wincing when his promotional funmanship succeeded, which was often. The only approval he got was in the form of a proclamation asserting him a good fellow after he sold the White Sox and was hospitalized for a neurological condition. "It was a memorial," he said. "They thought I was going to die."

Bill Veeck lives. The justice sought by Curt Flood in

his suit to do away with the reserve clause turned poetic with Veeck's appearance as his concluding witness. "A cleanup hitter," someone said, "batting ninth."

Capsuled, Veeck testified that several alternatives to the reserve clause system could be employed without endangering the game, perhaps making it work better. But his mere presence offered testimony that, to the great umpire in the sky, seemed more telling.

There was, first, the style of the man, that rare combination of intelligence and wit and passion. And Baseball had sat on him at every chance, and once purged him. What sort of calcified mentalities would be threatened by a man like that? Under cross-examination, Veeck admitted that he didn't think the owners were as bad a lot as he did when he wrote *Veeck—As in Wreck* in 1962, but he had an explanation for it. "I don't have to associate with them as directly."

He then quickly one-upped an attempt to discredit him as a rogue promoter. He was asked about the time in Milwaukee when he installed a movable fence in the outfield, movable, of course, to the best interest of the home team. Wasn't that breaking the rules? Well, he said, there were no rules against movable fences. "I try not to break the rules, but to test highly their elasticity."

Unfortunately Veeck was not asked about the time the lights blew out in Milwaukee, coincidentally at a crucial moment in a crucial game when the home team was about to lose its lead. He was ordered to appear before Commissioner Landis the next day. "It was," explained Veeck, "an act of God." Landis stuck a bony finger in Veeck's chest and warned, "There will be no more acts of God." There weren't.

All through the trial one of Baseball's defenses has been that it is equipped to meet changing needs and correct inequities, particularly in negotiations with the Players Association. There are equal parts of irony and gall in that because the players had to battle for years for recognition. Yesterday, along those same lines, Veeck was reminded that even some of his bold proposals had been adopted—the player draft, the minor league draft, the right of players to have agents.

Which served to dramatize Veeck as a prophet and add weight to his testimony. He also told how he had been the first to recommend moving major league baseball to California. He neglected to tell the reaction of Clark Griffith of the Senators when San Francisco was suggested as a companion franchise city for Los Angeles. "It's too foggy there," Griffith said. When was he last there? "Oh," Griffith said, "1903 or 4."

If the most damaging evidence in Flood's case was Flood himself—an obvious success, looking every bit the $100,000-a-year man; unhappy about being traded but willing to be traded under different circumstances—the most supportive evidence was provided by Veeck and his former partner, Hank Greenberg. Both obviously love the game, both have prospered in it, both testified in the spirit of constructive criticism.

Baseball, in contrast, put up a rather dispirited if persistent defense of its special position under the law. It could not match Veeck and Greenberg in experience and expertise; hell, it didn't even summon one of the two local owners in its behalf. It failed to demonstrate that chaos and one-sided competition would result if the reserve clause was modified. With the clause, a few teams have dominated the game; without it, other sports prosper.

Said Judge Irving Ben Cooper, who ran the courtroom with a fine sense of baseball drama and byplay: "We are resolved to call them as we see them cross the plate."

I win some, I lose some. Baseball's position was upheld, and negotiations indeed have modified the system. The real story was Flood, and I never followed up on him as diligently as I could have. He returned to the game after a year of self-exile, played part of a season, and fled to Europe in financial and personal distress.

The holdout is a more traditional baseball dispute. After Vida Blue's great rookie season, his acrimonious salary squabble with

Charley Finley made headlines right through spring training into May. I spent a day scanning microfilm in the public library and found out how little, and how much, the times had changed.

ANOTHER HOLDOUT

Did Henry Kissinger make a secret flight to Oakland to settle the Vida Blue matter? Has Charley Finley had a summit meeting with President Nixon? Was the Chinese Ping-Pong team about to recruit America's greatest left-handed server when he announced his intentions to sell plumbing fixtures rather than play ball?

Now that Vida Blue has made his first start and pitched his first shutout and won his first game, these questions must be asked because it is clear that never in the history of pitch-and-catch has a holdout created such a national furor.

What brings that into focus is the story of another holdout that isn't even a footnote to a pretty good ball-player's career. Joe DiMaggio's.

The Yankees had not won a pennant for four years when DiMaggio joined them in 1936. They won one that year and another the following year and DiMaggio had more to do with them than anyone else. Which made him think he should get paid at least as much as anyone else.

Wrong.

DiMaggio made $15,000 in 1937, when he hit forty-six home runs, an astonishing number for a right-handed hitter who called Yankee Stadium home. The next spring he was offered $25,000 and he held out for $39,000 because that's how much Lou Gehrig had signed for.

He held out and he held out and he held out. He held out through all of spring training. He did not play until the third week of the season.

If you think the world went on during Vida Blue's holdout, you should have seen it during DiMaggio's. It didn't miss a spin. The player who would become recognized as the best of his time wasn't playing, and hardly anybody but the player lost any sleep over it.

A check of three newspapers—*Post, Times* and *Mirror* —showed that none of their leading sports columnists thought the holdout was worth more than a passing mention. Dan Parker of the *Mirror* did not mention it at all. Hugh Bradley of the *Post* suggested that the Yankees would benefit by having two opening days, the official opener and the DiMaggio opener. John Kieran of the *Times* wrote: "Just think of the lordly Yankees being kicked around by minor league clubs in exhibition games. The lack of DiMaggio in the lineup had little or nothing to do with the humiliation though."

Sportswriters did not dig into the labor disputes of that day, and there were many of them. So many, perhaps, that one seemed like another. Red Ruffing did not report to spring training in 1937, after winning twenty games. Colonel Jacob Ruppert, owner of the Yankees, threatened to trade Ruffing and Lou Gehrig during holdouts that spring.

On the opening day of the season DiMaggio said from his home in San Francisco that the Yankees had not tried to contact him for five weeks. The Yankees, like many teams before and since, negotiated by not negotiating.

Ruppert said, "I haven't heard anything from him and I don't want to hear from him until he's ready to sign on our terms. I won't pay him a penny more than $25,000. I stake my word of honor on it."

DiMaggio signed right after opening day—for $25,000. Harold Burr wrote in the *Post:* "The sudden capitulation of DiMaggio didn't occasion any great surprise. . . . Joe's name appears on breakfast food, cigarette and toothpaste advertising. But his value is predicated only on his ballplaying. His picture in a Yankee uniform doesn't mean anything until he dons it."

After a five-day train trip, DiMaggio worked out for a week at Yankee Stadium. Al Schacht, the old pitcher and Clown Prince, threw batting practice to him. In his first game, on May 1 in Washington, DiMaggio got a single in three at-bats and spent the night in a hospital after colliding with rookie second baseman Joe Gordon. "DiMaggio showed no indication that he was more than shaken up," wrote Charley Segar in the *Mirror*, "occasionally breaking into song while waiting for the conveyance to take him to the hospital."

Probably "Brother, Can You Spare a Dime."

So much for the notion that only modern athletes are money-conscious. And on to another notion that is a favorite of mine, the notion that fans often can tell us more about baseball than the professionals. The next four columns are about baseball fans who, as gifted communicators, give us insights into the game and themselves.

SOMETHING TO DO WITH HEROES

Paul Simon, the Simon of Simon and Garfunkel, was invited to Yankee Stadium yesterday to throw out the first ball, to see a ballgame, to revisit his childhood fantasy land, to show the youth of America that baseball swings, and to explain what the Joe DiMaggio thing is all about.

Paul Simon writes the songs, Art Garfunkel accompanies him. They are the Ruth and Gehrig of modern music, two kids from Queens hitting back-to-back home runs with records. They are best known for "Mrs. Robinson" and the haunting line, "Where have you gone, Joe DiMaggio, a nation turns its lonely eyes to you." Joe DiMaggio and 100 million others have tried in vain to solve its poetic ambiguity.

Is it a plaintive wail for youth, when jockos made voyeurs of us all and baseball was boss? "It means," said Paul Simon, "whatever you want it to."

"I wrote that line and really didn't know what I was writing," he said. "My style is to write phonetically and with free association, and very often it comes out all right. But as soon as I said the line I said to myself that's a great line, that line touches me. It has a nice touch of nostalgia to it. It's interesting. It could be interpreted in many ways.

"It has something to do with heroes. People who are all good and no bad in them at all. That's the way I always saw Joe DiMaggio. And Mickey Mantle."

It is not surprising, then, that Paul Simon wrote the line. He is a lifelong Yankee fan and once upon a boy, he admitted sheepishly, he ran onto their hallowed soil after a game and raced around the bases.

"I'm a Yankee fan because my father was," he said. "I went to Ebbets Field once and wore a mask because I didn't want people to know I went to see the Dodgers. The kids in my neighborhood were divided equally between Yankee and Dodger fans. There was just one Giant fan. To show how stupid that was I pointed out that the Yankees had the *Y* over the *N* on their caps, while the Giants had the *N* over the *Y*. I just knew the *Y* should go over the *N*."

There was a Phillies fan too—Art Garfunkel. "I liked their pin-striped uniforms," he said. "And they were underdogs. And there were no other Phillie fans. Paul liked the Yankees because they weren't proletarian."

"I choose not to reveal my neuroses through the Yankees," said Simon, who was much more the serious young baseball sophisticate. "For years I wouldn't read the back page of the *Post* when they lost. The Yankees had great players, players you could like. They gave me a sense of superiority. I can remember in the sixth grade arguments raging in the halls in school on who was better, Berra or Campanella, Snider or Mantle. I felt there was enough suffering in real life, why suffer with your team? What did the suffering do for Dodger fans? O'Malley moved the team anyway."

Simon and Garfunkel are both twenty-seven years old. Simon's love affair with baseball is that of the classic big city street urchin. "I oiled my glove and wrapped it around a baseball in the winter and slept with it under my bed," he said. "I can still remember my first pack of baseball cards. Eddie Yost was on top. I was disappointed it wasn't a Yankee, but I liked him because he had the same birthday as me, October 13. So do Eddie Mathews and Lenny Bruce. Mickey Mantle is October 20."

Simon played the outfield for Forest Hills High, where he threw out the first ball of the season last year. Yesterday, after fretting that photographers might make him look like he has "a chicken arm," he fired the opening ball straight and true to Jake Gibbs.

Then Simon and Garfunkel and Sam Susser, coach of the Sultans, Simon's sandlot team of yesteryear, watched the Yankees beat the Senators 8–2 with some Yankee home runs, one by Bobby Murcer, the new kid in town. "I yearned for Mickey Mantle," Paul Simon said. "But there's something about that Murcer. . . ."

The conventional wisdom is that there are no more heroes who "are all good and no bad." Overexposure by the demystifying media is said to be the main cause. Much as I'd like to, I can't accept that flattery. Babe Ruth and Jack Dempsey were seen as antiheroes by many adults, as are Muhammad Ali and Joe Namath, but young fans always seem to make up their own minds.

POETRY IN MOTION

Marianne Moore, the poet, eighty years young, got up from the chair to fetch her baseball glove. It was in her bedroom, where every kid keeps his, or her, glove.

"It's a fielder's glove," she said, trying it on her right hand, then her left. Her hands are small and delicate, like fine ivory, and she laughed at the sight of that saddle-sized hunk of leather reaching halfway up her arm. "It's a little big for me. . . . Wait, I'll get my baseball too. I have two of them."

She disappeared into her bedroom again, fetching both baseballs, presumably from under her pillow. She called them "horsehide."

Marianne Moore is not in the habit of taking spring training in her apartment in Greenwich Village—"I like to go to Saint Petersburg," she said—but it seemed like a sensible concession to time. She doesn't have to cover as much ground as she used to. "I was a left fielder," she said. "I wasn't very good."

From out of left field though she has been given an honor she deems more astounding than all the honorary degrees and poetry prizes bestowed on her. She is going to throw out the first ball at Yankee Stadium.

"My goodness," Marianne Moore said. "I thought that was reserved for presidents and governors."

It was, when it was safe for presidents and governors to show up in public. It was, before Mike Burke took over the Yankees for CBS. Mike Burke has been trying to put the team together again and redo their image while he's at it. Last year there was that paint job on the stadium, powdery white with blue eyeshade for the old dowager. This year there are shrimp pink foul poles and Marianne Moore. It's hard to root against shrimp pink foul poles and Marianne Moore.

Mike Burke gave her the glove and the balls, to get her soupbone in shape, to work out the kinks, to be ready to go nine, in fact, Yankee pitching being what it is.

"He gave me everything but the mound and home plate," she said. She has a catcher, her brother. "My brother said I should return the glove after the game, but I'm going to keep it. He told me to throw the ball in a nice arc so the photographers can get their pictures, but I think I'll throw it around the knees; that's where they tell pitchers to throw it. You know what Campanella told the photographers when they asked him to smile? 'I haven't heard anything funny.'"

Roy Campanella was Marianne Moore's favorite ballplayer. Her brother took her to Ebbets Field. "Karl Spooner was pitching. Campanella went out to talk to him. He had an awkward look, but he moved with celerity."

Marianne Moore sees baseball with her own beautiful blue eyes. She doesn't see batting averages and strategy. She sees a game played by people. A very long time ago she taught commercial law at the Carlisle School in Carlisle,

Pennsylvania, and she had a student named Jim Thorpe. She watched him play football and do it all in track and field, but what she remembered was, "He was a gentleman. I called him James. It would have seemed condescending, I thought, to call him Jim."

There is a story, an anecdote, a piece of character exposure, that goes with all her favorites and unfavorites.

"A guard in the bank of Williamsburgh told me Campanella was thinking of his son, who had got in trouble, when he had his car accident.

"Elston Howard is my second favorite. I remember reading that he got $30 to play his first game and he couldn't believe anyone could get paid for doing what he loved to do. I named my pet alligator after him. Isn't that awful?

"I did a radio show with Mary Margaret McBride. She told me Willie Mays had been a guest too. He talked about his big new house in San Francisco. She asked him how he was furnishing it. He said, 'French Provincial.' "

She said that neither Mickey Mantle nor Babe Ruth appealed to her, although she admired them as athletes. Mantle seems "gruff" and "never hits a home run when I expect him to." Ruth was "boorish."

The game itself, as a thing apart, touches another sensibility in Marianne Moore.

"It's the dexterity and accuracy that I like most about it. The nimble movements of the first baseman, the way a ball lights in his glove. The way an outfielder catches one backhanded. But I don't like the double play; the execution is nice, but someone is always disappointed.

"Whenever I feel gloomy I watch a game. The people aren't sheep. The grass is so green. I'm annoyed only that I never get a foul ball; it always rolls down the screen."

Marianne Moore tapped her glove. Next Tuesday might be the day.

I have a special niche in my heart for Marianne Moore. At a luncheon for Larry Ritter's wonderful The Glory of Their

Times, *Fred Snodgrass—the Fred Snodgrass of Snodgrass's dropped fly ball in the 1912 World Series—overheard her talking about baseball and asked her if she was a sportswriter. "No," she said. "But I wish I were."*

THE SIX FITS

At a little after ten o'clock on Tuesday night a dirty red Volkswagen nosed out of a garage on 46th Street between Fifth Avenue and Madison Avenue with a cargo of despair. The Yankees had just scored three runs in the ninth inning to beat the Red Sox.

The car crept sadly to the corner of 46th and Madison, waited for a red light to turn green, then crept sadly to 47th and Madison and waited for another light change, then crept sadly to 47th and Fifth and waited for a third light change, then crept sadly to 46th and Fifth and waited again, having made a full spin of the block.

The car did this two more times—twelve light changes in all—before sputtering with resignation toward wherever.

"I was," explained Jonathan Schwartz, the cargo of despair, "having a baseball fit."

There is no known cure for such a seizure, though millions of ardent fans annually suffer from it. It strikes without warning and its symptoms vary. Jonathan Schwartz, musicologist, writer and Red Sox fan, began flipping out while ending his nightly show on WNEW-FM. Minutes later he found himself on that dazed cruise of darkened midtown streets.

He used to cry.

A "respected radioman," as Schwartz described himself, cannot cry on the air. But as the Yankees began to mount their rally, hit by bloody hit, he was stricken. Suddenly he began to have mechanical difficulties—a commercial on tape was botched. "I was aware of the hideous ending coming while trying to smooth the ship," he said. "I was aware of Bobby Murcer's imminence. I was shaking and fearful. The game had been built up by my delicious anticipation of a second straight victory and by the nature of the game itself. When Murcer singled in the go-ahead run, The Doors were singing 'Light My Fire.' I was aware that that was the beginning of a baseball fit." In ten minutes he was in his car. "I kept telling myself that this had no bearing on my life. Those people don't know me and I don't know them. But I was almost sick."

The origins of the illness, doctor, run deep. We are dealing here with a patient who thinks nothing of spending $50 in long distance tolls to listen to a Red Sox game on the telephone in its entirety. We are dealing with a patient who, during another excruciating ninth-inning Yankee–Red Sox hassle in early July, announced within the span of a few minutes, "This is the most important inning of the season. . . . This is the most important pitch of the season. . . . I have pennant fever."

Doctor, we are dealing with a patient from whom Hank Aaron's seven hundredth home run evoked this parochial response: "Ken Brett [a former Red Sock] threw the pitch. Tracy Stallard [as a Red Sock] threw the pitch that Roger Maris hit for his sixty-first home run." One gets the feeling that Babe Ruth is both redeemed and cursed by Jonathan Schwartz for starting but failing to finish as a Red Sock.

As President Nixon had his six crises, Schwartz has his six baseball fits. Doctor, this is his case history.

1949. "The Red Sox had a one-game lead on the next-to-last day of the season. With a 4–0 lead and Mel Parnell pitching, they lost to the Yankees. I was eleven years old. I cried uncontrollably, with my Red Sox hat on. I knew the Yankees would win the pennant the next day and they did."

1952. "Tommy Henrich beat the Red Sox with a home run in the ninth inning off Ellis Kinder. I walked down Park Avenue crying. A man patted me on the head and said, 'Son, are you all right?' "

1955. "The Red Sox led the Senators 3–0 with two out

and nobody on in the ninth, and the Senators won. I was in camp. I lay on my bunk, weeping, and refused to go to dinner."

1965. "Mel Stottlemyre hit an inside-the-park grand slam against the Red Sox before my very eyes. It was a meaningless game, but it seemed to have cancerous dimensions for me. It made me think, 'Is this going to happen all my life?' "

1967. "I was at my future wife's house. She lived on 75th Street between York Avenue and the river, the area of town that best receives the Red Sox games from Boston. Darryl Brandon, who should be set on fire, lost the second game of a double-header in relief. I left the apartment in silence."

Yesterday's exciting Red Sox win over the Yankees was nice, but it did not lift Jonathan Schwartz from the depression of his sixth baseball fit. "Only a pennant can do that," he said.

With the rise of Red Sox fortunes, Jonathan Schwartz, who is a friend, still suffers the exquisite agonies of the true believer, but he has been rewarded with more of the ecstasies as well. Still, it never ceases to amaze me that adults can wire their hearts and/or self-esteem into ball teams.

THE SOUTH SIDE

"If I was going to storm a pillbox, going to sheer, utter, certain death, and the colonel said, 'Shepherd, pick six guys,' I'd pick six White Sox fans because they have known death every day of their lives and it holds no terror for them."

The speaker is Jean Shepherd, monologuist and White Sox fan. The words are from an old radio show grafted onto an old record ("Jean Shepherd and Other Foibles"). With the White Sox suddenly storming the American League, there will be more of the same soon on WOR. When a baseball team has been down so long it thinks that's up and then suddenly does move up, it stirs tribal instincts as old as pithecanthropus erectus in the human breast.

In Jean Shepherd the instinct had its first stirring in the late thirties and forties. "My old man was a dedicated White Sox fan," he said. "That means he got mad every morning starting in early February when the *Tribune* would have a story about Bullfrog Bill Dietrich inking his pact. When he read that, he knew it was going to be another bad year. Bullfrog was a symbol of White Sox frustration. He had a 7–15 record one year and actually held out because it was a good year for him. The fans would watch him shake off two signs from the catcher and break up. They knew he had only two pitches—slow curve and wild fastball.

"Being a White Sox fan meant measuring victory in terms of defeat. A 6–5 defeat was a good day. A big rally was Wally Moses doubling down the right field line. Luke Appling led the league with a .381 average one year and knocked in about twenty-seven runs. There were no men on base. It was like he was the only human being in a jungle full of tigers, trying to keep the human race alive.

"The long-ball hitters were on the other side of town, in Wrigley Field: Hank Sauer, Ted Kluszewski coming in, Ralph Kiner. Nellie Fox was the typical White Sox player. If you wanted to see home runs you had to wait for the Yankees. My old man hated the Yankees. Anger would start building in him as soon as a Yankee series was in sight. My old man never saw the White Sox win a pennant."

In seventy-one years the White Sox have won five pennants, but just one, in 1959, since the Black Sox scandal of 1919. Yet they were remarkably consistent during a seventeen-year stretch from 1951 through 1967 when they finished out of the first division once and averaged over a million in attendance. A couple of bad seasons convinced short-memoried doomsayers that they were not long for Chicago. Fearmongers added their ghetto phobia. Now the White Sox are back, attendance is soaring, and Jean Shepherd isn't surprised at all.

"The White Sox mystique is fascinating," he said. "The people on the South Side identify with the White Sox the way Brooklyn fans identified with the Dodgers. All you had to do was turn on the radio, hear Bob Elson saying "*He's* out,' and you knew things were normal."

Shepherd demonstrated this tribal loyalty himself when he did a series of promotional commercials for the White Sox a few years ago. As a voice behind the current Rheingold beer commercials, he commands big money. From the White Sox, who couldn't afford his scale, he demanded only "an actual team warm-up jacket."

"Its value has been enhanced tremendously by the new White Sox uniforms," Shepherd said. "It's like a period piece now. I feel like Ty Cobb. But I think maybe the new uniforms have helped the White Sox. Makes them look tougher."

Will the new White Sox rule the world? Their fans will settle for Chicago.

"In New York fans look at all other baseball teams like the chorus line in a Barbra Streisand movie," Shepherd said. "They don't know what it's like in Chicago. The White Sox didn't represent Chicago—they represented the South Side. If you were a White Sox fan, you would no more go to Wrigley Field than a guy in the Bronx would go to Cleveland to see the Indians. You hated the Cubs. Hated them.

"Our big thing was the intercity series. If we beat the Cubs our season was made. They played in Wrigley Field and Mike Kreevich, our center fielder, got lost in the vines for fifteen minutes."

And if the White Sox should play the Cubs in the World Series? The thought leaves Jean Shepherd speechless, which is no small thing.

"I can't even imagine it," he said. "It would be the biggest event since they closed the coliseum in Rome."

That sense of place people get from the home team materialized on another occasion, the 1974 World Series. It seemed like the right time to take a look at the big picture.

OAKLAND, CALIFORNIA

Late into the night the empty Alameda County Coliseum was still lit up like a birthday cake, plain vanilla with no icing and three candles for the successive championships won by the Oakland Athletics.

Downtown in Jack London Square the party was still going full blast, young people honking horns, baying at the fog, congratulating each other for living in such a wonderful town.

That's what it's all about, Alfie.

The Oakland Athletics confirmed once again that they are the best team in California or any other state when they beat the Los Angeles Dodgers 3–2 to win another World Series. The only thing the Dodgers could say was that at least they were going back to Los Angeles. The Athletics had to stay in Oakland.

Oakland is the Newark of California, the butt of jokes from insular San Franciscans across the bay, a thousand variations of Gertrude Stein's "there's no there there." The reason for Oakland, they say smugly, is to hold up the end of the bridge that connects them, although they wouldn't be caught dead on it. Oakland is, like its ball park, a colorless, functional place.

A place that needed two hustling mavericks to put it on the map. Al Davis built a football team, the Raiders, and got the county to build a stadium and an adjoining arena. Charles O. Finley made it home for the Athletics. The Raiders have eclipsed the 49ers and the Athletics have eclipsed the Giants.

And folks in Oakland now look at San Francisco as

though it is an over-the-hill heavyweight. Magnificent San Francisco shrugs and tries to ignore tough welterweight Oakland.

The cost of the sports complex was $26 million a decade ago. Was it worth it? Whom has it benefited besides the fellows who poured the cement?

There are fewer than 400,000 people in Oakland proper, a fourth of the population of the area known as the East Bay. Most of those people are black. The ball teams have not affected the high rate of unemployment and long welfare rolls. Few blacks go to football games, not many more to baseball games.

A handful of businessmen and employees benefit directly. But the same civic enterprise that got behind the sports complex is responsible for a construction boom and a surge in port business that has virtually drowned San Francisco.

Said Al Davis in his box seat last night, "When I came here people would never say they came from Oakland. There seems to be more pride in the community today."

Yet every year during the World Series, as sure as Rollie Fingers coming in from the bull pen, stories appear in the local newspapers suggesting that the Athletics may move on. They turn a tidy profit—said to be over $1 million annually—but attendance sagged below 1 million this season, half of what it would be elsewhere.

Despite the players' complaints about the small crowds and cold winds, they are beginning to take root. About half of them have bought homes in the area. Reggie Jackson said, "The town can't afford to support us, but it's proud of us and would miss us if we left. The Oakland Athletics and Oakland Raiders have given it something. The Raiders are a strong, tough team, and they make the town feel strong and tough. We're a money team, and we make the town feel that it can come through. I feel I'll be here the rest of my life. I'm an Oakland A. I'll always be identified with Oakland and Oakland with me."

"If you lived in the East Bay," said Claudell Washington, who grew up here, "you lived nowhere. Now you live somewhere."

At Jack London Square a young black man watched the passing parade with a benign grin. It was a parade of blacks and whites, hippies and dippies. He said his name was Thomas Howard and he was a sociology major at Cal State. "Oakland is like anyplace else—it likes a winner," he said. "It doesn't give people jobs, but it does something for them psychologically to be associated with a winner. There isn't a kid in the East Bay who doesn't want to be Reggie Jackson."

Thomas Howard broke into a big smile as a white kid came by shouting nothing but "Oakland, California; Oakland, California; Oakland, California."

The sense of place can be reduced to a street in New York. After writing a column about stickball, I was inundated with mail from stickball players past and present. It resulted in this column.

115TH STREET

They are going to honor Casey Stengel with an old-timers celebration at Shea Stadium tomorrow. Joe Di-Maggio will be there. Whitey Ford will be there. Yogi Berra will be there. Sunday there will be another old-timers celebration, this one on 115th Street between Park and Madison avenues. Hector Pacheco will be there. Philip Rivero will be there. Alfredo Rojas will be there. They are great old-timers too—in stickball.

The old stickball teams of East Harlem and Harlem still live, largely through the efforts of Pedro Velez, a letter carrier who has lived on 115th Street for most of his forty-one years. Velez is an original member of the Young Devils —who now have a fancy "Inc." attached to their name— running baseball and football programs for youngsters and a summer stickball tournament for the teams of his own generation.

"We started in 1943," Velez said. "We were the kids on

the block, thirteen, fourteen, fifteen years old, and we had to play in backyards because the big Devils wouldn't let us use the street. Then we challenged them and beat them, twice. We could play on the street after that."

The street today is an official play street on Sundays, with teams named Prestos, Home Relief, Robins, Viceroys, and others showing their wives and children what great street athletes they were. "Some of the teams, like Home Relief, were formed during the Depression," Velez said. "The Viceroys were the hoods of the neighborhood, but they could play stickball. They're all married and respectable now, and they can still play. A lot of the guys who play haven't lived here for twenty years, but they still come around. We got about a dozen policemen, seven or eight guys working in the Transit Authority and a couple of lawyers."

Also a former player for a team called Swanee, Basil Patterson, who happens to be running for lieutenant governor of New York. "Good speed, fair hitter," said Velez.

The game, like the players, hasn't changed much. But they no longer steal brooms and mops for their handles because, according to Velez, modern brooms and mops are too skinny; he buys the sticks for 69 cents. And spaldeens have gone the way of the Roxy and the Paramount; Velez said they have to settle for the inferior British Bouncer at 35 cents. "We break two a game," he said. Progress is built-in obsolescence, even for stickball.

Of the original Young Devils two have died, one in a shooting. Velez gave a partial pantheon of the neighborhood immortals who should be there Sunday.

"Alphonso Castro was Mr. Outfielder. He would leap over a moving car for a ball. He went through windows chasing balls.

"Peter Rojas. He started us off as a 'slugging' team. Slugging a ball is like a Baltimore chop in baseball. He would deliberately slug the ball down and by the time it came down he'd have a single or double. Sometimes he'd whistle before he hit the ball and the runner would score all the way from first. They heard about our slugging all the way in Brooklyn. We had to rule it out.

"Hector Pacheco. He's the Willie Mays of stickball. He could do anything. Incidentally, we don't believe Mays ever played stickball. We think it was for publicity. A guy from Alabama, how could he?

"Alfredo Rojas, Pete's brother. He was the greatest clutch hitter in the history of stickball. When the money was on the table we wanted to see him up there."

The money was always on the table, as much as $2,000 for a game. Velez said, "We'd chip in $5 per man at the beginning of the season and keep doubling our bets. We rarely lost. Usually we'd split the money three, four times a season, like for Mother's Day so we could buy presents. One time, believe it or not, we dumped a game. We let some guy bet most of the money, about $150. We figured he'd at least buy us sodas after the game, but he just laughed at us. So we deliberately lost the second game and he lost it all back."

Casey himself would have done the same.

Over a period of a month I ran two more columns on the affectionate reminiscences of retired stickballers. It's fun to get readers involved with fun things. This next trifle pulled in four columns worth of wacky name dropping, and a man waiting for a green light on Fifth Avenue yelled "Coaker Triplett" at me.

NAMES

Henry was always careful about names, for they were what gave the league its sense of fulfillment and— failure, its emotion. Names had to be chosen that could bear the whole weight of perpetuity. Brock Rutherford was a name like that; Horace Zifferblatt wasn't. . . . Call a player Sycamore Flynn or Melbourne Trench and something starts to happen. He shrinks or grows, stretches or puts on muscle.

—From Robert Coover's *The Universal Baseball Assn. Inc.*

Which brings up the most important question of this young baseball season. Is Burt Hooten another Clint Hartung or another Vida Blue?

Names, good names, are vital to public people. Vida Blue was in the tradition of great baseball names as a rookie last year. America knew it instantly. Vida Blue! Vida Blue tripped off the tongue like Babe Ruth and Ty Cobb and Lefty Grove. No way that a pitcher named, say, Sonny Siebert could get on the covers of *Time* and *Newsweek* and draw crowds like the pope. Sonny Siebert would have to win forty, strike out 400 and whistle "Flight of the Bumble Bee" to do that.

Consider Babe Ruth. The name Babe Ruth is so derivative that we can't even imagine any other name doing the things he did, much less becoming the greatest name in our sporting folklore. The Japanese in World War II were said to have launched attacks screaming, "Bleep-bleep Babe Ruth." No way they could have screamed, "Bleep-bleep Lynn Lovenguth."

Conversely, Ted Lepcio. His manager once said, "He's the worst ballplayer I ever saw." No way if his name perchance had been Goose Goslin.

Consider the names of that mythical all-star team: Pie Traynor, Rogers Hornsby, Lou Gehrig, Honus Wagner, Babe Ruth, Ty Cobb, Tris Speaker, Mickey Cochrane. Those were names. To say nothing of Christy Mathewson, Grover Cleveland Alexander, Napoleon Lajoie, Mel Ott, Zack Wheat.

And Joe DiMaggio. Is there any doubt that a Joe DiMaggio would outdo a Dom or a Vince DiMaggio? There is only one Musial, one Feller, one Kiner, one Spahn in the record book.

Mickey Mantle—straight out of central casting. Yogi Berra, Sandy Koufax, Hank Aaron, Willie Mays, Al Kaline, Ernie Banks, Roberto Clemente, Pete Rose, Rod Carew, Johnny Bench. Harmon Killebrew—it speaks of power. As Phil Rizzuto and Pee Wee Reese speak of shortstop and Bobby Doerr of second base. Can we forget Country Slaughter, Van Lingle Mungo?

Tom Seaver is a name to be reckoned with. It has a ring, a strength. Not as flashy as Vida Blue. Nor as cunning as Warren Spahn. But solid, always there.

And what of Burt Hooten? Will we forget whether it was Burt Hooten or Hoot Burten five years from now? In other towns, where the promise of Clint Hartung failed to catch hold, perhaps he is remembered as Hart Clintung.

Burt Hooten. It has possibilities. It has hope. A Burt Hooten could be a great one. A Burt Hooten could have pitched a no-hitter in his first start of the season. It's a name that Robert Coover could have conjured, a name that could have come out of the old pulp magazines. A name that could be throwing the mysterious knuckle-curve.

There used to be a candy called a Hooten. Tasted like a Baby Ruth.

Fear not, sports fans, Mickey Mantle and Willie Mays are coming. But first a few lesser names.

CHARLEY PRIDE

The baseball field in Pompano Beach, Florida, where the Texas Rangers are hyping themselves for a pennant run, looks like it was set down on the banks of the Rio Grande during the drought season. The infield is a bright, stony orange. The stands must have been slapped together out of old fencing. It's a good place for a team named the Texas Rangers to train. It's a good place for Charley Pride to try to piece together his busted dream.

A guy with a handle like Charley Pride has a right to think he could have been a big leaguer. "Now batting for the Texas Rangers, the pitcher, Charley Pride." Yup, it sings. Like Charley Pride.

We will hear more of the Texas Rangers for the next six or perhaps seven months. Unless we tune in to a country music station, we aren't likely to hear more about Charley Pride.

Charley Pride is one of the top country music singers

in the country. He would trade his dozen gold records for a mention in the *Baseball Encyclopedia*. Would Charley Pride vs. Vida Blue ever pack them in?

"I'm here because this is what I love, hanging out with ballplayers, feeling the sweat run down my body," Charley Pride said. "Deep down what I want out of it is to hear them say, 'Dadgummit, he coulda helped us.'"

Baseball is going home for Charley Pride. Not to the big home in Dallas, the chartered jets, the Grand Ole Opry. Home to Sledge, Mississippi. Sledge was too small (pop. 526) to have its own school team so Charley Pride went down the road to Byrdie, "a general store with a view," to play with the older men on the Byrdie Blues. He was twelve years old.

"My folks wanted me to get an education, become a chemical engineer or something, but you didn't see any blacks who were chemical engineers," he said. "You saw Jackie Robinson. Playing ball was a way out of Sledge.

"I made it as an outfielder and a pitcher with the Memphis Red Sox of the Negro League. In the middle of my first season they traded the left fielder and me to the Birmingham Black Barons for a bus."

It was a pretty good bus though, Charley Pride recalled, straight-faced. There isn't much laughter in country music. A tall, good-looking man, he ambled plaintively in his snakeskin boots toward the stands for the start of an exhibition game.

"My big chance came when we played the Willie Mays All-Stars on a barnstorming tour. They had everybody—Mays, Aaron, Banks, Gilliam, Howard. I had them beat 1–0 in the ninth inning and there were four Dodger scouts watching. They beat me 2–1. I walked a man and Aaron hit a ball through the shortstop's legs. The count was 0–2 on George Crowe. I'd struck him out three times. Struck out twelve altogether. The catcher called for a pitchout, and they had the double steal on. But I threw it over the plate and Crowe hit it over shortstop. I came close to crying."

Elston Howard remembered, "He had a Hoyt Wilhelm knuckler. It was damn impressive. Struck out quite a few. Got me. I beat him the ballgame in the ninth inning."

After a hitch in the army, Pride answered an ad in the *Sporting News* for a pay-your-own-way tryout with the Missoula (Montana) Timberwolves. He made the team, got his money back, but was released after a few weeks. For the next five years he worked in a smelting plant, sang in road-houses for $3 a night, and played semipro ball. Still hung up on baseball, he got a tryout with the Angels and lasted two weeks. Jim Fregosi loaned him $100 to get home.

"An old man in Sledge said to me, 'Have you ever thought just possibly that you weren't cut out for baseball, that you're here to sing?' I've been singing ever since. But it didn't work out the way I had it planned. I was going to break all the major league records by the time I was thirty-five and then go into singing."

So every spring Charley Pride plays what might have been. Last year he got a pinch single off Jim Palmer. The other day he pumped a ball over a fifteen-foot fence 360 feet away.

Dadgummit, Charley Pride. You coulda helped someone.

Spring training is among the best of times for sportswriters. The weather's nice, the living and working are easy, confirming the illusion that even if a sportswriter can't be rich he can live rich. I used to spend six weeks or more at this seasonal rite, but now ten days are enough, if I go at all. I don't bother much with preseasons because the in-seasons usually are coming to a climax then and because the seasons are long enough as is.

SLUMP

Ron Hunt is in a slump.

Last night he was not hit by a pitch for the seventh game in a row.

He has not been hit by pitches in twenty-four of Montreal's twenty-six games.

"The damn pitchers," he explained, "their control is too good."

If Hank Aaron had only two homers at this stage, there would be cries of anguish. Did the baseball strike ruin his timing? Has the ghost of Babe Ruth cast a spell?

Ron Hunt deserves our anguish no less. Last season he was hit by fifty pitches, breaking the great Hughie Jennings's seventy-five-year-old record. He is only fifteen behind the career mark of 192 held by the immortal Minnie Minoso.

With Montreal fans cheering every black-and-blue mark on his body, Hunt managed to get hit eleven times in September alone—as stirring a stretch of clutch getting-hit-by-pitches as the game has ever seen.

While pitchers grumbled obscenities, and ballplayers in general thought he should be committed, Hunt shook off the hematomas and pointed to the meaningful part of his record: the Expos won thirty-two of their seventy games when he was hit. In appreciation the Montreal press guide features a photograph of Hunt sprawled on the ground after one of his tape measure HBPs.

Inside the guide there's an honor roll of Hunt's victims, from Jim Bunning on April 10 to Milt Pappas, who threw the immortal fiftieth on September 29. The Mets led the league in hitting the ex-Met with nine. Tom Seaver, who put Hunt in the hospital with a concussion in 1969, backed down last season, failing to hit him even once. Bob Gibson hit him twice, yelling after one of them, "Next time I'll stick it in your ear." Hunt replied sweetly, "That junk?"

But to people who ask him how it feels to get hit by a lethal five-ounce blur at ninety or more miles per hour, he replies honestly, "It hurts."

Or, when the business side of his hard body is exposed, welted and bruised in a blaze of discoloration, as though he were an Indian fakir risen from a bed of hot coals, he yawns, "I'm just a dumb German."

Some dumb. The fifty HBPs pushed Hunt over the

.400 mark in the get-on-base department, tops in the league for a lead-off man. Where it didn't hurt was in his contract negotiations.

"I'm not proud of the record," said Hunt, who could have fooled you last September. "It's part of what I do to try to win games. Awards go to guys who hit bleeping home runs and get a lot of bleeping RBIs. Those are the important things."

In a notable coincidence of symbolism, Hunt does wear a Medic Alert medallion around his neck, to promote its use for people who are allergic, have blood disorders, heart conditions, etc. He does not wear it during games, although no one needs it more. He is playing with a leg that looks like it won a battle with a land mine.

"Little Leaguers ask me about getting hit," Hunt said, "and I tell them it's nothing to be proud of, but it shows I'm not afraid of the ball. I've been hit everywhere—the head, jaw, neck, elbow, wrist, ankle. It's important that they shouldn't be afraid of the ball."

Hunt claims he gets hit so much because, besides crowding the plate, begging for it, he has "slow reflexes." So slow that he was hit by a pitching machine three times and by pitchers who weren't even trying in spring training. Now a nation turns its lonely eyes to Ron Hunt as he pursues Minnie Minoso, hoping that his reflexes weren't fatally speeded up during the baseball strike, hoping that he breaks out of his slump soon.

Characters like Hunt are a columnist's best friend, as are characters like the character who gets off on records.

THE RECORD KEEPER

The thing Seymour Siwoff loves more than anything else is "a nice quiet day when somebody breaks a record." It is a religious experience for him, like a good soufflé for a gourmet. Yesterday was such a day.

Seymour Siwoff owns the Elias Sports Bureau, which

assembles statistics for baseball and football. Records are to statistics as a good soufflé is to a hard-boiled egg.

"I'd like to see a guy hit five homers on a nice quiet day," Seymour Siwoff said. "Five homers—wham! Headlines. Everybody talking. Wham! On a nice quiet day."

So yesterday, Earth Day, a day of meaningful quietude, Tom Seaver went "wham."

Seaver struck out ten Padres in a row, breaking the modern record by two, and nineteen overall, tying Steve Carlton. He did it with a dramatic flourish, getting the last ten men to face him. It was, in the ninth inning, a game between Tom Seaver and that great record keeper in the sky, Seymour Siwoff. At his office on 42nd Street, said Siwoff, "there was a mighty roar" when Seaver got Al Ferrara to end the game. Siwoff and his six assistants, whom he calls "my busy bees," conjuring visions of Disneyesque dwarfs skedaddling over columns of numbers, watched it on television.

"I don't care what or who," Siwoff said, "a record is a record, a triumph, something to be cherished. The other day Steve Whitaker struck out five times and hit a sacrifice fly. Holy mackerel! All he needed was one more. Nobody ever struck out six times in a game. I have nothing against the player, but what a record."

To Seymour Siwoff the meaning of Seaver's record is clear. Max Surkont, Johnny Podres, Jim Maloney and Don Wilson, who struck out eight in a row, will be stricken from the record book. More important to Siwoff, so too will Michael Welch be banished. "The tenth strikeout was the big one," he said. "I hate them old-time records." Welch struck out nine in a row in 1884.

This promises to be a big season in the records-to-be-cherished department. Hank Aaron and Willie Mays will become the ninth and tenth players to reach 3,000 hits. "We're on the brink of a real breakthrough," Siwoff said. "We're going to see how great modern players are. Aaron may catch Ruth in homers and Musial in his National League records on hits, runs and runs batted in. In 1968 Aaron drove me crazy. He needed 100 runs to break a tie with Lou Gehrig for scoring 100 runs in consecutive seasons (thirteen). He missed. I said to myself, 'Oh my God, how can you do this to me.' It killed a streak.

"I went to Musial one year and told him I needed some doubles and stolen bases from him. He looked at me kinda funny. It was like I was ordering off a shelf."

But records are more than numbers to the record keeper. "They're people," Seymour Siwoff said. "The human element. What gets into a Roger Maris? How does he get psyched to hit sixty-one home runs? How does Dale Long hit homers in eight consecutive games? Why him suddenly? And Jim Gentile. He hit grand slam homers in consecutive innings. I remember it so well. It was a nice quiet day."

There's a man happy at his work. Here's a man who isn't. My approach to him was suggested in a conversation with John Ford Noonan, a playwright and former athlete, on another subject.

THE OUTSIDER

The return of Dick Allen to the Phillies—a rapprochement as unlikely as Solzhenitsyn and Russia—is fraught with dramatic possibilities. They can come to an end that can only be tragic or ecstatic.

Knowing Dick Allen, he will arrange for some of each before they split again.

Knowing the Phillies, bringing him back to Philadelphia is the death wish that is parent to the pennant wish. Historically, pennant is a big underdog.

Dick Allen is an outsider. Like Duane Thomas and Bobby Fischer, he is enormously talented at a game, but he has enormous difficulty playing the game of life. An outsider is like a child who perceives all the lunacies and none of the realities of a situation. He is not mature or hip enough to deal with them.

It may seem loony to Dick Allen to have to show up at a ball park two and a half hours before a game, to have to travel with teammates, to have to endure the whims of managers, to have to put up with boos as well as cheers, to have to sit still for dumb or probing questions from the media, to have to finish a season that is lost. And, isolated, loony some of that may be.

But if you love to play ball, as Dick Allen professes to, and if somebody is willing to pay you $250,000 to play it, then you make believe the lunacies aren't oppressive and you take the money and run. Or society is likely to conclude that you are the loony one.

Dick Allen has what can be generously labeled amateur ideals in a professional world. They are expressed in strange, almost demented twists in logic, on and off the field.

Last season he brought a claque of relatives to the All-Star Game in Pittsburgh, showed up minutes before it started, singled to drive in a run in the first inning, and disappeared two innings later, leaving his relatives and the American League bewildered. His explanation: he didn't want to face reporters after the game.

With thirty-two home runs going into September, Allen said he could hit forty or fifty but didn't want to because he then would be considered a home run hitter rather than an all-around player. A few days later he announced his retirement. This spring, having been traded to the Braves, he said his contract with the White Sox was still valid, implying a lawsuit on the grounds that they quit him.

Allen's business dealings were equally bizarre. He got $10,000 to do a book and neglected two appointments with an author who traveled thousands of miles to see him. His agent landed a $50,000 contract with a sporting goods firm, and Allen neglected to show up at a meeting to tie that up. "I don't want to be a commodity," he said. Who put a gun to his head?

Allen has come back to baseball, agreeing to play by all its loony rules, because he is in deep financial trouble. Creditors have filed a number of suits against him.

Perhaps the fear of losing everything will turn him into a professional overnight. Perhaps a pennant contender will do the same. When things go right, nobody much cares what you do wrong, and he can be an immensely appealing, personable fellow under those conditions.

But his attitudes run deep and make him vulnerable, and things do not always go right. His test will come when the Phillies lose and he gets lost in traffic and the fans funnel their wrath at him, all of which have been known to happen.

Only the Phillies would rehire an outsider to remind a good young team of the storied, bitter past it has to overcome.

The key to this column is the disclosure of Allen's financial dealings, which came to me through a source close to his advisers. The disclosure suggests the depth of Allen's confusion. The Phillies did fail to win the pennant, in no small measure because Allen had his poorest season. He behaved reasonably and played abominably. Perhaps there's a psychological connection there, but it may fall into the realm of a John Ford Noonan, who says he "explores the wilderness of the mind."

Athletes, like people, are trying to cope with the wilderness in many ways these days, as I discovered one day.

INTO THINGS

The Dodgers are leading the Western Division because they got Jim Wynn and Mike Marshall in trades for Claude Osteen and Willie Davis. But, also, they are into static stretching.

Static stretching, whatever its importance may be, is not as important as being into it is. Being into things is crucial in this humdrum world, and modern athletes are into a lot of things.

A group of Mets are poking around the dreamy edges of transcendental meditation. Yoga appears to be making converts elsewhere. Willie Davis was into Buddhist chanting before he found himself reincarnated in Montreal. Hypnosis, astrology, even old-fashioned religion have their champions. Davey Johnson of the Braves is into computers: a slump, he explains to himself, is just a negative chance variation. Don Sutton of the Dodgers may be the last of the vitamin pill poppers; vitamins, it can be said, are into him.

Static stretching, to get the suspense over with, is a way of stretching muscles without flexing them. Dodger after Dodger at Shea Stadium yesterday bent over at the waist and hung there. A few of them added refinements, like looking through their legs. Andy Messersmith blew a terrific bubble gum bubble.

A team with Mike Marshall, who has been described by Don McMahon of the Giants as "a professor of every muscle in the body," figures to be into something like static stretching. But Marshall didn't put the Dodgers up to it. Another professor of muscles did.

Being into something, anything, has its own rewards. Tom Lasorda, a coach, put music into that category. Tape recorders apparently are therapeutic. Ballplayers used to be into superstition, Lasorda said. "Guys thought that if they saw a pregnant woman it meant they would get base hits. They'd rub a hunchback's back for good luck. And if they were going good they'd eat the same food, wear the same clothes."

There are still players who observe elaborate rituals to relieve pressure, anxiety, fear. John Hiller of the Tigers starts chewing gum when he is called into a game, then discards it after exactly ten warm-up chews.

But more and more young players are experimenting with exotic disciplines as a path to everlasting happiness and .300 batting averages. They are trying to solve a riddle of much greater moment than which-came-first-the-chicken-or-the-egg. It's how do you bear down and relax at the same time. Mike Schmidt of the Phillies has an answer that defines the dilemma better than solving it. He says he "concentrates on relaxing." Which is one of the neatest tricks this side of going up and down at the same time.

George Theodore is one of the Mets into transcendental meditation or, as it is known, TM. He meditates twice a day for twenty minutes. The theory is that it provides rest far beyond the time invested, clearing the mind. "Sometimes you wonder if it does anything for you," he said. "But if I get two hits a season out of it, it's worth it."

Marshall, whose field of study is the psychology of physiology, is a skeptic. "Yoga and TM are philosophies, not sciences," he said. "I believe they're both expletives."

Yesterday Marshall made his seventy-ninth appearance, coming in to protect a 2–1 lead in the sixth inning. He refuses to reveal the theories that enable him to pitch so often, but he did sneak in a five-second static stretch when he arrived at the mound.

Oddly, going into the ninth inning, 33,000 Met fans made not a move toward the exits, as though they knew something. Possibly Marshall's pitching hypnotized them. Possibly they were meditating on the Mets' pennant chances. Whatever, the Mets promptly scored two runs to sweep the series from the Dodgers. The Mets have a new thing. They're into winning.

I did my own kind of meditating before I wrote the next column. I found myself getting angrier as the day went on. The only question was how I would treat the matter, with deft ridicule or a blunt instrument. I decided the occasion demanded an unmistakable response.

THE WRONG APOLOGY

Cleon Jones's father fled Mobile, Alabama, because he knew what kind of justice he would get after he beat up a white man who humiliated Mrs. Jones.

Would that Cleon Jones had beat up M. Donald Grant at that vile press conference and fled the plantation in Flushing. M. Donald Grant would have got what he deserved and Cleon Jones would be left with a shred of dignity from the humiliation of his clumsy affair in Florida.

Cleon Jones made the sort of dumb mistake we have come to expect from him from time to time, and he will

have to live with it. But he did not with malice afore-
thought mutilate a helpless human being's feelings in public.

M. Donald Grant did that obscene thing. It is he, not
Cleon Jones, who owes us an apology.

How dare this supercilious blowhard put a man on the
rack for the entertainment of presumed moralists in Met-
land?

How dare Mrs. Joan Payson permit this outrage, as
though she were gelding an obstreperous thoroughbred.

Cleon Jones owes them and us one thing: professionalism. He has performed here professionally, if not always
passionately, for eleven years. Being found by police in a
van with a woman at five o'clock in the morning in downtown Saint Petersburg is not professional, though it does
suggest passion.

Upon learning of the incident, veteran Cleon watchers
responded in several ways:

Couldn't he wait to get to Shea Stadium before he fell
asleep in public?

How did his damaged knee hold up?

Some years ago a major league star was caught by
police rolling with a woman on the sands of Lake Michigan
in Chicago. He emptied his pockets and said, "I'm a married ballplayer. I'm going to give you this money ($60) and
start running. If you want me you'll have to shoot me."
They took the money and let him go.

That, alas, is not Cleon Jones. If it were, he would hit
.340 every season.

A ball team, being a very public enterprise, has to take
disciplinary action when a player acts unprofessionally. An
appropriate action by the Mets would be to announce a
modest fine of $250 to $500, order him to get his ass ready
to play ball, and let him deal with his private misery as best
he can.

M. Donald Grant orchestrated a flogging and seized
the airwaves to assure Mets fans that he had "restored our
image" and that Jones was properly penitent.

What he was saying, of course, was, "Don't worry,

folks, Cleon will be fully dressed when he gets into the lineup. It's okay to bring out the kiddies."

They gave Jones a prepared statement of remorse to read at a press conference in which he all but got down on his bum knee and sang "Mammy" and thanked the boss man for fining him only $2,000. A thirty-two-year-old adult, palpably fearful of losing his job, was cowed into pleading for forgiveness and mercy. And he brought his wife to play the faithful heroine to his fallen weakling. Which really should have got him arrested for indecent exposure. We're not as dumb as we look.

A slip of his paternalistic heart, made while discussing Jones's physical condition, revealed what M. Donald Grant was up to. "Cleon has to go out and suffer a little," he said.

Adding assininity to injury, Commissioner Bowie Kuhn, protector of our morals, revealed that he was clearing Jones of the suspicion of smoking funny cigarettes.

How dare these people—in our name—play God with a human being's self-respect.

How dare they put a price on his spirit.

How dare they.

It pays to be subtle. They told me Grant cried like a wounded ego when he read that. But three days later I received an invitation from some organization that was honoring him as its Man of the Year.

There are better days at the ball park. Here are a few.

PETE ROSE

The ball rose in an arc toward the clock. The clock sits high atop the scoreboard in right field at Shea Stadium, and, as clocks will, it was moving on, past five o'clock on a gray Tuesday afternoon. Pete Rose, who threw an elbow the other day that nearly touched off World War III, would like to throw an elbow that could turn all clocks back. He gets base hits in the present and lives in the past. He should be dancing the Charleston, drinking sarsaparilla, and wearing a big-brimmed fedora.

The ball rose off Pete Rose's bat in the twelfth inning of an excruciating tie, the Mets staving off one Reds' threat after another in the fourth game of the play-offs. The ball fell short of the clock, but, for the Mets, not short enough. Pete Rose, the first $100,000 singles hitter, hit a home run.

"Yesterday I was Charley Hustle," he said, alluding to the pejorative nickname and the near riot his hustle triggered. "Today I'm the Big Brute."

Villain, thy name is Pete Rose, and the only trouble is that there aren't enough of him to go around. In the movies he would push old ladies downstairs. Villainy isn't fashionable anymore, but Pete Rose grew from a Cincinnati kid to a Cincinnati Red with an old-fashioned sense of my-town-can-beat-your-town and the passion that goes with it. He drives a snazzy 1934 Ford. He thinks 1930s clothing styles are peachy. He said, "I feel like I know Babe Ruth and Ty Cobb."

Having hit just five home runs all season, Rose didn't have the Ruthian gall to point to the spot where he would hit the home run, but there could be no doubt he had something like it in mind. He had been on base three of the five previous at-bats. He had a big red raspberry on his left hip where he had gone after Bud Harrelson again, missing him. Now, crouching pugnaciously in that balled-fist of a stance, he was swinging with uncharacteristic bravura, like a boxer going for a knockout.

"When I get excited," Rose said, "I swing too hard." The Reds had stranded eight runners in the last three innings. Rose had been ducking eggs, apples, and other objects of affection from Mets fans for three hours. He had refused M. Donald Grant's ridiculous request to shake hands with Harrelson at home plate before the game. His only disappointment, he said, was that he didn't get a base hit the first time up to shut up the rousing rabble. "I would have given a week's pay ($5,000) to go four-for-four and score four runs," he said.

Rookie Harry Parker replaced Tug McGraw in the twelfth for the Mets. McGraw had given the crowd some thrills, loading the bases twice, running all the way out to right field to thank Rusty Staub for holding onto a drive before thudding into the fence. Parker thrilled Rose. Excited, Rose swung and missed at two high pitches, then tried a third. That one became the home run. He pumped a fist triumphantly as he circled the bases.

"I love to play baseball," Pete Rose said. "I can't wait to get out there tomorrow. I wish the play-offs were sixteen out of thirty. I'd play for nothing—if someone paid my bills."

That sounds more like 1937 than 1973. Is that Ernie Lombardi catching and Bucky Walters pitching for the Reds? Will Franklin Roosevelt be in a box seat today for the fifth and final game? Who's playing in the stage show at the Paramount? Is the NFL a new government agency?

There's no tomorrow in these play-offs, but there's always a yesterday for Pete Rose. He turns the clock back —to a time when there were no Mets.

ONE MORE TIME

Did Thor loose one more bolt of lightning after he lost the zip on his high hard one? Probably not. Did Shakespeare compose a last sonnet on his deathbed? Unlikely. But Willie Mays got a hit yesterday to win a World Series game. Even when he has nothing left, Willie Mays doesn't let you down.

Willie Mays has nothing left. "That's not Willie Mays," said Reggie Jackson. "It's him in name only."

In different ways, Willie Mays has been telling us that for a couple of years. No more lightning in his bat, no more sonnet in his step. But only recently has he told it to himself. The mad dash of the Mets from last to first in September left him, like everyone else, an admiring spectator. "Willie," he said on his farewell night, "say goodbye to America."

For the last month and a half he has graciously deferred to and cheered his younger teammates. He made it clear he didn't want to hurt them or embarrass himself on the field. What happened to him, then, up to the twelfth inning of the second game of the World Series was infinitely sad. America doesn't want to see a Willie Mays who can't pick up a ground ball, as he couldn't in the 2–1 win by the Athletics Saturday. America doesn't want to see Willie Mays falling down in the outfield and on the basepaths, as he did yesterday. His sun has set. Let the darkness roll in.

Rusty Staub led off the ninth inning with a single, and Mays ran for him. When John Milner singled, Mays tripped rounding second. He said he missed the bag and slipped. Willie Mays missing the bag and slipping? It was like hearing a sour note from Jascha Heifetz.

Deron Johnson hit a line drive to center field to lead off the ninth for the Athletics. Once upon a time Willie Mays would have caught it in his teeth. He made a belated lunge, and Johnson had a double. "The sun was in my face," Mays said. Good outfielders had been playing like they had blinkers on for two days. But Willie Mays? Willie Mays was a force of nature who overcame other forces of nature.

"He didn't misplay the ball, but Willie Mays used to catch those," Reggie Jackson said. "When he looks mortal he looks bad. You used to think if the score was 5–0 he'd hit a five-run homer."

In the twelfth inning, with the score 6–6, Willie Mays came to the plate with runners on first and third and two out. Relief pitcher Rollie Fingers had overpowered the last two batters. Rollie Fingers throws hard, and Willie Mays can't hit hard stuff anymore. By all that is holy in baseball, Mays had as much chance against Fingers as Molly Klutz.

Fingers knew that as well as anyone, which was why his glove was sailing majestically over the infield moments later. The Wonderful World of Willie Mays had replaced the Wonderful World of Walt Disney on early evening television. To the consternation of Fingers. Mays had bounced an 0–1 pitch just beyond his reach, through the infield and into the storybooks.

The nervous effort it took for Mays to get around on Fingers sent him sprawling in the dirt. He picked himself up and ran to first, adjusted his cap, and stole a glance into the Mets dugout as the winning run scored.

"I never showed them the real Willie Mays," Willie Mays said. "They haven't seen me when I was young. Two out and a man on third. That's clutch hitting. Seeing those guys in there, being in a World Series, that's my reward."

Gods may not write letters, as John Updike wrote about Ted Williams, but they do reach you. Here are three more whose poignant glances in the rear-view mirror reached me.

SUMMER WISHES, WINTER DREAMS

In their bright summers, Mickey Mantle and Whitey Ford hit home runs and pitched shutouts. On an appropriately mellow winter day, they were sent skipping like boys into the Hall of Fame.

They are no longer boys—country boy and city boy—but the Hall of Fame is dedicated to the fantasy of eternal boyhood. It is the original museum of summer wishes and winter dreams.

"The trick," Casey Stengel once said, "is growing up without growing old," but for the great athlete the trick, as Mantle told us, is simply growing up. Baseball was "one thrill after another," and where do you go from there?

"I dream almost every night," Mickey Mantle said, "of making a comeback."

Making the Hall of Fame, the seventh player so acclaimed in his first year of eligibility, seemed like the end of a long climb for Mantle. Suddenly he was expansive, running downhill breathlessly after so many years of blocking us, and perhaps himself, out.

He talked about two recurring dreams.

"In the first one I pull up in front of Yankee Stadium

for a game. I hear 'em saying over the loudspeaker, 'Now hitting, No. 7, Mickey Mantle.' The guy at the door won't let me in, so I try to crawl in through a hole. But I'm stuck. I can't get in. I hear Casey asking, 'Where's Mickey?' The players say, 'He's coming.'

"In the second dream I'm up at bat, hitting left-handed. I'm always hitting at fastballs and I always foul the ball back over my head. I say to myself, 'That's it. I can't hit anymore.'"

Mickey Mantle has been retired for five years and he played five of his last six years as a semi-invalid, his strength breaking his body down. Yet, so far removed from his prime, he lives in a reverie.

"I never used to read scrapbooks," he said. "In the last three years I've gotten about fifty of them from fans who grew up and didn't have any use for them. I keep one in my toilet. I read it every morning."

The innocence of the country boy, spelled out so ingenuously here, attracted him to Whitey Ford, the streetwise city boy.

"I was nineteen, from Commerce, Oklahoma," Mantle said. "I was nervous and backward. Whitey was brash and outspoken." They had in common large talent and large thirst. The city boy complemented the country boy's insecurity and naiveté; the country boy complemented the city boy's brass and smarts.

Because they were Yankees, with the national glamour they earned, Mantle and Ford were the only ones voted into the Hall of Fame this year. The timing that brought them together on an occasion so important to them was impeccably sweet. Their remembrances of things past sang with affection.

Mantle: "He'd ask me where the hell over yonder is, and he'd say vodka and soder."

Ford: "We shot some quail. The next day his mom's got quail on toast with gravy for breakfast. And I'm a ham-and-eggs kid from New York."

Mantle: "We figured out once that I struck out 1,700 times and walked 1,800 times, so if you came to bat 500 times a season I played seven years without hitting the ball."

Ford: "Mickey's the same, he's never changed."

They hit home runs and pitched shutouts, the stuff of summer wishes and winter dreams.

STARDUST

The bells of Christ Church in Reading, Pennsylvania, sing out with Hoagy Carmichael's "Stardust" at five o'clock every evening. This spring it is Robin Roberts's song.

Robin Roberts, as always, is reaching for the stars with his right arm. Robin Roberts, age forty, winner of 286 big league games, a certain Hall of Famer, is pitching for the Reading Phillies of the Eastern (AA) League.

"I am," he said last night before going out to face the York Senators, "a very interesting case."

Stubbornness—uncommon, glorious, hard-headed stubbornness—the quality that made him great and then not so great, makes Robin Roberts an interesting case. He was one of the most stubborn of competitors in his prime, and he stubbornly resisted change when he staggered past his prime. But he came back once and now, a stubborn corpse, he wants to come back again.

"I'm not here to pitch in the minors," he said. "I'm going to give myself two or three more shots and then call up all the general managers in the majors. That will be it. I think I can pitch two or three more years. That's all there is to it. Winning 300 is secondary. In fact it's a drag. People think that's the only reason I want to come back. I'd like to win 300, but that's not the objective. I just want to pitch."

Roberts had just made the hour's drive from his home in suburban Philadelphia to Reading Memorial Stadium. He was sitting on a training table in the dressing room. Laundered sweatshirts hung overhead. The manager's office was partitioned off in a corner, a match box inside a cigar box. Roberts looked the way he always has, boyish, the blue eyes like perfect marbles, the smile right off a Wheaties ad.

"Nobody liked the idea too much, including my wife," he said. "But they know how I am. They knew I had to try. I have nothing else. I'm in good shape financially, but I don't have a business. I was never very organized. All there was was baseball. That's all I thought about."

He had eight starts before last night in places like Pittsfield, Massachusetts, and Waterbury, Connecticut, and Pawtucket, Rhode Island. He won five and lost two (1–0 and 2–1). He didn't mind the bus trips. The $4 a day meal money amused him. The mounds confounded him. After an inning in Waterbury he went behind the stands for a shovel and landscaped the mound.

"You can't believe how fabulous he's been," Frank Lucchesi, the manager, said. "You know what he said in spring training? 'I'm having more fun than ever.' He was like a kid. He'd carry bats out to the field. I couldn't get nineteen-year-olds to carry bats, but Robin Roberts carried bats. I'm pulling for him like crazy. I'm usually very calm in the dugout, but with him I'm saying under my breath, 'Come on, Robbie, come on, Robbie.' Maybe someday I'll write a book and I'll be able to say I managed Robin Roberts."

Roberts aside, Reading is made up of never-wases and never-will-bes. There isn't a major league prospect on the team. Their broken dreams seem ennobled by Roberts.

"Being with Robbie is one of the high points of my career," said Charley Shoemaker, twenty-eight, second baseman. "I bust my neck for him. He doesn't moan or groan or ask for special favors. He's just Robin Roberts, ballplayer."

Richard Billings, an outfielder for York and, like Roberts, a Michigan State graduate, was skeptical about his chances. "I don't think he'll make it back," he said. "I wonder what he's doing here, a superstar. What does he need this for? He can get any kind of job he wants. I guess he loves to play. You can't knock that."

There was a rock 'n roll contest at home plate as Roberts warmed up. There were 803 fans in the open stands.

Roberts gave up a bunt single and a walk in the first inning. He kept the ball low and he seemed surprisingly quick. He gave up nothing in the second inning, but he conferred with Lucchesi on the sidelines afterward. In the third inning he gave up two ground ball singles and a walk for a run, and he took himself out of the game. He repulled a muscle in his back that he had injured falling off a bad mound in Pittsfield.

"Isn't that a shame," Roberts said, lowering himself into a whirlpool. "First time I've had trouble. I was throwing good too. . . . Something will happen yet. I'll take two more starts, in Williamsport and Elmira. Things will work out."

York won 4–2. Robin Roberts was the losing pitcher.

BUBBLE GUM CARD

The dean looked at the student, who was fifty years old, and said that, well, it would be necessary to take some physical education courses in order to graduate from City College.

The student said, would it be all right if I had an equivalency outside of school.

The dean wondered what in the world the student could mean by that.

The student whipped a bubble gum card out of his pocket. "See, look, I was a major leaguer," he said. "That's worth at least two credits."

The dean checked the picture on the bubble gum card, and sure enough it was the man sitting opposite him, fifteen years earlier, in a Phillies uniform. The dean agreed that was worth two credits.

And Saul Rogovin matriculated.

There was a story going around that Saul Rogovin, at fifty-three, was graduating today, but it turned out to be premature by a semester. Saul Rogovin is a name from the past that evokes a particular response every time a pitcher discusses his craft in pedantic detail. Laughter.

Rogovin was a big right-hander who threw hard during a short and happy career with the White Sox, then soft during a shorter stint with the Phillies. So soft that his ability to get hitters out, when he did, seemed magical.

"I throw the ball right down the middle," Rogovin would say. "The high-ball hitters swing over it and the low-ball hitters swing under it."

Rogovin's other talent was sleeping in dugouts, which was as negotiable outside baseball as his bubble gum card. He became a liquor salesman, decided after eight years that the only thing he hated more than the work was the taste, played golf on his savings for a few years, and enrolled in Manhattan Community College. He had graduated from Lincoln High School in Brooklyn thirty years earlier.

"The kids in college never heard of me," Rogovin said, bemused by his fled fame. "Even when I whip out my bubble gum card, they don't believe me. It's strange. I feel like a young man.

"I've kept in good shape, but I haven't thrown a ball since the day I retired. I'm afraid that I'd think I'm throwing it harder than I am and wonder why I didn't give it another shot. It's hard to be realistic when you get out of the game. I was surprised no one would take a chance on me. I didn't realize what good is a thirty-six-year-old pitcher.

"Now I look in the mirror and I don't believe myself. It's hard to look at myself. I still feel I could throw. I feel like I missed a few years since high school and now I'm back in school. My friends tell me I'm gray, but I still believe I'm brown."

Rogovin is majoring in education and English. He used to fantasize about being a sportswriter, he said, a career that doesn't end at thirty-six.

"I wrote a paper once on the batting stances of Di-Maggio and Musial, how two successful men approached

their work in different ways. The instructor gave me an
A for organization, but not content. I didn't put my feelings into it.

"I had an experience with DiMaggio I still think
about. It was at the Stadium. I had him two strikes, no balls.
I thought I'd surprise him with a crossfire right down the
middle. All I heard was the crack. It whizzed right by my
ear. First I was glad it didn't hit me. Then I figured it was
a base hit. Then I turned around and Busby caught it waist
high in center field. That one pitch instilled more respect
in me for DiMaggio than Musial. It's what's known as
self-preservation."

Rogovin gets a pension of $300 a month for his seven
years in the majors. His wife is a student too. "I met her
with my bubble gum card," he said.

*Old ball parks never die, they just fade away with the memo-
ries of those who inhabited them. It was a labor of love, a dozen
or more telephone calls, to piece together this one.*

HIT SIGN, WIN SUIT

Abe Lincoln was born in a log cabin, studied law by
candlelight, split rails for spending money and became
President of America. Abe Stark did nicely too. He gave
away a few suits to baseball players and became president
of the City Council and of Brooklyn.

Abe Stark, who died Monday, was the man who made
famous and was made famous by the "Hit Sign, Win Suit"
sign at Ebbets Field.

Cartoonist George Price captured the essence of the
offer in his celebrated *New Yorker* panel showing a little old
man standing between an outfielder and the sign, wearing
fielders gloves on both hands.

Abe Stark never went to those lengths to defend his
suit racks from wholesale raids, but only because he didn't
have to. The sign stretched across the bottom of the score-

board in right field, was only four feet high, and had such masters as Dixie Walker and Carl Furillo defending it.

"I saved him a lot of money," Furillo said with a chuckle from Reading, Pennsylvania. "I remember Walker saying he was guarding his suits for so many years he was going down to the store to get something."

The store was at 1514 Pitkin Avenue in Brownsville. Above the store was a poolroom where you could make a bet on baseball. Not a few giddy parlay winners would shoot downstairs and buy a suit from Abe Stark.

Perhaps that is how Abe Stark got the inspiration to put his only billboard in Ebbets Field. His son, Dr. Stanley Stark of Palm Beach, said, "From the day the sign went up in the thirties we had a box behind the third base dugout. We shared it with Sam Abrams of Esquire Shoe Polish; they had a sign too. Next to us was a fellow who owned a restaurant and blew up balloons with the players' names on them.

"I'm sure the sign had a lot to do with my father's political success. Everyone knew him. The Dodgers were frequent customers in the store. When someone came in for a suit, he usually had a friend or two who would buy things wholesale. They didn't know it, but they were paying for the free suit. Reese, Reiser, Furillo, Lavagetto, Medwick, Robinson, they were all there.

"Hack Wilson was the first player to hit the sign. The official scorer had the final decision on whether the ball hit the sign on the fly. Sometimes if a player hit it on a bounce my father would give him a pair of pants."

Generations of Dodger fans were certain that a fly ball could hit the sign only if a sniper shot the right fielder first. But five players collected suits in twenty years.

Tommy Holmes, as a baseball writer for the *Brooklyn Eagle*, notified the store that someone—he forgets who, but it could have been Wilson—hit the sign. "A guy there—not Stark—gave me an argument," Holmes said. "But they gave the player the suit."

Lee Scott, who covered the Dodgers for the *Brooklyn*

RINGSIDE SEAT AT THE CIRCUS

Citizen and now is their traveling secretary, said he was the official scorer when Mel Ott hit the sign. "Stark didn't believe it and he hung up on me," Scott said. "Then he called back and gave Ott the suit."

Jim Gilliam won one suit and Carl Furillo two. "You were supposed to get a 3Gs suit, the best suit they had, an $85 suit," Furillo said. "Stark tried to lead me to the cheaper suit but he gave me the 3Gs."

Red Barber, the Dodger broadcaster from 1939 through 1953, didn't recall any suit-winning hits. He said from Tallahassee, Florida, in pure Barberese, "My money is on Walker and Furillo, who were such superb right fielders, and on the astuteness of Abe Stark for putting the sign grasstop high."

II.
Strange Bedfellows

Only in tumultuous times like the last decade does sport become openly political. Richard Nixon, an avid fan, used sport for political purposes. Muhammad Ali was dethroned. Political violence marred the Olympics. Billie Jean King became the lightning rod of the women's movement for equal rights.

There were fun and games too. This section includes boxing, track and field, and tennis everyone.

PING-PONG POWERS

This mad world has permitted itself a small chuckle because a dialogue between America and China has started across a Ping-Pong table. In the heart of the Upper West Side of New York, where political intrigue is a way of life, a couple of men have permitted themselves a much larger chuckle. They knew it all the time.

Their names are Bill Marlins and Marty Reisman, and they operate out of Reisman's seven-table Ping-Pong Palace at 96th Street and Broadway. Reisman is a former two-time national champion and is famous as a trick shot artist. Marlins is his manager. Marlins also is an amateur political scientist.

Four years ago Marlins put together his interest in Reisman, Ping-Pong and politics and wrote two articles in *Table Tennis Topics*, the bible of Ping-Pong, on how America and China could resume diplomatic relations. Ping-Pong, of course. You were expecting fortune cookies?

"The thought struck me," said Marlins, "that (1) there is no historic basis for conflict or antagonism between China and the U.S.; (2) the American people like the Chinese people; (3) the Chinese people like the American people; (4) the Chinese words for America are still *mei gwo*, which means 'beautiful country'; (5) having observed Reisman doing fantastic things playing the Chinese in Hong Kong and Taiwan; (6) with table tennis a very serious business in China; (7) with America so superior in most tangible things that the two countries could discuss, China was in danger of losing face; (8) except in the field they are superior in, table tennis.

"So it occurred to me that there would be no problem in setting up a dialogue through table tennis because they would operate from a position of strength and we would operate through a position of weakness that we wouldn't care about. So the world has just taken a turnaround—and table tennis has played a role."

Marty Reisman said, "If somebody had proposed this

plan two weeks ago they would have taken him to an institution." Marty Reisman is, among other things, the original political Ping-Ponger.

"In 1951 I was touring Europe with the Globetrot-
ters," he said. "The American embassy asked us to appear
in West Berlin after a big May Day celebration got a lot of
publicity for the Communists. Seventy-five thousand people showed up at the Olympic stadium on a few days'
notice. I played an exhibition at the intermission. I'm sure
most of them were so far away they couldn't see the ball,
but they cheered anyway."

Because it is an inexpensive game to play and perhaps
because it is one of the few international games that the
Chinese could quickly win championships in, Ping-Pong
has become the national sport of China. Although it was
invented as a spin-off of tennis just ninety years ago, politically it has its roots in ancient Chinese custom. David
Brinkley of NBC related the other night that centuries ago
when Chinese warlords declared war on one another they
assembled their troops at an appointed location, then sat
down at opposite ends of a table and debated the merits of
each other's armies and negotiated a settlement rather than
spill blood.

In that spirit, Marty Reisman, who says he is apoliti-
cal, had arranged weeks ago, before the Chinese said "How
about a game?" to the American team touring Japan, to let
the West Side Peace Committee use his Ping-Pong Palace
for a fund-raiser this Sunday.

Next thing you know, Howard Samuels, the Off-
Track Betting commissioner, will put a few tables in
Grand Central Casino and start booking the action, really
bringing Ping-Pong into the big time.

BASEBALL DIPLOMACY

If track and field diplomacy helped defrost the cold
war between the U.S. and Russia, and if Ping-Pong diplomacy reopened the door to U.S.–China relations, can base-

ball diplomacy between the U.S. and Cuba be far behind?

Or, as the inscription on the Statue of Liberty urges, "Send us your poor, your huddled masses, and your short-stops, your outfielders and your pitchers."

Senator George McGovern returned recently from Cuba with the flash that Fidel Castro wants a team of professionals to come on down for a few games. The state department rejected the proposal, as it did previous over-tures from Bowie Kuhn. Americans compete against Cu-bans in many sports, including amateur baseball, on neu-tral fields, but the pin-striped suits who approve passports aren't ready yet for a home-and-away series.

Inevitably that will come to pass, and when it does the man who will play the position of ambassador will be Pres-ton Gomez, the manager of the Astros. Gomez was a na-tional hero in Cuba in 1959 when he managed the Havana Sugar Kings to the International League championship. "I got a big laugh out of Castro last winter," he name dropped at Shea Stadium, "when I told him we both could get rich as agents for the big league prospects down there."

It's been nearly thirteen years since the U.S. and Cuba stopped talking, a terrible blow to our cigar smokers and baseball teams. Cuban major leaguers—Luis Tiant, Tony Oliva, Bert Campaneris, José Cardenal, Tony Perez, Cookie Rojas, Mike Cuellar, et al.—are all in their thirties.

"They have six, eight, maybe ten kids who are sure major leaguers," said Gomez. "It's hard to say whether they will get the chance. I think someday they will. Baseball is very important to Cubans."

It is the official policy of Communist Cuba not to have professional athletes as we know them, although the best amateurs get paid to play their games and are in effect professionals. These, shall we say, scholarship athletes have done well in international competition. Gomez said Castro has been rebuffed in his attempts to make baseball an Olympic sport. So, despite his policy on professionalism, Gomez speculated, he may relent on baseball.

A few years ago Castro, who has his own autographed bat, asked Gomez for his opinion on Cuba's vast amateur program. "You have advantages and disadvantages," Gomez said. "You don't lose ballplayers to the big leagues, and that's an advantage. But your players reach only a certain level without professional instruction."

Gomez, whose two brothers, one of whom was a political prisoner for three years, still live in Cuba, was allowed to leave the island with his mother.

Pride, curiosity and even public demand seem to be behind Castro's softening attitude toward baseball professionalism. It obviously would be a highly popular move to enable prospects to come to the U.S. "If Tony Oliva gets three hits today," said Gomez, "everyone in the country knows it tomorrow. They listen to the games from Atlanta. They get the Voice of America. Word gets around."

Last year Cuba issued a set of stamps commemorating the one hundredth anniversary of baseball there (imported, undoubtedly, by José Doubleday). A factory that manufactures bats, gloves and balls was opened because Cubans can't get equipment from the U.S. Balls are at such a premium that fouls hit into the stands must be returned. Gomez said that the policy of free admissions to play-offs in Havana may have to be scrapped because the 30,000-seat stadium is too small.

In the great tomorrow, Havana, like San Juan, Caracas and Mexico City, may have a major league franchise. Progress right now is baseball diplomacy that says, "Yanqui, come back."

POLITICAL SPORT

It's been a long four years since Eugene McCarthy told us that Hubert Humphrey would be the kind of pitcher who would lose 1–0 or 6–5, or by whatever close score it took to lose, while Richard Nixon would throw slow curves and sliders and even spitters, or whatever it took to win.

Eugene McCarthy elevated the sports metaphor to its loftiest heights during the 1969 presidential primaries, reminding us of the richness of the language. He likened his campaign against different opponents in different states to a runner competing against a relay team. Of newcomers to the antiwar movement, he asked, "Where were they when the puck was in the corner?" He mused that "politics is like coaching football—you have to be smart enough to understand it and dumb enough to think it's important."

If McCarthy was a four-letter man of letters, President Nixon was a two-letter man and George McGovern is a no-letter man. Whether the country is ready for a non-sports nut in the White House remains to be seen, but the primaries that come to town tomorrow have not been without their jockular moments.

More athletes than ever, for example, have aligned themselves with candidates. Senator McGovern's team includes such stalwarts as Deacon Jones, Steve Carlton, Leroy Kelly, Lem Barney, Jan Stenerud, Arthur Ashe, Phil Jackson and Jim Bouton. Bouton was elected a McGovern delegate in New Jersey and has been named vice-chairman of the delegation. The McGoverns have virtually eliminated the Edmund Muskies, who boast of Tom Heinsohn, Bobby Murcer and Hank Aaron. In the fall they will all take on the President Nixons, who have Arnold Palmer, O. J. Simpson, Wilt Chamberlain, Roger Staubach, Ted Williams and George Allen.

The influence of this sporting life on politics is manifest in many ways. One of the new ones is the statistical demographics now in high favor, the art of determining the emphasis of a campaign. Pat Cadell, who graduated from Harvard last week, is the young whiz behind McGovern in this area. And it all began with baseball.

"I hated math in school, but I was fascinated by its application to baseball," said Cadell, echoing many a boy's experience. "I was intrigued by percentages and trying to judge the potential of people through numbers. When I was twelve I wrote to the league offices to get as much background in statistics as I could. I suppose my parents thought it was a waste of time. Later, when I got fascinated with politics, I applied my interest in baseball stats to that."

Jimmy the Greek, another kind of statistical whiz, is

applying his art to politics too. Hired by columnist Jack Anderson as a pollster and oddsmaker, he has been sending down the odds on the primaries from his Mount Olympus with the same fallibility as his point spreads.

Sportswriters traditionally have exposed themselves to ridicule with their predictions, but we deal in games of chance as well as strength and weakness, while political pundits theoretically deal in cosmic truths. It is hilarious then to observe some of them squirming and rationalizing as Senator McGovern defies their expertise. We haven't had anything like that on the sports pages since Muhammad Ali, Joe Namath and the Mets defied their doubters.

Finally there was the little matter this weekend of a Republican functionary caught trying to steal Democratic secrets. George Allen or a good third base coach could have shown the poor fellow a thing or two about that.

The "little matter" turned out to be Watergate.

Although the next three columns were written over a span of eight years, with no direct connection, they brushed against one of the more bizarre events of the times—the kidnaping, radicalization and disappearance of Patty Hearst.

MAKE POINTS, NOT WAR

They played a game of political football at Princeton yesterday and its repercussions will be heard long after today's noise over UCLA–Southern Cal and even Princeton–Yale dies down.

The Army and Navy ROTC Hawks played the Students for a Democratic Society Doves.

On a field as muddy as a Vietnam rice paddy, under a gray November sky, the Doves upset the Hawks, three touchdowns to two.

The star for the Doves was Steve Weed, a bearded philosophy major. In keeping with the growing spirit of antiwar militancy, he ran, passed and demonstrated out of the shotgun formation.

An ROTC defector played for the Doves. So did a freshman team linebacker. Jim Tarlou, one of the Dove coaches, said several varsity players volunteered their services, including Ellis Moore, who set an Ivy League record by scoring five touchdowns against Harvard. But they are not allowed to play touch tackle and, besides that, the Doves wanted only to disarm the militarists, not dismember them.

A crowd of about a hundred students, many of them turned out as mock hippies, a few wearing toy army helmets and brandishing toy weapons, cheered and jeered both sides. The Doves had the only organized cheering. One of their favorites was, "Kill for peace."

Tarlou credited the victory to stronger convictions, organization and a razzle-dazzle offense. "We prepared for the game with only one day of practice, but many days of political discussion," he said. "We discussed the reasons why Rotsy [ROTC] was abominable and had to be destroyed. The coaches were the steering committee of SDS. Some of us, like myself, never played football. We felt that political spirit should pervade the team, not athletic qualifications. The coaches led the cheering. The players ran the game. The most effective political movement is from the bottom up. People doing the work should make the decisions."

Larry Kelley, an ROTC student, challenged SDS to the game after it led a sit-in at the Institute for Defense Analysis at Princeton. "They like to make martyrs of themselves," he said. "This game will help remind them that they are part of the student body."

The challenge was quickly accepted. "We think this is a great way to channel aggression," said Jerome Hoffman of SDS, "a much better way than sending boys off to fight a meaningless war."

The result of the game undoubtedly will confuse the football community, which, like military and political leaders, equates physical courage with patriotism, long hair with bolshevism and dissent with a breakdown in team discipline.

Vince Lombardi has noted that "We need followers who will accept authority . . . too much freedom has had an adverse effect."

A. M. Coleman, commissioner of the Southeastern Conference, said, "Next to home and the church, the greatest influence for good today is to be found in our athletic programs. Look at the campuses where there's trouble. It's with the bearded, long-haired, tennis-shoed element. You don't see athletes involved in that."

Rip Miller, assistant athletic director of Navy, said, "Those pinkos can't touch football."

To which Jim Tarlou responded triumphantly, "We were seen as curiously non-Princetonian. We showed them that we aren't that different from other students, just that our views are different."

At Southern Cal the play "student body left" means an end sweep. At Princeton, as the ROTC learned to its sorrow, it has a double meaning.

Steve Weed came to the country's attention seven years later. He was engaged to Patty Hearst before she was abducted by revolutionary elements.

Hair length and changing attitudes about the athlete-coach relationship became hot issues. The establishment was threatened. Sportswriters drew up sides, most siding with the hair-is-discipline hard-liners.

HAIR

Two years ago, when asked how he felt about competing against a certain long-haired shot-putter, Olympian Dave Maggard replied that he simply didn't look at him because "he makes me sick to my stomach."

Last weekend the University of California won the NCAA track and field championship in a startling upset; it did not score a single point last year. But it was not the kind of team that President Nixon would make one of his famous congratulatory telephone calls to. It was a team with goateed and mustachioed sprinters, sideburned and long-haired middle distance runners and jumpers, and even a few crewcuts. And who was the coach of these campus bums in short pants? Dave Maggard.

It undoubtedly came as a surprise to many that California had a track team at all or that the boys from Berkeley competed in regular events. Considering the ferment there, one might have imagined that they excelled only in the hurled insult, the heaved Molotov cocktail, the 110-yard hurdles over police barricades, the steeplechase run through tear gas.

What is interesting is that Maggard replaced an old-line disciplinarian named Sam Bell this year. Bell kicked kids off the team because they joined campus revolts, and he destroyed morale with a heavy-handed approach to training. Maggard, in the aftermath of the Kent State massacre, told a meeting of concerned athletes: "Do what your conscience tells you." Spring football was curtailed, the wrestling team withdrew from some events, but the track team decided to make its statement through competition.

Watching this phenomenon from the sideline with the greatest of interest, along with J. Edgar Hoover, was Jack Scott. A former sprinter at Syracuse, Scott taught a course at California last semester called "Intercollegiate Athletics and Higher Education: A Sociopsychological Evaluation." He said, "We are in a battle to create a humane, just society in which sport would flourish as a meaningful, joyous activity." It is his contention that intercollegiate athletics can only be justified as a fun learning experience, that coaches should be teachers rather than drill sergeants, motivating by inspiring young men to self-discipline rather than by imposing blind obedience.

"Coaches have always lied, connived and manipulated instead of related and educated," Scott said, "because it's easier that way. It's harder to teach on a one-to-one basis." He said Maggard showed "intelligence and foresight" by adapting to a situation at a school plagued by trouble.

Dave Maggard couldn't have done it without the players, as Casey Stengel used to say, but he helped.

"Coaching has changed," Maggard said. "You can't

separate the athlete from the outside world today. You must take into consideration his problems, academic and personal. You have to treat them and respect them as individuals.

"That doesn't mean you have to pamper them. We don't have rigid rules and we don't have laissez-faire. We try to avoid the extremes. We try to use common sense and understanding. You have to be flexible. You have to build trust.

"I don't stress winning to them—win, win, win. We talk about doing your best. I encourage them to discipline themselves. When they're out of college that's what they're going to have to do. I'd like them to wear blazers when they travel, but they don't have to. I don't give them a curfew; I tell them to get their rest. You try to create a feeling of wanting to do, not having to do.

"This doesn't mean it's an intramural thing or recreation. We're trying to excel. I lay down guidelines but I don't believe in sacrificing everything to win."

Scott later achieved notoriety for his views when several pro football players who were attracted to him quit the NFL. Later he materialized as an adviser to Bill Walton, and both of them were questioned by the FBI about Patty Hearst, making front-page headlines.

TALL IS NOT GROWN UP

There are two things to remember about Bill Walton, the wealthy young man who is stirring up the natives with his revolutionary rhetoric.

One is that he is terribly young.

Two is that being wealthy does not automatically make him healthy and wise.

Like many young people politicized by the war and great social issues of the day, Walton blends sweet idealism with anger and cant. It is to his credit that he feels strongly about injustice despite the fame and fortune that give him a stake in the status quo. But that does not qualify this giant of a kid as a giant of an intellect. Tall is not grown up.

Perhaps if he had been able to test himself as a public speaker in college, rather than being quarantined like a rare plant, he would be able to deal with his celebrity status. He would not spit inflammatory abstractions, as he did when questioned by the FBI about the Patty Hearst case. He would, when compelled to discuss the state of the nation, say his say so well that he would turn people on to rather than off his cause.

When you call the government "sick" and "corrupt" and "the enemy," as Walton did, you call attention to yourself rather than the issues. Even in liberal Oregon, where fans have been very supportive toward Walton during the travails of his rookie season, some people are going to take exception to such stuff. It sheds heat, not light. Compared with Walton, as a political philosopher Muhammad Ali comes off as Bertrand Russell.

Yesterday, following an urgent statement by Portland's management to the effect that it deplores the view of its twenty-two-year-old maverick, a statement meant to appease the more hysterical season-ticket holders, Walton lowered his voice to reasoned dissent. He is distressed only by "the trend, the practices and actions of recent government." He has a lot of company there.

The current flap brings into focus the controversy Walton attracted to himself this season as though he had to have it. Much of it could have been avoided had he been able and willing to arrange his thoughts in simple sentences.

Contrary to his ideological harangues about the establishment conspiring to get him, his own teammates were the first to find him a puzzlement. He was uncommunicative, and they interpreted that as arrogance.

Then it took weeks for Walton to not quite clarify the confusion about his injured foot and the accusation that he was trying to con his way out of his contract. There was no reason to believe he wasn't hurt, for he has a history of leg injuries. He had undergone a knee operation before the season, leading to a series of setbacks that kept him out of action for long stretches.

The problem turned out to be that management and teammates expected him to take pain-killers, which he rightly refused to do. But he remained silent while they all publicly doubted his commitment. A normal person yells when he is stepped on. Walton seems to enjoy it. It confirms his demonology about the evils of the system.

Similarly, when his former legal adviser stated that he was trying to use the injury to collect his $2 million and fast-break back to California, Walton responded elliptically to inquiries. He said, "Selected parts of that discussion were told to the media." Because he did not deny the selected parts until it was too late to stop the furor, he encouraged the furor. He is so convinced "people are not going to like me because of what I say and do" that he seems determined to make that a wish fulfilled.

Walton is fighting the last war, a war won by athletes like Bill Russell and Joe Namath, who established their rights of self-expression in team sports.

There is the matter of Walton's vegetarianism. Management tried to get him to beef up. He refused. That's all there was to it. No undue pressure was exerted. But Walton saw it as a Capitalist plot. Needing meat, he explains in the magazine *Crawdaddy*, "is just a myth that is perpetuated, I feel, by the ruling class. I believe they want a good segment of the population to be ill so that, you know, doctors can prescribe drugs and make a lot of money and perform a lot of needless operations."

There's a dunk shot here that is spinning out of the basket. But Bill Walton is, remember, terribly young.

Although the record seemed clear, had he been reachable I would have preferred to discuss my perceptions with Walton. More important to me, I was signaling the end of the political decade in sport, a time to move back to people and away from symbols. Many

doctrinaire liberals who had come to expect confirmation in my
attitudes were upset. That pleased me no end.
  I would have preferred to discuss his change of heart with
George Sauer, one of the politicized defectors from the NFL and
another Jack Scott protégé, but he too was unavailable. I chose to
have some fun with him, paralleling the controversial, much-dis-
cussed movie The Exorcist *in a semifantasy. It must have been*
gibberish to those who missed the movie, the book, or the contro-
versy, but at the time I felt you had to be on another planet to be
that tuned out.

THE EXORCISM

George Sauer, the former Jet end, is coming back to
football.

This is the true story of how he decided that the game
wasn't as dehumanizing as he felt it was when he quit three
years ago.

Some of Sauer's teammates began to notice his strange
behavior about the time of the Super Bowl in 1969. He
turned up at a meeting reading *The Plague* by Camus instead of his playbook. Asked about it by an assistant coach,
he replied, in an eerie hoarse voice, "None of your bleeping
business."

No one had ever heard George Sauer curse before. It
was attributed to Super Bowl jitters.

In the exuberance of the postgame locker room, after
the Jets upset the Colts, people swore they saw Sauer's head
spin 360 degrees around his neck, but they laid that to an
illusion induced by mass hysteria.

When the Jets regrouped for pre-season practice the
following August, there was no mistaking what George
Sauer did. But the Jets laughed it off as a prank.

With the team gathered in a circle, as Weeb Ewbank
was about to send them off on a two-mile run, Sauer relieved himself. Even Ewbank chuckled over that one, inter-
preting it as a commentary on the rigors of getting in
shape.

Nobody laughed after that.

One night in the Jets' dormitory, Sauer's bed levitated, with Sauer sleeping in it, and ran a fly pattern down a hallway, faked right and cut sharply left into Joe Namath's room.

"George, I love you, but what is this all about?" Namath wondered.

Sauer spit a vile green liquid right in Namath's eye.

For the opening game, Sauer put on his uniform in a peculiar fashion. He wore his shoulder pads around his waist. His helmet was on his right foot. His jock hung from his left ear. A sock was pulled over his head.

Questioned by Ewbank, Sauer replied hoarsely, "Kiss my kneecap."

The Jets sent him to a psychiatrist.

Sauer told the psychiatrist that when he was very young he quit the Cub Scouts "because I didn't think it was a big deal to get stars for taking out garbage." Then he leaped out of his chair and karate chopped the psychiatrist.

The psychiatrist reported to the Jets that Sauer could be cured with sympathetic toilet training.

The Jets sent him to Pete Rozelle.

Sauer told Rozelle that football was an extension of social Darwinism (the survival of the fittest), that the violence reflected our involvement in Vietnam, that he didn't see why opponents had to be enemies, that it was degrading for adults to be tucked into bed at 11 P.M.

Just as Sauer was about to kick Rozelle below the belt, the front four of the Vikings pinned him down. Sauer was taken to a hospital for a spinal tap.

Rozelle reported to the Jets that Sauer could no longer distinguish between good and evil—winning and losing.

The Jets reluctantly accepted Sauer's resignation.

For the next three years Sauer tried to write a novel. One day a man appeared at his home in San Francisco. He said he was an exorcist. Sauer recognized him as one of the country's top football fans, Henry Kissinger. Kissinger chanted ancient chants for twenty-one days.

Last week George Sauer said he wanted to play foot-

ball again. He couldn't remember anything that happened
to him since the Super Bowl.

*Politics and sport collided most dramatically and violently in
the 1972 Olympics. The sudden shift from athletic combat to guer-
rilla warfare traumatized not a few sportswriters on the scene. All
of us, after all, had to some degree chosen sportswriting as a pleasur-
able dodge from reality. Instantly we were transformed into war
correspondents.*

THE TWENTY-THIRD SPORT

The lives of seventeen persons and the last spark of
innocence in the Olympic flame were extinguished in Munich yesterday.

Eleven members of the Israeli team, five Arab guerrillas and one German policeman are dead. The Olympic
movement, its ideal of promoting international amity exposed tragically as an illusion, is in critical condition.

In an Olympics vibrating with historic and political
irony—the return of the games to Germany thirty-six years
after the Nazi Olympics in Berlin, the expulsion of
Rhodesia on racial grounds by African nations that haven't
condemned the racism of Uganda—the final irony is that
Israelis, of all people, felt they were on safe ground.

Either because of a naive faith or uncharacteristic neg-
ligence, the Israelis did not secure themselves adequately.
Seven guerrillas had no trouble invading their quarters at
about four thirty yesterday morning.

"We could expect something like this in Frankfurt or
even Munich," said an Israeli tourist, "but not in the Olympic village."

The Israelis reportedly had requested extra security
measures before the games and were refused by the Germans, who were determined to maintain an image of non-
militarism. There, unfortunately, the Israelis let it stand.
The Russians used to provide their own security when the
political climate was tense for them.

Further, according to Israelis, they were alerted last week by boasts of guerrillas that they would terrorize Jews in Germany on Rosh Hashanah weekend.

Once the guerrillas struck, their politics of terror turned into a bizarre and probably inevitable dance of death when the Israeli government refused to yield to demands to free 200 political prisoners. Two Israelis were killed during the break-in. Nine hostages were in effect abandoned.

The midmorning drama was being played out in a gray, flat three-story building within a few hundred yards of thousands of spectators. The politics of terror had become the twenty-third sport of the Olympics.

Spectators stood two to ten deep around the fenced perimeter of the village, which is at the bottom of a natural bowl, where the Israelis were housed. Several hundred athletes were spectators themselves, clustered on terraces and half hidden behind abutments, watching vague, almost surreal movements. The men in the red and blue sweatsuits tiptoeing across rooftops with rifles and machine guns were police.

As insular as the Olympics tries to be, it is a reflection of the outside world. Life was going on too. Spectators could see athletes sunning themselves by a pool and running and jumping on a practice track.

The Olympic Park, built on the site of the airport where Neville Chamberlain came to arrange "peace in our time," overlooked by a grassy hill of World War II bomb debris, resembled a battlefield. Police and army trucks rumbled down the wide street adjacent to the park. The name of the street is Dachaustrasse.

Bulletins on the progress of negotiations were issued at the press center as batteries of television sets showed equestrian, volleyball and boxing events. Avery Brundage, who assured the triumph of Adolf Hitler's propaganda machine in 1936 by bulling through widespread opposition to the Games, said that these games would go on as scheduled. Brundage regards interference with the Olympics person-

ally, as though someone urinated in one of his priceless
Ming vases. Not until 4 P.M., seven hours after the first
announcement of the murders, was it decided to postpone
the evening's schedule.

The Olympics that the Germans had brilliantly and
sensitively planned as a celebration of youth and humanity—and as a $1 billion public relations gesture to
dramatize that the Germany of great German culture
had emerged from the rubble of German militarism—
was coming apart.

At 11 P.M. it crumbled. The guerrillas and the hostages
were helicoptered to an airport as a ruse to isolate them.
When two guerrillas left the helicopter to investigate a jet
they thought would transport them to North Africa, police
opened fire. Presumably they hoped some hostages would
escape in the dark and confusion. But hand grenades blew
up the helicopter and with it the remaining hostages.

Whether or not the Germans had any way out of the
dilemma, they seemed certain to reap a whirlwind of criticism that could have political repercussions. Germans said
that the government of Willy Brandt might be toppled in
December elections.

When fun and games get that big, they are too big.
Gigantism has destroyed the Olympic ideal. Gigantic costs
and gigantic exposure. The costs require government participation. The exposure makes it vulnerable to exploita-
tion. No one expected yesterday to happen—until it happened. Then it seemed logical.

You can't turn the Olympics into an armed camp to
prevent such tragedies. The alternative seems clear.

*I wonder now if the last line wrote itself, in the sense that in
trying to recreate the events in a broad context I simply had to come
to a strong conclusion. I cannot judge whether the tone of the piece
suggests how deeply wrenching the experience was.*

*I did not attend the previous Olympics in Mexico City, where
blacks demonstrated on the victory stand. These columns deal with*

events leading up to that action and its impact on two of the demonstrators.

HARD TIMES

These are hard times, and honest men differ on how to make them easier, on whether they can be made easier, on what the priorities are. Even a nation's toys have been drawn into the passions of the day. It has been inevitable since it first became obvious that Black Power no longer meant Jim Brown going off tackle, Willie Mays hitting one upstairs, Wilt Chamberlain stuffing.

The singular reality of the threatened black boycott of the Olympics is that it won't work. It won't work because Negroes themselves are divided on whether it is the right protest at the right time for the right reason. It won't work because if Tommie Smith or Lew Alcindor decides he must make his moral stand here, a kid will fall out of bed in Bogalusa, Louisiana, who can run the 220 a tenth of a second slower than Smith and decide he'd like to go to Mexico City and win a Gold Medal, and another one will amble off a playground in Indianapolis holding a basketball between two fingers thinking cool thoughts too. And if America wins a few less medals, that won't destroy the union, or add $10 billion to poverty programs, if that is the answer, either.

It won't work on almost any terms imaginable, or negotiable, and yet it is not an ignoble gesture. It comes from an anguish that white men can only guess at. Some young athletes who have escaped the ghetto because they can run and jump are willing to stand up for those who have a smaller chance of escape because they can't run or jump. Whether or not we feel they are mistaken, misguided and misled, there will be many Negroes who will be more uplifted by such a gesture than by yet another soul brother designated "world's fastest human."

Harry Edwards, the San Jose State sociology professor trying to organize the boycott, says, "This is our last chance to avert racial catastrophe in this country." He overdramatizes, but this is a point of view that must be heard. The fact that a Smith and an Alcindor would consider such a gesture suggests the depth of feeling among many Negroes.

The Olympics certainly seems like the wrong place and time for such a protest because it is the one parliament on earth where a man is truly judged on what he does, not on where he comes from or what he looks like.

But Edwards says we use the Olympics "to propagate the hypocrisy that the Negro is equal," that we try to sell our way of life to undeveloped countries, and that the threat of a boycott would be another lever in the fight for equality in underdeveloped inner America.

Maybe so. But how can it be measured? By what drop in what bucket?

There are others with different answers. You can't win if you don't run. You have to compete, to work through the institutions. Win enough races on tracks and ultimately you will win the race race.

Perhaps the issue can be defined through a secondary boycott proposed by Edwards, a boycott of the New York Athletic Club meet. Because the NYAC has never been, shall we say, eager to recruit Negroes as members, he asks, why should they compete in its meet? No Negroes, no meet. A track meet without Negroes would be like a flower show without roses. Who would go?

These are hard times and honest men differ, but only a few would aver, as one writer did, that in this society "a man can walk away from his environment, a black man or a white man." The walking is a lot easier if you are white. If you are black, it is easy only if you can run and jump.

JUST RUNNING

However much beer and gemütlichkeit are served up in Munich, the return of the Olympics to Germany will evoke bitter memories of the politically charged Nazi Olympics of 1936. Appropriately, as one of the central figures in the politicalization of the last Olympics, Lee Evans intends to be there.

He does not intend to get mixed up in politics.

In 1968 Lee Evans, Tommie Smith, and John Carlos, track stars at San Jose State, came under the influence of a professor there, Harry Edwards. The fire of black and white militancy was sweeping the country, especially on campuses, and Edwards and his pupils dramatized the burning issues for athletes. The flames engulfed and razed the New York Athletic Club meet. Lew Alcindor refused to try out for the Olympic team. Muhammad Ali already had been made a political victim.

Only days after the riots at the Democratic convention in Chicago, the black movement had its Iwo Jima in Mexico City. Smith and Carlos raised their fists in the Black Panther salute on the victory stand during the playing of "The Star-Spangled Banner."

That demonstration triggered the wave of black athlete protest that has yet to abate.

It also got Smith and Carlos hustled out of Mexico City by U.S. Olympic officials, further martyring them. Evans, after winning his race, was content to bow his head.

Only Evans remains in the Olympic picture.

The other night at the AAU meet Evans was reluctant to look very deeply into the 1968 scene and its aftermath. He said a few things that suggested that Smith, Carlos, and he felt they had been used, or that, at the least, they had to pay much more dues than anyone else, meaning Edwards. Smith and Evans, both split from their wives and teaching in San Jose, share a house. Evans said he visited Carlos a few weeks ago while he was in Canada for a meet. He has not seen Edwards, who lives 100 miles away from him, in nearly a year.

"I don't like to talk about it; I don't want to hurt anyone," Evans said. "It changed my life. It was a heavy learning experience. I was kind of naive. I found out a lot about people. . . . I'm glad I went through it, but I'm glad it's behind me. Some of us had to make a lot of sacrifices. Overall it was beautiful."

Shooting for an unprecedented repeat in the 400 meters, Evans said, "If you like to run, and I like to run, there's no reason why you can't keep going. I had adrenaline in Mexico City. I'll have adrenaline in Munich."

This time the adrenaline will be pumping for a political unit of one—himself.

UNDERDOG, UPPERDOG

Among life's little complexities is the problem of the dedicated underdog who finds himself in danger of becoming the upperdog. It can be a very unsettling thing. Consider John Carlos.

John Carlos, the sprinter and Olympic protester, is a natural-born underdog. He is black and he is involved and he is impatient. Also he is a natural-born upperdog. He can run like hell.

Bud Winter, the track coach at San Jose State, suggests that the natural-born underdog and the natural-born upperdog in Carlos are having one terrific dogfight with each other.

"John Carlos," Winter said, "is one of the strangest people ever put on the planet. He is potentially the world's greatest sprinter of all time. The only drawback he has to immortality as a runner, the only thing that can keep him from breaking world's records is that he likes the role of underdog. We call that the will to fail.

"He wants to be behind in the relay races. He wants to have the sympathy of being the underdog. I wonder what's going to happen when he sets that record in the 100. Once he gets it he isn't the underdog anymore."

Since his negative triumphs in the Olympics—a record in the trials dismissed because of his footwear, eviction from the team after his protest—the upperdog in Carlos seems to have taken over. He predicted that he would run 100 meters in 8.9 seconds—when 9 seconds flat hasn't been done yet. "No one since Adam has run 9 flat," said Winter. "But I like him thinking that way."

Winter has coached for twenty-five years. He has had many supersprinters: Tommie Smith and Ray Norton to name two. Smith was celebrated as the ultimate speedball. Carlos is on the verge of becoming the new ultimate.

"He has great inherent talent that has blossomed," said Winter. "He can break every sprint record there is. But it's going to take the right kind of motivation. He's like a powerful force that's ready to be unleashed, but you don't know if it's going to blow. You don't know where he's going from one moment to the next."

Carlos came off the starting blocks in Harlem, tried junior college in Texas, then gravitated to the track mecca of California. He's twenty-three, but only a sophomore. He still makes speeches up and down the coast for black causes. According to Winter, he's looking for a new direction to funnel his energy.

Despite Carlos's anger, despite the emotional if plaintive outbursts that make headlines, there is a solid side to him too. Winter doesn't baby sprinters, and he says Carlos is one of the hardest workers he ever had.

This weekend Carlos will run in a big coast relay meet and then jet to Philadelphia for the Freedom Games in honor of Martin Luther King. It may be time for the upperdog to put down the underdog for good.

Carlos never fulfilled his goals in track. Or did he? Track and field athletes are among the more fascinating studies for sportswriters. They are individualists, often introspective, given to running private races within themselves in public places.

SOME FINISH

At eleven twenty last night two dozen workmen began to dismantle the track at the Garden for the last time. It was easier than usual. An hour earlier Jim Ryun, running the last mile in the doomed barn, running with a stride as big as Kansas, running with a roar in his ear and a smile on his lips, tore it apart for them.

It took Ryun 3 minutes 57.5 seconds to loosen the boards and bolts and perhaps some of the bricks and girders too.

The mile is the glamour event of footracing, and Jim Ryun is the glamour boy, twenty years old, the world record holder. So when the NCAA advertised to come "see Jim Ryun run" in the last meet at the old Garden it was an invitation to a small piece of history. A crowd of 15,002, biggest of the season, came.

The appearance of a supermiler and the prospect of a good race transforms the hurly-burly carnival of indoor track into a theater in the oval. The national anthem is sung just before the big race. The introductions are lavish: "Jim Ryun, the golden boy from Kansas." The ovation is thunderous.

At least it seemed thunderous. In a few minutes it would swell from one hysterical crescendo to another and another, thousands of tenors and sopranos waking the ghosts of Nurmi and Cunningham and Santee and O'Hara.

"Ninety-nine percent of the time you don't hear anything," said Ryun, who is hard-of-hearing. "But I heard it. It was exciting."

There were five others in the race, two of them serious competitors. Sam Bair, 120 pounds, out of Kent State, as tall as one of Ryun's legs. Dave Patrick, the powerhouse from Villanova who had beaten Ryun in their only confrontation, at the half mile.

Check that. There was one more starter, the only real competition for Ryun—the clock.

Ryun broke out on top with Bair right behind and Patrick fifth. Bair took the lead on the second lap. Ryun loped on his heels, and Patrick was fourth. The time for the quarter was a pedestrian 61.2.

"It took me a long time to learn that if you want to run a fast time you have to do it yourself," Ryun said. In an unpretentious way that was a great athlete or great artist saying he has to compete against himself. Ryun began to race himself, and the clock, in the second quarter.

He sprinted into the lead and held on there, not extending himself yet, duplicating the first quarter for a 2:02.4 half. As Ryun gradually stretched his lead to fifteen yards, there was a feeling that he had something in mind and the crowd started a sustained roar. Patrick sprinted into second place, and the roar rose to a shriek. His move flattened out, but the din didn't.

It hit some decibels that shook the seismograph at Fordham when Ryun, after passing the three-quarter mark in 3:00.5, blasted off. He was grinning. "You could see he was stimulated by the crowd," said Bob Timmons, his coach. "He felt like he had it."

The rest of the field resembled a string of valets chasing Danny Kaye out of a hotel. Imperially alone, Ryun opened up that Kansas stride and chased the clock. Lifted by the frenzied crowd, Ryun said, "I was surprised I was going that fast."

The gun sounding the last lap was nearly drowned out by the bedlam. Athletes urged Ryun on, bouncing up and down in their brightly colored track suits. "Run, Jim, run," yelled the Garden in attitudes of arm-waving frenzy. He wobbled coming out of the last turn, straightened out and went for the tape.

I like that. It's a narrative about an event written under extreme deadline pressure, in an hour and a half or so. Which is lightning for me because I am notoriously slow, taking as much time as I have and then some. The guy who picks up the paper, including me, doesn't care how long I took, although editors have been known to get exercised.

RUNNING FOR FOURTH PLACE

If Ben Jipcho was an hour, Sam Bair would be a minute. Ben Jipcho is the best of the professional distance runners, an international star. Sam Bair runs professionally too. He's considered hot stuff at Allegheny County Community College in Pittsburgh.

Ben Jipcho and Sam Bair will run in the mile at the Garden tomorrow. Jipcho has won the mile so routinely that it has become a race for second place. Except for Bair. "I'm running for fourth place," he said. "I can use the money."

Fourth place will be worth $550 to Bair—$50 for the finish and $500 for the cumulative points that would give him for the season's tour. His earnings since track and field went legit last year are "about $1,000."

Sam Bair is what running for supper is about too. His rewards are a round-trip plane ticket, a hotel room, $20 a day for food, and a chance to indulge his muse. "I just love to run," he said. "A guy I worked for once told me, 'You can't keep running with that silly smirk on your face all the time.' I don't believe him."

To support his running habit—"I feel guilty if I don't put in twenty miles a day," he said—the twenty-eight-year-old Bair has sold insurance, dug ditches and graves, worked in a nuts-and-bolts factory and taught school. He lost one teaching job because he skipped classes on Fridays to get to a starting line somewhere, somehow. By turning pro he could do something he couldn't do as an amateur—coach. He is an assistant at Allegheny.

"In a way I don't regard myself as a professional," Bair said. "I'm running mainly for the satisfaction and recognition. I'm not really groping for money. But people do respect you more as a professional. If you go to an employer and tell him you'd like to run in an amateur meet, he looks at you like you're crazy. If you're a pro he looks at you differently. Kids look up to you more. You have status."

That's a commentary on our changing values, for pro track hasn't achieved much status in the upper-tax-bracket world of play yet. Its pay scale couldn't get an NBA scrub out of bed. Only if it survives long enough to get graduates of the 1976 Olympics and then provide incentives for record breaking in events like the mile will its top performers be able to move up to the Rolls Royce standards of modern athletes. Bair, running in the draft of Jim Ryun, ran a 3:56.7

mile five years ago, but like Jipcho and Ryun he hasn't approached his best time as a pro.

"In college you have a better background in cross-country, and you're anxious to find out how good you are, so you get mentally ready for big meets," Bair said. "As a pro you have to run in big meets week after week. You sort of get into a rut after a while because you're running against the same guys. It's hard to get superpsyched every week to go out and lose."

With the proper incentives, Bair believes, the pros will start to set records. But right now fourth place is all the incentive he has. He said he can use that $550 to help buy a new car. A little car.

THE LAST AMATEUR

Nobody has come out of nowhere—besides the fictional Joe Hardy—to engage Babe Ruth in immortal combat.

Nobody has walked out of a tryout camp and beaten out Jim Brown.

Nobody has come out of a schoolyard and gone one-on-one with Oscar Robertson.

Nobody does those things in the real world. They are the stuff of adolescent fantasy.

But Dr. Delano Merriwether has done it.

This is an Olympic year, when runners and jumpers and throwers are said to materialize out of the woodwork. This means that a young athlete who has been running, jumping and throwing in relative obscurity is thrust by termite dedication and ambition into prominence. Dr. Delano Merriwether is not such a product. He materialized out of a medical laboratory—out of a test tube perhaps.

Track and field, a menagerie of the tall and short and fat and skinny and crazy and crazier, has never known such a phenom. He burst on the scene last season, a put-on apparition in yellow bathing trunks, a flowing white hospital shirt and suspenders, looking like an eager intern making a house call. He wobbled out of the starting blocks as though he had medical bags in both hands. Yet in short dashes that are virtually all start, he won some and was close some. And then, at the age of twenty-eight, in his first major outdoor meet, he won the 100-yard dash in the National AAUs with a spectacular though wind-aided nine seconds flat.

Walter Mitty was alive and well. Frank Merriwell seemed like an impostor. And the best part of it was that Dr. Delano Merriwether was doing it just for fun. There were no foreign trips or public relations jobs at the end of the runway.

"Running is just a healthy option for me," he said the other day. "I don't run to compete. I run for exercise and fun. I haven't thought about the Olympics. I don't have the time to worry about it.

"And I can't wear a sign that says I won the AAUs and make it on that. It's what you do next time that counts. It's like a pathology clinic. If I examined fifty-five gallbladders and analyzed them perfectly I still have to examine the next one."

Dr. Delano Merriwether is a hematologist, a blood specialist. He is with the Harvard staff at the Boston City Hospital, teaching and doing research. He runs a couple times a week after work. (Dr. Roger Bannister trained for the first four-minute mile on his lunch hours.) Sometimes his wife takes movies of his starts with the family camera. "I still forget everything as soon as the gun goes off," he said. "I've got to go with what I've got."

What he's got are long legs, a smile to match his sunny perspective and a curiosity rather than a yearning for blood.

"I'd like to emphasize something besides the cockiness and aggressiveness that so many people associate with sprinters," he said.

He is The Last Amateur.

My favorite event is the Boston Marathon. This is why.

THE ZOO WONDERFUL

They opened the pens of Animal Farm again yesterday, loosing herds of strange and wonderful creatures on the countryside and cityside. Twelve hundred and twenty primates ran in the seventy-sixth Boston Marathon and hundreds of thousands of affectionate zoo keepers lavished love and food on them.

There are many beautiful vantage points to watch the menagerie pass by on the serpentine route from suburban Hopkinton to downtown Boston, none more beautiful than Wellesley College.

Wellesley is about halfway through the race, just before the smiles and hopes of the starters begin to turn to pain and jellied insides. The girls of Wellesley line both sides of the road to provide orange quarters, water and good cheer to the runners.

Last year a few of the girls donned togas and plopped grapes in each other's mouths while sprawled on a divan, a sign above their intellects warning, "The Last Temptation." Others waited in ambush for a noted author with the sign, "Erich Segal, This Is Your Penance, Male Chauvinist Pig." Yesterday they singled out an obscure burgher from Milwaukee because of the following advertisement that appeared in the *Wellesley News*:

> Dear Girls: A good friend of mine, John Archer, and I have been running in the Boston Marathon—he for the last four years—and whenever he runs past the Wellesley girls he lets out with a cheer, "Yea, Wellesley." John will be fifty-eight years old in July, his nickname is Black Bart (for his jet black hair) and his number this year is 251. He should be running by Wellesley about 1:30 and I'd appreciate it if you would give "Black Bart" a cheer.

It was signed "Syd Ludington No. 248," and, of course, the girls of Wellesley prepared an appropriate welcome. A Burma Shave sequence of signs went: "Half a Race/ In Half an Hour/ Fallen Archer/ Wellesley Power . . . Black Bart." When Black Bart himself hove into view, the girls squealed. He replied with a raised fist and a "Yea, Wellesley," and when he saw the special welcome he reached out to touch them and did a half pirouette in full stride.

This rite-of-spring spirit bathes the Boston Marathon in a country fair glow. The runners get high on liniment, high on pain, high on love. "The spectators are fantastic," said Nina Kuscsik. "The applause goes right through you."

Nina Kuscsik, the thirty-three-year-old housewife by way of Brooklyn College, won the race-within-a-race for girls, the first time they have been officially entered. Running between two big men, she received no special notice at Wellesley, but at Boston College, eight miles up the road, she was given a rollicking cheer that momentarily anesthetized her stomach cramps.

The girls of Wellesley had healing powers too. "They pick you up," one middle-aged jogger said, "just when you need it." A younger fellow ran the gantlet of affection blowing kisses and panting, "I love you, I love you, I love you." Erich Segal greeted them with a smile and wave, and for being a good sport after last year's hazing he got a lusty reception. Dick Gregory, the former presidential candidate, flashed a peace sign and heard a chorus of "right-ons" in return. Blind Joe Prado, the former St. Louis Browns farmhand, carrying a red and white cane, sped through grinning.

On and on they came. Dr. George Sheehan and three of his sons. Frank Stranahan, the former socialite golfer. Chuck Davey, looking worse than he did after Kid Gavilan finished with him. Seven cops from the Los Angeles Police Department. Emmett Eastman, a Sioux Indian from North Dakota. Ted Corbett, a legendary figure among long distance runners, having run in races up to 100 miles. Larry Boise, a handsome kid who sent one Wellesley girl into rapture.

"No. 121," she cried, "is mine."

A Finn won the race, a Colombian was second, a Mexican third. There were no losers, only winners and survivors. The idea isn't to beat the guy ahead of you or the guy behind you as much as the guy inside you. Or girl.

Four years after she started jogging for exercise, Nina Kuscsik, a mother of three, had the green halo of a Boston Marathon laurel wreath set on her head by Mayor Kevin White. She seemed on the verge of collapse and later she cracked into tears. "I don't have plans to put out ever again like today," she said. "But that's until tomorrow."

Spoken like a true strange and wonderful marathon creature.

That was one of the early breakthroughs of the women's movement into male preserves. Of all the movements, this one probably is the most meaningful, on and off the sports page.

THE MS. MILE

On television from the Astrodome last weekend a lady on a motorcycle vroomed up a ramp, soared over ten parked cars, vroomed down another ramp and, with her blond hair ducking a low-hanging pipe, disappeared under the stands. It was an inspiring performance, proving that women have as much right as men to risk their fool necks.

Not everyone agrees with that notion, however, which is what makes the Ms. Metric Mile at the Olympic Invitation Meet so provocative.

The Ms. Metric Mile, featuring Francie Larrieu, who broke the indoor mile record last weekend, has been underwritten by *Ms.* magazine, the house organ of women's liberation. *Ms.* donated several thousand dollars to the U.S. Olympic Committee to pay for the expenses of the six entrants, including two Europeans. *Ms.* also has invited dozens of schoolgirl track stars to the meet.

That, according to *Ms.* publisher Pat Carbine, is just for openers. *Ms.* plans to support women's track at the regional level and eventually run its own meet. Presumably there will be a special men's invitational mile at that one.

"This is the beginning of something," Pat Carbine said. "We want to encourage young women—as Billie Jean King has—to know that their efforts to be excellent will be recognized and rewarded."

That's the provocative part, for the goal of *Ms.* is to get young women a fairer share of the monies allocated for sports in schools and colleges. When the crunch comes, entrenched interests cry a lot. Typical is the Oklahoma University athletic department, which has a $3 million budget. Recently it yielded to pressure by siphoning a whole $1500 for women student-athletes. Call us the unfair sex.

Call George Gilder the unfairest of the unfair. George Gilder has written a book, *Sexual Suicide,* challenging the women's movement. "Sports," said Pat Carbine, "reflects the seismic change we're all into," and Gilder is shook by the earthquake.

Gilder contends that sports for boys and men are essentially masculinity rites and a "moral universe" where we pursue "noble ideals." Sports for girls and women, he suggests, should be rites of grace and beauty celebrating femininity. *Da* Olga Korbut, the bird of a Russian gymnast. *Nyet* Tamara Press, the whale of a Russian shot-putter.

Replied Pat Carbine, "By whose light is Olga Korbut more feminine than Olga Connolly [the American discus thrower]? We're not all diminutive. Why should the rest of us be made to feel abnormal?"

As a clever polemicist, Gilder swats the sillier polemics of women's lib like a hitter jumping on a fat pitch. The best women athletes will never measure up to the best men athletes in speed and strength sports. The issue is not men vs. women. The issue is whether women have a right to play anything they want to play.

"Why is it all right for women to get sweaty and hot picking fruit and cleaning offices," said Pat Carbine, "but not playing games?"

Gilder can be silly too. He asks, "Am I wrong to observe that a great many women's sports events are boring for spectators, unless one of the girls is pretty?"

In a word, yes.

When Francie Larrieu went for her record, fans stood and cheered as though she were Jim Ryun.

The women's pro tennis tour is playing to sellouts, because the tennis frequently is more interesting than men's tennis, and because the women are frequently more interesting than the men as people.

In Iowa, girls high school basketball was, and remains, a popular rage before anyone heard of women's lib.

Gilder would conjure visions of a world populated by Tamara Presses who reduce truck drivers to sobbing, impotent hulks by invading their saloons and beating them at wrist wrestling. That's not the way it's going to be at all. They simply want the right to order a shot and a beer.

THE OCEANSIDE SOLUTION

A tomboy used to be a girl who wore dungarees instead of skirts, played with boys instead of girls, and grew up to be the most popular and perhaps the prettiest and most feminine woman in the class. Today some folks regard her as a threat to the moral order, the male order and the batting order. She's come a long way, Abner.

It's hard to say which is the more significant event for baseball, Hank Aaron breaking Babe Ruth's record or record numbers of babes wanting to break into the Little League.

Lawsuits to open up Little Leagues to girls have inspired a variety of responses, many of them emotional, a few of them sensible. One of the suits was filed in behalf of the daughter of Dallas Green, a former pitcher for the Phillies who now runs their farm system, who reminded the Gullivers of Lilliput that the idea, after all, is for the kids to have fun.

But even women are fudging on that proposition now. Some feminists who used to argue that Little League was overorganized and overcompetitive have decided that is exactly what the next generation of career women should have.

While Little League headquarters in Williamsport, Pennsylvania, carries the banner of boy chauvinism to court, and while Congress ponders an equal rights amendment to the Little League charter, the game goes on. It goes on in Oceanside, Long Island, separately and perhaps equally. It goes on in New Jersey angrily.

Sam Cooperman forestalled a crisis in Oceanside by bringing back the sweetest name a defunct minor league ever had—the Sally League. It is, of course, a Little League for girls. When tryouts were held, 160 ten- to twelve-year-olds threw away their Barbie dolls and came running.

"It's been beautiful, unbelievable," said Cooperman, a Little League official. "We knew they could catch and throw, but much to my surprise some of them are very good players. None of them requested to join boys' teams, but three or four are capable of it and in a year or two there'll be a whole lot more. The most amazing thing is the enthusiasm. We're getting larger turnouts for their games than for Little League games."

The Oceanside solution suggests two things. Those men threatened by infield-grass-roots demands for equal opportunity can relax. Given another choice, it isn't likely that girls will invade the boys' den in large numbers. But they must be given a choice. As much as one is gratified by the squeals of enthusiasm for baseball, the fact remains that many girls don't have a choice. Half the girls who showed up for tryouts in Oceanside were shut out because there weren't enough facilities.

After the courts forced the Little League in New Jersey to take in girls, it was too late for a compromise Sally League. In Ridgefield, where one spirited girl insisted on playing with boys, she took a brutal ribbing from the town punks when she finally made it. Ray Platoni, a Little League official, said, "If too many girls came out we wouldn't have room for them."

The issue is so highly charged that defenders of the

true faith make irrational claims. Girls might get breast cancer or be permanently disfigured. They might be touched on private parts by boys. How would it look for a manager to pat a girl on the behind after a game-winning hit, or rub a sore spot after a mishap? (They have women coaches for that in Oceanside.)

Ray Platoni is one of a group of dedicated men who raise $20,000 annually for structured baseball programs in Ridgefield. They are so disturbed by girls' liberation that they vow to quit after this season. They are as hurt and confused as tribal elders told they have to teach girls to hunt for food. Not only would that spoil the masculine rituals of the hunt, but why bother if the girls are only going to grow up to have babies?

"I feel in my heart that I don't want to do it with girls," Platoni said. "They won't stick with it. With a boy, one of them might make something of himself and you could say you were a part of it. They say it's only kids and let them play, but that isn't the way the organization is set up. It's a social thing with the men too."

What do we do now, Abner?

We segue to Billie Jean King, the jock queen. With one spectacular show biz stunt that grabbed people where they breathe, her coronation as a legend and a leader was assured. Herewith my before and after.

SHE IS WOMAN, HE IS MAN

Right here in Houston, Texas, where fortunes have been made digging into the ground and fortunes spent exploring space, where men are men and they never let each other or women forget it, Billie Jean King and Bobby Riggs will meet tonight in the biggest floating hustle of all time.

Right here in the Astrodome, that monument to the modern mix of sports and show business, Billie Jean King and Bobby Riggs will pat tennis balls at each other in front of a record crowd—locally, nationally and internationally —for a record jackpot.

She is woman, he is man.

She is the one woman, besides Gloria Steinem, most closely associated with women's liberation in America. She single-handedly elevated women's tennis to equal pay if not equal play.

He may be the first athlete in history to be a legend in two different times, as a world champion player and world champion hustler. He has become an elfin spokesman for the terror that strikes men's hearts.

That is an overly serious assessment of what on the surface is an underly serious match. The tennis boom will explode tonight with a circus cacophony of "ladees and genelmun . . ." and nobody can get hurt. The loser has a $100,000 guarantee.

And indeed the promotion has been worth its weight in smiles, in good dirty fun, in passionate debate and in identifying.

Bobby Riggs has earned the lion's share of credit for that. Without lioness Billie Jean King's leadership there would be no women's movement in pro sports for Riggs to rail against, but his antics have kept the thing fizzing like a natural spring.

His Lob vs. Lib put-downs of women begin to pall from repetition, but they are still worth laughs in Texas, where Riggs is seen as a latter-day cowboy more comfortable on a horse than in a parlor. At a party an old friend of his grabbed a microphone and gave a drunken harangue about the glory of women in "frilly dresses." Nearby sat a doll on a pedestal marked "pedestal."

So beneath the symbol of male chauvinism that Riggs has adopted and exploited beats the heart of real chauvinist piggery. Seriously, folks, there are a lot of folks taking him and the match seriously. The grimmer males of the species identify with his bluster and his dreams of conquest. After he humiliated Margaret Court, Riggs was taken to the bosom of Hollywood, literally. His spree included a wench who hustled $1,800 out of his wallet as he slept. He mused recently, "I wasn't really good with the girls. I wasn't smooth. I made the move too soon."

Billie Jean King has paid a separate but equal kind of dues. A lifetime of competition seems to have toughened her with calluses. Her battle for equal rights has put a scratchy shrillness in her public voice. Her marriage apparently has cracked up, although her husband remains her business partner. Yet she blossoms as a woman.

But the play is the thing. In common with millions of others, I've been hustled by Bobby Riggs again because I think it will be a real match. And I think she will win, for when the revolution comes it eventually gets us all. Even in Texas, home for a woman is no longer at the range.

HUSTLER OUTHUSTLED

All right, men, quit brooding and get to the dishes. Make sure the beds have hospital corners. And on the way to the supermarket why don't you stop off at the doctor's office for a little vasectomy? We've been the unfair sex for millennia. Last night we surrendered unconditionally.

Bobby Riggs, carrying the banner of male chauvinism, went down in flames.

Billie Jean King, carrying the banner of women's liberation, shot him down.

In a once-in-a-lifetime promotion that would have made P. T. Barnum and Tex Rickard swoon, she-is-woman beat he-is-man in straight sets 6–4, 6–3, 6–3.

Before the largest audience ever to witness a tennis match, or a circus—30,472 in the Astrodome and many millions on television, in thirty-six countries—Billie Jean King reduced the oinking Bobby Riggs to a ham sandwich. She ate him up and picked her teeth with his racket.

"I said I was a fifty-five-year-old man with one foot in the grave," Riggs said. "It's one and a half now."

Billie Jean King was simply too good for Bobby Riggs. He had taken his magnificent "Battle of the Sexes" hustle as far as it could go—until it got to a woman who could play the game and not the stakes. A hustler is someone who isn't intimidated by the stakes. That is a definition of a great athlete as well. Billie Jean King is a great athlete. She was raised in a competitive environment to do exactly what she did last night—be at her best when the money, a $100,000 jackpot and lots of commercial "fringies," as she calls them, was on the table.

"There's something in my psyche, my personality," Billie Jean King said, "that gets me up for the main event."

"Under the pressure and tension," admitted Riggs, a legendary money player, "she did better than I did."

Riggs knew it was a game on the second point, a textbook rally of lobs, volleys, drop shots, backhands and forehands. Riggs hit enough good shots to win a set against the country club suckers who love to lose to him. But he lost the point to Billie Jean on some amazing recoveries. "Her quickness," he said, "was too much for me." And he wasn't wearing galoshes or holding a dog on a leash or doing any of those exotic handicaps he dreams up for his hustles.

His only handicap was her. The only thing he beat her at was huckstering.

When they arrived at center court, she borne like an Egyptian queen, he wheeled in a rickshaw, as though it was a summit meeting of Cleopatra and Confucius, she could only sigh a "God!" at the hokeyness, but he rose to the occasion by remembering, "Where's my Hai Karate aftershave?" She stripped off a blue sweatsuit and emerged resplendent in a pastel blue dress with rhinestones and sequins across the shoulders. He, shameless, wore a windbreaker with "Sugar Daddy" (a candy sponsor) emblazoned on the back. The two plugs were worth a reported $95,000 to him.

A couple of hours later Billie Jean King looked like she could run the Boston Marathon and Bobby Riggs looked like he had both feet in the grave. She toyed with him, like a daughter now tweaking her father's cheek, now jabbing him in the ribs, now mussing his hair. His entourage of trainers and medicine men rubbed ice on his legs and arms and forehead as though he were a beaten fighter. What he was, was a tired old man.

"I feel this is the culmination of my career," she said. "Ever since I was eleven years old and I couldn't get in a tennis picture because I didn't have tennis dress, and I thought tennis was a game only for the rich and the white, I wanted to change the game."

So the short and happy resurrection of Bobby Riggs comes to an end and the folk herohood of Billie Jean King begins. For his farewell he leaned over and nibbled on her ear.

It was a culmination for me too. I won $165 in the writers' pool for picking the score closest to the result. She was woman, he was man, I am tennis nut. And consumer advocate.

RACKET RACKET

Man walks into Herman's sporting goods emporium on 42nd Street, goes to the tennis department, asks for a look at the newfangled C-6 graphite racket. Man says, "I'm not much of a player but I've got a lot of money and I want something nobody else has."

This actually happened, according to a salesman, Craig White. The purchase was made. The price, including stringing and tax, came to $175.

The racket racket strikes again.

For conspicuous consumers who need Gucci and Louis Vuitton labels to advertise their chic, next on the list no doubt is the pearl-handled, chrome-coated, radar-directed, leopard-skin-cased number that guarantees backhand winners down the line.

If you have to ask how much it costs, as the saying goes, you can't afford it. Maintenance alone is staggering. You'll need a jeweler to polish it, a physicist to tune it up, and a game warden to protect it.

"There seems to be a competition to see who can make the most expensive racket," said an unlikely skeptic, Skip

DeWald. DeWald runs about the most chic, i.e., expensive, tennis shop there is, Feron's.

The C-6 (C for carbon, which graphite is derived from; 6 for its atomic number) is not the most expensive racket on the market, it develops. The Chemold graphite job gives you another $10 worth of snob appeal.

The Herman's in the Wall Street area sold six of the C-6s this week after an ad appeared in the *Times*. Salesman Dave Butler said, "One of two types buys it. Somebody who is so rich he doesn't know what to do with his money, and addicts who have to scrape it up."

Graphite is a very hard form of carbon. The manufacturers claim that, unlike wood and metal rackets, the graphite won't bend on impact with a tennis ball, thereby giving it a larger solid hitting area. How many suckers it creates remains to be seen.

There are graphite shafts on golf clubs now, selling for more than $100 apiece. But they are said to demonstrably add yardage to drives. Distance is not a factor in tennis, unless you are Ilie Nastase and you want to swat a ball out of the stadium.

Remember when metal rackets were going to make Rod Lavers of us all? "I wish I had a dollar," said Skip DeWald, "for every person who has come back to wood. Metal isn't trendy anymore."

Before the carbon era came to get us, the big prestige racket was the Head. It cost about $75 strung. Today they are getting as hard to find as Buicks with tailfins.

So too is the Chemold aluminum racket, which was introduced with a major advertising campaign. It was endorsed by Rod Laver and other pros. When Laver lost a few matches with it, he gave it up and offered to return his fee. To avoid embarrassment, Chemold permitted him to use a wood racket that was painted the same metallic color as the discarded one. Laver posed a lot with Chemold racket covers.

The thing about metal rackets is that they weren't a great leap forward in form or function, only in price and profit. They may serve a useful purpose to some women, old folks and tender elbows. But to the hordes of new tennis players who are trying to learn how to stroke a ball correctly rather than trampoline it wildly, they are as fast food is to eating.

For $40 to $50 you can get all the wood racket you'll ever need. Wood is as comfortable as an old rocking chair. As Stan Isaacs, the Long Island columnist says, wood is good.

CHRIS

Chris Evert is sixteen years old and she hasn't even won her first major tennis championship yet. She may end this scandalous state of affairs this weekend at Forest Hills.

There in the U.S. Open little Chris Evert has been behaving like a fantastic Barbie doll for the last ten days. She walks, she talks, she changes costumes, she hits tennis balls.

Wind her up and she gives cute little interviews with cute smiles and cute modesty, cutely amazed over her forty-five straight victories and her emergence as the darling of fuzzball and the savior of the biggest tournament in America. She probably would cutely faint if she knew about the fuss she was causing on Madison Avenue, where advertising executives, troubled over the defection of top men stars, have been making offerings in the memory of Maureen Connolly in hopes that Chris Evert beats Billie Jean King in the semifinals so that cute things will happen to the TV ratings for the finals.

But on the tennis court, while she cuts a cute little figure, little Chris Evert plays a game of tennis that is about as cute as Ernie Terrell standing behind the baseline, carefully pumping jabs at the other guy. She stands there cutely and pow-crash-boom, the other gal winds up with a tennis ball lodged in her face.

Margaret Smith Court is a big lady with a big game, but she gives the appearance of soft feminine vulnerability. Chris Evert, for all her cuteness, plays with a brass metronome ticking inside her. Playing her is like playing a wall. She goes to the net for one reason: to accept congratulations.

This is how her father, a pro in Fort Lauderdale, Florida, taught her to play, as though she came out of a primer. She serves in sections, or panels, so deliberately that you can count the illustrations. Her racket goes back almost militarily on her forehand. Her two-handed backhand is a holdover from infancy. (There are three more tennis prodigies at home, and a three-year-old sister who has shown promise with a flyswatter.)

The thinking at Forest Hills is that Chris Evert just might make it to the net two more times. Margaret Smith Court said, "She's got all the girls quaking."

The tournament regulars regard her with mixed emotions. She has attracted the focus of all tennis to those who play in skirts and pantaloons, which is nice. But her pure defensive style is exposing them as players. "Some of the girls don't think she's that good," said Billie Jean King, who is willing to be shown. "But if you have the stature to be great, it shows at that age."

Losing, Chris Evert would still be a winner because there would still be Everests to climb. Winning, well, that would be a fairy tale, it was suggested to Billie Jean King.

"That's what sport is about, isn't it?" she said.

THE STATUS INJURY

The fashionable injury is tennis elbow. The urban gamesman can get a lot of terrific injuries, but if it isn't tennis elbow it's Bridgeport.

A broken leg is déclassé. Once upon a time a broken leg meant something. During the winter it indicated a glamorous fall down a snowy mountain and pretty girls offering therapy. Now a broken leg is a bore.

Strained ligaments and a trick knee bespeak good breeding, and a pulled muscle has a solid utilitarian quality about it. But these are minor injuries. So too is a tacky ankle sprain. Strained ligaments would no more talk to an ankle sprain than eat at Howard Johnson's.

A torn hamstring muscle is something else. That

crosses class lines. The unmistakable pop in the thigh reveals to the urban gamesman that he indeed has such a muscle, a muscle he thought only blue-blooded Mickey Mantles and Kyle Rotes had.

The up-and-coming injury is the ruptured Achilles tendon. It's an injury for stars that hasn't trickled down to the rest of us yet.

Tennis elbow has trickled down and become a giant status wave. Tennis elbow is so big that you don't have to play tennis to get it anymore. Pitchers complain of tennis elbow. Quarterbacks complain of tennis elbow. If Isaac Stern fiddles too much he complains about tennis elbow.

"Violinists, conductors, housewives who iron too much, typists who type too much, golfers, they all get tennis elbow," Dr. Daniel Manfredi said in his Park Avenue office.

It is not for nothing that Dr. Daniel Manfredi has his office on Park Avenue. The resident physician at Forest Hills tournaments for twenty-five years, he probably is the biggest tennis elbow doctor around. He certainly is the best known. With the tennis boom on, he has very nearly cornered an important market.

People come from all over the country to be treated by Dr. Manfredi. This is the pinnacle of tennis elbowdom, like being gowned by Dior. Fully one fourth of his practice is devoted to tennis elbows, about 200 cases annually, of which, he said, 90 percent are cured.

Small wonder. A tennis elbow feels relief immediately upon entering Dr. Manfredi's office because instead of the usual medical paraphernalia lying around he has—a tennis racket. The essentials are a table, a cabinet and an old wood tennis racket.

Tennis elbow is a fancy label for stretched tendons or damaged ligaments. Dr. Manfredi, a wiry athletic-looking man in his fifties, a tennis player naturally, said that in years gone by it usually was diagnosed as arthritis because it is most common to players who are thirty-five or older. He defines the precise nature of the injury by having the patient swing the racket against an opposing force—himself—and by the use of a Japanese finger cot and a hand-strength tester. The finger cot is a weight attached to coils that fit around the fingers. When the patient says "ouch" to the applied pressure, Dr. Manfredi replies "backhand" or "forehand." And the patient can return to his or her tennis game, violin, ironing board or typewriter.

"When it hurts on the outside, it's the backhand that causes it," he said. "When it hurts on the inside, it's the forehand. Usually you get it by trying to put too much top spin on the ball."

The cure can include some or all of the following: he recommends that players hit the ball flat for a while, without rolling their wrists. For older players he may recommend a light metal racket. To speed recovery he injects the elbow with hydrocortisone. He uses Japanese acupuncture. He prescribes muscle-relaxing pills and liniment and razzle-dazzle exercises.

The reason tennis elbows love Dr. Manfredi is that, unlike doctors less experienced with tennis elbows and tennis heads, he doesn't recommend too much rest, seven to ten days at most. "The tennis player can't conceive of rest," he said. "He'd go crazy if you told him to stop playing."

And himself? "I've had mild problems. But I don't treat myself. I can't afford my prices."

Tennis has supplanted boxing as our main one-on-one game. Muhammad Ali has been what is left of big-time boxing in America for the last decade, so all these columns are about Ali and his opponents, who for several years included much of polite society and its elected and appointed politicians.

ALI BABY

It is said that truth is the first victim of war. The furor over Muhammad Ali at least grievously wounds a few truths about him.

Those who view him as evil incarnate, as a threat to Western civilization and as a poor misguided child, those who interpret his every move or statement through a one-dimensional Muslim prism, miss the essential Ali Baby. They have blinded themselves to the fun that still gushes from him.

One of the interesting sidelights to his predraft physical this week was the remark of one of the young men with him that he seemed so entertaining and down-home because "he was away from the Muslims." Why must we believe that the bogeymen we create are as humorless as we are?

The Muslims in their undertaker tidiness are indeed a grim lot in public. But they could no more gag Ali Baby than they could convert Floyd Patterson. They are, in fact, his best audience. Membership in the sect does not automatically exclude laughter—except among the nonbelievers who never laughed at him to begin with.

This is in evidence any time Ali Baby can be observed for, say, ten minutes. He still makes people laugh. When the professional cynics see this, they shake their heads and murmur, "Tsk, tsk, he could've been a credit to his race."

When he was in town to fight Zora Folley, Ali was asked some nonsensical questions simply to measure his mood. Willie Mays, asked the same questions once, was suspicious and uncooperative. Ali Baby took off on wild paper-plane flights of fantasy.

What's your favorite number?

"Nine. Yes, nine. I used to like to write nines in school. I like the way nine looks, a circle and a curl. My favorite two numbers are sixty-six. I believe there's a prophetic meaning in numbers."

If you had to give up ice cream or steak, which would you choose?

"Steak. You can always eat hamburger, roast beef, lamb and veal. I like ice cream too much. Chocolate and vanilla. Integrated."

Which would you rather have, a big dog or a little dog?

"I had a little dog when I was young, a little white dog with spots. We called him Spot. He was a sick dog. He died. If I got a dog now I'd want a big dog, a great big dog. Woof, woof."

A second essential of Ali Baby that is generally missed is that while he may be relatively unlettered he sees things less as a child than with a child's open curiosity, an unadulterated adult. Thus, when he was matched with George Chuvalo, he identified him as a "White Hope," scandalizing the boxing community, which acknowledged it privately. Thus, when Howard Cosell patronized him with, "You're a bright boy, Muhammad," he shot back, "You're not as dumb as you look."

Dumb Ali Baby isn't. Naive maybe, especially about some aspects of the Muslims, but doesn't naiveté and/or faith go hand in hand with all religious conviction? What makes him "brainwashed" while others are merely pious or zealous?

He is not an intellectual. It is easy target practice to shoot his arguments full of holes. But that doesn't mean he can't make more sense than respected muck-a-mucks on some issues. "We are fighting for the freedom of the Vietnamese. Why can't I have freedom of religion?" Argue with that.

He challenges our values. He makes us uncomfortable. Which is why the American Civil Liberties Union had to come to his aid this week, charging he was being punished by boxing authorities who stripped him of his title because of his unpopular political and social beliefs.

Ali Baby isn't wise beyond wisdom and good beyond goodness. He has shown flashes of the ugly side of himself. But in sum he is a young man of the times who is making a mark on the times that the times are better for.

I called him Ali Baby in those days to suggest that he wasn't the grim religious fanatic he frequently was pictured as. Two years later, in 1969, Ali appeared on Broadway.

SONNY AND ALI, AGAIN

The bizarre careers of Sonny Liston and Muhammad Ali touched once again Saturday, briefly and obliquely.

Liston was knocked out in Las Vegas. Ali Baby was knocked out on Broadway. Perhaps there's a moral there someplace.

A tough heavyweight named Leotis Martin demolished the last of the Liston myths with a knockout in the ninth round. A tough theater audience scored a TKO over Ali Baby after seven performances in *Buck White.*

The last of the Liston myths was connected to all the previous ones—the myth, ironically, of the invincible black buck, the malevolent, ignorant, antisocial black animal out of the cotton fields or coal mines, a threat to our women and our jobs. It implies that he never really was beaten by Ali Baby. That he gave away a title worth millions for conspiratorial reasons. That for the last five years he has stalked the earth, fighting for paltry thousands, as the uncrowned heavyweight champion.

Sorry about that. Sonny Liston lost in Miami because he was out of shape and because he couldn't cope with a remarkably gifted tyro then known as Cassius Clay. The result was confirmed in Lewiston, Maine, when he went down as though he had been poisoned after walking into a flash right hand. It didn't seem like much of a punch, but apparently it didn't have to be much of a punch. The ponderously slow Liston had been so lethargic in training that his handlers gave a sparring partner $100 to make him look good so he might feel good.

Martin was the first fighter of substance to meet Liston since that memorable fiasco. He nearly killed him—with right-hand leads. And Martin is not known as a fast puncher.

Liston was unconscious for what seemed like minutes after the knockout. When he got up, his lips puffed, his nose bloody, his eyes glazed, he wasn't malevolent or invincible or any of those terrible things he used to be. He was human —old and defeated, another guy busted in a Las Vegas casino.

A few hours later Ali played himself as Buck White for the last time in the George Abbott Theater. There can be

no quarreling with the verdict of theater economics that
this show didn't have to go on.

But of course one must quarrel with a society that
permits a prizefighter to sing and carry on on Broadway
but does not permit him to fight in Madison Square Garden. A society that permits theatergoers to decide whether
they want to support a performer, but doesn't permit fight
fans to decide whether they want to support a fighter. This
is a schizophrenic society. It deprives our rights as much as
his.

Ali Baby was on stage for an hour in the role of a black
militant and martyr. His performance was a miracle for an
athlete, but he has always played himself well.

There was one final disquieting note. Jack Johnson, as
the story is told in *The Great White Hope* elsewhere on
Broadway, also took a role in the theater when he was
driven into exile. Johnson went to flab while he waited out
the government, and Jess Willard did him in. It would be
nice if Ali Baby got to fight again before he is as old as
Sonny Liston.

SPORTIN' LIFE

There are brightly plumaged birds in the lobby of the
Regency Hyatt House in Atlanta. Last Monday afternoon,
a few hours before Afro-thatched Muhammad Ali and Irish
warbler Jerry Quarry were caged together, the birds cawed
and squealed a plaintive song of protest. They were being
outfeathered by homo sap peacock.

A few words about the hotel and its other-worldly
lobby, center stage for the incredibly rich and colorful, and
meaningful, fight spectacle.

The hotel is the ultimate edifice complex: it faces in-
ward. A great square plaza is surrounded by twenty-five
stories of introverted balconies and Babylonian vines,
topped by a sky of glass and a rotating cocktail lounge in
a blue plastic bubble. The elevators are exposed spaceships

that glide like Coney Island parachutes on a massive column.

The birds are in an aviary that starts one level below the lobby and fans through the lobby into another cocktail lounge, which is shaped like a cocktail glass and covered by a spectacular Tiffany-like lamp that hangs from the roof by a 250-foot cable.

But the people were better.

If the hotel is a monument to a dynamic city, the fight promotion was a symbol of dynamic black power. The return of Ali Baby to the city was a signal of cosmic significance. Blacks of the South and North merged for what was a black political convention, in the sense that it was a demonstration of power and unity and wealth undreamed of only a few years ago.

The presence of the Rev. Jesse Jackson of Chicago and Whitney Young of New York, along with Coretta King and the Rev. Ralph Abernathy and Julian Bond of Atlanta, and entertainers Bill Cosby and Sidney Poitier, was a phenomenon not likely to go unnoticed in important places. Nor the invasion of black tourists with money to throw around.

But the color of their money was the least colorful aspect of their invasion. Blacks transformed the lobby into one big aviary of haute couture. It was an Easter Parade in Harlem with guys in two-tone jumpsuits and fur-edged ensembles and snakeskin hats and satin and lace and suede and leather, with dolls in fantasmagoric numbers and uninhibited skin and modern art hairdos. Soulsville on Peachtree Street.

Ringside was a gallery of black society and power. Politicians and businessmen in dark suits, hustlers and pimps in white and pastels, the sublime to the garish.

It was a black version of what a major fight used to be as a social event for paleface Sportin' Life with its gaudy cars and silk suits and lacquered ladies and pinky rings.

And Ali not only inspired it, he dug it and luxuriated in it. In the last few days before the fight he was all over the place, rolling his eyes with glee as he checked the fashion show, dazzling his constituency with his charm. An hour and a half before his second coming, he collected a few dozen people around town who couldn't afford the price of a ticket and ushered them into the arena.

He is some piece of work, Ali Baby. In a country that equates winning with character and self-sacrifice with heroism and clean living with godliness, he has surely confused the professional patriots. Like Sherman, he took Atlanta. The rest of America can't be far behind.

That is your basic postevent wrap-up piece, the scene taking precedence over the contest on that occasion. The next three pieces zeroed in on the second Ali–Frazier fight.

RERUN

In the fourth round of Super Fight, Muhammad Ali hit Joe Frazier with twenty-nine clean punches (twenty-one jabs, eight hooks and crosses) and Joe Frazier hit Muhammad Ali with seven clean punches (all hooks). Joe Frazier won the round on all three official cards.

In the fifth round, Ali hit Frazier with twenty-four punches (sixteen jabs) and Frazier hit Ali with two (hooks). One official gave the round to Ali.

Three years ago I promised to dissect Super Fight punch by punch, but by the time the film became available months later I decided to wait until Son of Super Fight to confirm or retract my original impressions. I was among a small minority of writers who scored the fight for Ali.

Like the other astigmatic dunces, I had no serious quarrel with the decision. Frazier fought bravely and well, and he won two one-sided rounds to Ali's one and scored the only knockdown. But, having always felt that sheer aggression is often overvalued, I was curious about the scoring anyway.

Yesterday my colleague, Vic Ziegel, who thought

Frazier won, and I dissected the film. Vic counted Frazier's punches and I counted Ali's—only the solid, unobstructed ones—and afterward we compared totals.

Admittedly this scientific method is not a threat to IBM, but there is no science less exact, as our findings showed, than scoring fights. It is often more like theater criticism than judging an athletic contest. Styles and timing, and even personalities, seem to count as much as content.

Admittedly too, a fight cannot be broken down punch by punch and put together again in a neat package any more than Humpty Dumpty could, any more than an opera can be broken down note by note or a painting stroke by stroke. Still, there ought to be standards. And you must wonder about the standards if a fighter can land eighteen punches to his opponent's two—as Ali did in the tenth round—and lose the round on one official's reckoning.

There are two main problems in scoring. One is the implicitly subjective judgment of the effectiveness of punches. Do six jabs neutralize one hook? Seven? Eight? Do two lefts and a right equal a solid shot to the body? You might as well ask for the directions to Oz. There are no guidelines.

But, secondly, the rules are so vague that they encourage subjectivity where it isn't necessary, where it invites emotion and bias.

What a fight is about is who puts more hurt on the other guy—round by Marquis of Queensberry round. One-sided rounds are not supposed to count more than close rounds in this state unless the rounds add up to a draw, when points and aggression should and do come into play. It is, of course, understandably human when an official rewards a fighter who has won a round big by giving him the benefit of the doubt in a close round.

What is not understandable is the rule stipulating that, in addition to clean punching, such abstractions as ring generalship, effective aggressiveness, and defense should be used in the equation. It is, in my judgment, a contradiction in terms to be rewarded for any of these when you are outpunched. Your ring generalship wasn't good enough. Your aggressiveness backfired. Your defense was defeated.

Which is why Vic and I tried to reduce Super Fight to its basic components—punches. This is what we found, round by round:

(1) Ali 20, Frazier 12; (2) Ali 30, Frazier 10; (3) Ali 27, Frazier 13; (4) Ali 29, Frazier 7; (5) Ali 24, Frazier 3; (6) Ali 10, Frazier 8; (7) Ali 24, Frazier 7; (8) Ali 12, Frazier 10; (9) Ali 24, Frazier 2; (10) Ali 18, Frazier 2; (11) Frazier 12, Ali 9; (12) Ali 15, Frazier 10; (13) Ali 18, Frazier 8; (14) Ali 23, Frazier 6; (15) Frazier 19, Ali 10. Total: Ali 293, Frazier 129.

Obviously these numbers represent the fallible judgment and arithmetic of two people looking at fallible film. Nor do they measure the impact of the punches. Ali got hit more than he had ever been hit before, his jaw swelling to the size of a cantaloupe. Frazier was disfigured and spent two weeks recuperating in a hospital.

Vic now says it was a very close fight that Ali could have won. I think he was robbed.

I wish I had left off the last line, letting the rest of it speak for itself. But what that column really was about, it is clear now, was the craziness of sportswriters. My craziness was matched by another sportswriter who claimed that the column influenced judges to give the decision in the rematch to Ali, who clearly won.

MUHAMMAD'S MOUNTAIN

The mountain wouldn't come to Muhammad Ali, so he bought it. He bought this Pocono mountain in Deer Lake, Pennsylvania, and built a training camp on it to indulge and recapture his adolescent fantasies. The question is whether, after the rematch with Joe Frazier, he will be as dead as Humphrey Bogart in *The Treasure of the Sierra Madre* or as triumphant as Edmund Hillary on Mount Everest.

Three years ago Muhammad Ali and Joe Frazier gave each other and us a night of sustained fury and theater unmatched in heavyweight history. Ali, deposed champion, martyred social conscience, boxer and showman, vs. Frazier, new champion, straight arrow, slugger and pure fighter. Both unbeaten. It was billing impossible to live up to. They surpassed it.

Something has gone out of them since that night, as though they gave too much. Frazier lost the championship, listlessly. Ali went through the motions of a dozen fights, losing one. Like exhausted armies, neither could muster the will to rejuvenate their bodies and their spirits to the highs of that night. Perhaps they can't. It took them this long to get it on again because they needed time and space to gather their forces. Now they have discovered that they need each other. They want that night again.

Ali's way of trying to find it was to construct a fanciful world of self-denial, a primitive castle in the sky to remind him that the name of the game has become survival. "It is," he said, "like all those preparations to get a rocket ship off."

Ali has invested $200,000 in his log cabin retreat. He has given up his two Rolls-Royces and companion baubles for the moment "to get back to how things were." He sleeps in a one-room cabin that has two unusual features consistent with his inconsistency. Two stonemasons were breaking rocks yesterday to make a modest little $4,500 fireplace. And in one corner there is an indoor replica of an outhouse. "You can get too rustic," Ali explained.

Ali's workout consisted of seven rounds of shadowboxing and rope skipping. Once as a young man he preferred sparring to the drudgery of calisthenics. Yesterday his sparring partners were extras in a gym scene. The log cabin training room is decorated with dozens of magazine covers and photographs of the once and future champion. Glistening with a coat of oil, he looked as sleek and as beautiful as any of them. He is, impossibly, thirty-two years old. One of the rules of the log cabin kitchen, set down by his father, seems to apply: "Don't criticize the coffee. You may be old and weak yourself someday."

"A fellow gets great and forgets what he did to get

great," Ali said. "The next thing you know you're behind in points and you can't get back.

"I've never really trained hard. Just as hard as I had to. I dreaded going through what a Rocky Marciano did. Now I'm suffering. Staying away from temptation.

"It took a million-dollar fight to get me off sweets. I love sweets. Hamburger and french fries. Double malteds. Pancakes and butter. Half a whipped cream pie. Three, four scoops of ice cream. I was like a horse in a stable. Run, come back, stick your face in the trough and eat hay.

"You don't know what it is to be me in the city. A pretty girl comes by and says we're having a party. You say no. She's in room 612 and you're in ᴜ18. You're sleeping and you hear the music. Bum-bum-de-dum-dum. You get up and say, okay, five minutes. . . . Here all they got is Pennsylvania Dutch and coal miners."

No man has suffered more for his art.

A MATTER OF STYLE

It is very much like Muhammad Ali, the mystic and dreamer, to build a mountain retreat for training, to go back to romanticized beginnings when he tries to go back to what he used to be.

It is just as much like Joe Frazier, the farm boy with feet planted solidly on the ground, to go back to his beginnings as a fighter, to a Philadelphia gym, to get ready for Son of Super Fight.

Reaching into the past is what the rematch is about, but any similarity between Ali and Frazier beyond that is purely coincidental. It is their differences in personalities and styles that tantalize us. The difference probably means more to Frazier than Ali.

Joe Frazier is the kind of fighter who lives fast and dies young in his career. Short and ornery, like a warthog, he has to take two punches to get close enough to land a harder one. In the heavyweight division that usually is a brainaddling ratio. Before Frazier only Jack Dempsey and Rocky Marciano got to be champions with that style. Snarls Ali with contempt for the breed, "Ya hurt Frazier's feelings if you don't hit him." The masochistic training required for survival, to say nothing of the punches, makes early retirement necessary. Dempsey won one major fight after his twenty-eighth birthday. Marciano retired after eight years as a pro. Frazier, at thirty, is in his ninth year.

With enough money in the bank to never have to punch a time clock or an opponent again, with the strains of Super Fight behind him, Frazier decided not to torture his body anymore. "We have a tendency to look for little shortcuts," he said. The result was three lackluster wins and one devastating defeat that made him a former champion. An out-of-shape warthog quickly becomes a butchered piglet.

Can the clock be turned back?

"I'm trying," Frazier said the other day after going about his chores with the old masochistic glee.

Asked the same question, Ali replied, "The clock is back. But when Frazier's clock was back he was taking punishment. That clock was built to take punishment."

This is a difference in style that we have come to know and love, or endure. But it suggests a deeper difference that helps explain why Frazier has put himself on the torture rack again. When he says, "We don't get along," he means, "I hate the mother."

If by some genetic miracle a replica of Muhammad Ali should be thrust on us and matched with the original, the original would abuse him with wit and verse and impunity. He would call him an imposter, a spy for the Ku Klux Klan. That is Ali's game. Joe Frazier understands this, but a target that understands is still torn by a bullet.

When Ali abuses Frazier and Frazier sputters feebly, he is seething with the rage of a short man overmatched by a tall man, a plain man overmatched by a witty man, an ordinary man overmatched by an extraordinary man. He is reminded that while he is admired, Ali stops traffic. That when he was the champion, Ali was still the hero.

So when Joe Frazier huffed out of a television studio yesterday because Ali called him ignorant, he seemed mad enough to want to turn Ali's magic mountain into Boot Hill. He will get the chance.

With two veteran athletes whose tics are familiar, and who perform as nakedly as fighters do, you can attempt to get beneath the skin, as I did in those two cases. Most often, I suppose, we are caricaturists.

Following is the nucleus of my coverage on Ali's fight with George Foreman in Zaire, a spectacle I became a toenote to.

ALI'S PEOPLE

As Muhammad Ali runs alongside the great green grassy Zaire (aka Congo) River in the morning, children pop out of huts chirping and flapping like birds from cuckoo clocks. "No television, can't read, but they know me," Ali muses in one of his frequent reveries on the wonder of himself.

It is true. Nothing like Ali has ever descended on Zaire, a primitive country ruled by colonials for nearly a century, torn by civil strife for five years, cauterized by revolutionary zeal for a decade. He is Mickey Mouse, one of the enduring international symbols of America, alive in living color.

Chants of Al-ee, Al-ee, Al-ee, no different than the chants that fly from the rafters of Madison Square Garden, greeted him on his arrival at Kinshasa airport two weeks before his date with George Foreman. A troupe of native dancers in bright yellow and green and purple danced a spear dance to tribal rhythms. "I can still see that African dance," he said a week later. "It brings tears to my eyes. Go up to Harlem and see them dance. This is where it started."

The identification of Zairos with Ali is a kinship from the top of his handsome head to the tip of his elfin toes.

A postcard with a ceremonial dancer pictured on one side was inscribed: "My Dear Brother Ali, I wish you a beautiful fight/ You come in our own land/ With all your family/ I think it is also the family of us/ All sons of Africa."

A woman at Ali's workout said in trembling French, "He is too beautiful to be a man."

A manager of the resort where Ali is training said, "Ali is loved by everyone, even by women who don't know he's a boxer. We admire him because he stood up for black men everywhere. We admire higher intelligence and cleverness over brute strength. If he loses we will be very sad. It will seem as if a man died."

After his workouts, Ali conducts question-and-answer sessions with Zairos. Reserved by nature, they bust up as he plays and politics with them.

Can Foreman win? "I can never lose to a man who is so slow and ugly." Where are your ancestors from? "My parents don't know neither. But after looking at you it might be here."

Questions done, Ali conducts a collegiate pep rally for himself. One day a man piped up with a cheer in the native dialect that caught Ali's ear. It pricked like a thoroughbred's, much as it does when he picks up the latest street wit in black neighborhoods back home, and incorporates the good stuff into his act.

The cheer went *naku-boom-ah-yay*, which means "knock him down and kill him." Ali asked the man to repeat it several times, mouthing the words with him. A group of workers peering through lattice walls improvised in unision, "Ali-boom-ah-yay," meaning "Ali, kill him." Now he finishes each workout by pumping his right arm as he leads the crowd in a succession of Ali-boom-ah-yays. His fertile mind ever plotting, he envisions 100,000 Zairos Ali-boom-ah-yaying on fight night.

Not everyone seems thrilled with Ali's godlike popularity. The government forbids him from going into Kinshasa, the capital, because it fears he might touch off a riot. The government is concerned that an ugly scene could follow an Ali defeat. Apparently that is why it planted a crude statement in the press attributing remarks to George

Foreman that he couldn't possibly have said, criticizing Ali because he has white people in his camp, in a transparent attempt to build a following for the champion and favorite. What if he should knock out Ali? That may be the reason why President Mobutu, whose prestige is at stake in the fight, as his money is behind it, is going to watch it on television from his palace.

It is clear that the government, though a dictatorship, is in over its head against Muhammad Ali.

BANNED IN ZAIRE

A funny thing happened to me on the way back to Zaire. I didn't get Zaire.

In fact I didn't get out of town. With a hot plane ticket in my hand, I was informed at Kennedy airport that my visa was not renewed by the Zaire consulate. No explanation given, or needed. It seems that I'm a political undesirable in Zaire.

In retaliation, I have decided not to invite President Mobutu Sese Seko (which translates out to "the all-powerful warrior who, because of his endurance and inflexible will to win, will go from conquest to conquest, leaving fire in his wake") to my Halloween party.

I am flattered, of course, by the attention. Sportswriters have been belted by ballplayers, ostracized by owners and abused by illiterates, but how many of us have been banned by a whole country? In the broad sweep of human history, none, before this.

The reason my visa was not renewed, as near as I can figure, is that I wasn't censored when I was there last month before the George Foreman–Muhammad Ali extravaganza was postponed. Several sportswriters' stories were censored. My stories got through, and the government didn't like what was getting through.

Apparently the government was most put out by the story about Rosemary Severance, the librarian from Michigan who paid more than $2,800 for a tour and found that it covered transportation and little else. At a press conference in New York recently the minister of tourism reported that tours had been cut-rated by $1,000 from their inflated prices, and he implied that Rosemary Severance's claim of fraud was a hoax. Sorry, not only did she show me her phantom travel itinerary with the price printed on it, but I have to believe her because, unlike the promoters, she hasn't lied to me lately.

There is no tradition of a free press in Zaire. The media is the message sent out by the government. The government, humorless as all one-party governments are, even was urged by some pooh-bahs last year to fire a sportswriter because he suggested that local officials contributed to a victory in soccer over a team from Brazil. The sportswriter kept his job because he had relatives in high places.

The astonishing obtuseness of the government in my case grieves me. I qualified my reports without being judgmental about Zaire's values. They are making a heroic effort to pull the thing off. If a primitive country with problems that dwarf ours thinks it can stimulate growth with a highly visible sports event, much as advanced nations do with the Olympics, good luck to them. I resisted the temptation to say they are giving the people circuses instead of bread.

It was easy to sympathize with the Zairos too because they had no experience promoting an event of such magnitude, while the Americans, who didn't have the experience either, were getting uglier by the minute. They put on a music festival that was a disaster, misled the government into preparing for an invasion of tourists that never materialized, ripped off the few tourists who did appear, and botched travel arrangements and communications for the press. For good measure, they advised Zaire to censor reports on George Foreman's disabling cut and the subsequent postponement.

I'm disappointed that I won't be at the fight because I wanted to be there for Ali's last hurrah and because we are not likely to be engaged by a fight of this dimension for a long time. My road to Zaire was paved with good intentions. I feel like a liberal who has been mugged.

I also canceled a contract for a book on the fight, for which I had done several months of research. It wasn't a total loss. I didn't have to feel guilty about withholding stuff from the column that I had obtained for the book. When it came down to a decision, I didn't cheat on the column, but I vowed never to create that conflict again. Books may grow out of columns; they shouldn't interfere with the column.

I covered the fight on closed-circuit television at Madison Square Garden. It saved me about 14,994 miles of travel, another plus.

AS HE WAS SAYING

In one of the sublime moments of this sporting life, Muhammad Ali turned what was believed to be an electric chair into a throne last night.

A right hand, prefaced by a right and a left, and seven rounds of calculated terror, sent the fatal juice through George Foreman instead.

Six years after he had been unseated as champion by the guardians of our morality, Muhammad Ali reseated himself.

At age thirty-two he was still wiggling his ears at convention and dropping banana peels under propriety, but when the bell rang he reminded us that beneath the bombast he had bombs, beneath the showmanship he was a very great athlete.

The decisive clue, it developed, was his remark several weeks ago that "if George don't get me in seven his parachute won't open." Ali was convinced that Foreman could not sustain his invincible act past the middle of a big, tough fight.

Sure enough, late in the eighth round, George Foreman was on his back, his red satin trunks resembling an unopened parachute.

It is one thing to perceive the flaw in Foreman's armor, quite another to survive until it could be pierced. Never in the history of championship head bashing had Ali's survival plan been employed. He leaned against the loose ropes and invited a devastating puncher to "go ahead, punch."

There was a punch line though. It was sotto voce, "If you can."

This was a fail-safe tactic because Ali found in the first round that he couldn't fight Foreman with his legs. "I'm gonna dance," he cooed from his corner, but Foreman was an unwilling partner. He went at Ali like a cop pushing an obstreperous suspect against a wall.

In the second round it appeared that Ali was throwing himself on a butcher block. Angelo Dundee, his trainer, had said that the one way he couldn't fight Foreman was on the ropes. Ali replied that, well, he might try it for a while because a guy could punch himself out trying to put him through the ropes. Foreman tried to put him into the Zaire River. He hacked at Ali's sides with those terrible-looking blows that have paralyzed lesser men. Ali discovered he could live with the few that got through his guard and decided to stay there.

It wasn't until the third round that Ali's strategy was clear. He was matching his will, nerve and professionalism against Foreman's strength. His logic, and necessity, escaped the crowd at the Garden, which pleaded with him to do something, anything, else.

The pattern continued through the fourth and fifth rounds, Foreman hacking, Ali shooting quick little combinations from time to time. Unbeknownst, Foreman was preparing himself for slaughter. He seemed surprised when Ali lashed at him. The steak was jumping off the butcher block at the butcher.

Foreman became arm-weary. His punches were longer, slower. He was entering the realm of fatigue for the first time as a champion and he had no resources to escape. In the sixth round Ali sounded him out with a series of heavy jabs, then returned to the ropes to let him soften himself up some more. Foreman had no choice but to follow. In midring he couldn't match Ali's hand speed.

In the eighth round Ali saw Foreman was spent. "Foreman has confidence in his power and that's good for him," Ali had said. "But it's good for me too because it will bother him when he doesn't hurt me." It broke him. When you break a man's strength, the rest crumbles.

George Foreman crumbled, his brute strength outwitted, what was left of him outpunched by Muhammad Ali. In Africa, once known as the Dark Continent, the light of dawn was not far off.

Ernest Hemingway purified the language and wrote about losers, for which sportswriters are much in debt to him. Herewith a couple of losers.

A GREAT BUM

As the bell rang for the fifteenth round last night, the boys from Bayonne stood and cheered Chuck Wepner. He was their bum and they loved him, and they were relieved. He was standing up to the great Muhammad Ali, making him know he was in a fight.

It took a great bum to do that, and Wepner proved he was worthy of such sainted bumhood. He won the only fight he could win, the fight for himself. He missed going the distance by nineteen seconds, done in by the exhaustion of his effort as much as by Ali's punches.

"I feel no shame in losing," he said.

It was a fight between a house painter and an artist, and the artist was sloppy enough to make it look like a contest. It wasn't. It just lasted so long that you couldn't be sure. Maybe dull solid walls were the new thing in the art world.

Ali was a dull solid wall for much of the bizarre night in the Cleveland Coliseum. Then, at the very end, determined to redeem his losing fight with himself, he flung some color on the canvas. Chuck Wepner. The end resembled George Bellows's classic painting of Dempsey walloping Firpo, the battered, pulpy Wepner smashed through the ropes by a killer right.

"Usually I back off, but I tried to annihilate him," Ali said. "I had no mercy. It was an eye for an eye and a tooth for a tooth."

Ali, as is his custom with bums, had not even bothered to take Wepner lightly. He trained in the first thirteen rounds and fought in the last two. Al Braverman, Wepner's manager, took the fight saying, "The whole world is a mismatch," and Ali prepared accordingly.

The crowd did too. The usual electricity before a heavyweight championship fight was reduced to candlelight. Everybody was waiting for Ali to blow Wepner out.

But as Ali played his no-punches game in the first round, serving notice that he intended to stay awhile, bar brawler Wepner came at him with everything but the stools, as advertised. He rabbit punched Ali, inspiring Ali to return the illegal shots with a flourish. Once Wepner started to come up with a terrific left knee. You do not expect a Nijinsky to dance out of Bayonne, New Jersey.

In the middle rounds Ali rested on the ropes, checked himself out on the television screens, and fought about ten seconds per round. There was alarm in his corner—the ultimate tribute to Ali's acting ability—which suspected that he may have been carrying Wepner but feared he was too fat to carry the sweat on his brow.

"Champ, champ, champ," soothsayer Bundini Brown cried just before the ninth round.

The champ turned to him casually and said, "What?" A minute later he found out. He was sitting on the floor, put there by a sweeping right under the arm pit that caught him off balance. Ali claimed that Wepner was standing on his foot at the time. "I shoulda stood on his head," cooed Wepner.

It was like seeing a museum guard deck the *Mona Lisa.* Ali got serious in the tenth round, and seriouser and seriouser through the fifteenth.

By that time Chuck Wepner looked as though he had been hit with the bottles of whisky he sells for a living. It was a hard if gritty way to earn an easy $100,000. "I'll be back on the route in a week or ten days," he said.

PUNCH ME

The little speed bag is used by prizefighters to sharpen reflexes and build stamina and drum out a rhythmic rat-a-tat-tat that makes them feel good. The heavy bag puts muscle into their punches and combinations into their heads. The European slungballen swings in erratic arcs, simulating a moving target. And then there is the easiest punching bag of them all—George Chuvalo.

George Chuvalo hits your fist with his head wherever it may be, a gift that promoters and opponents value highly. Throw a jab, George Chuvalo hits it. Throw a hook, George Chuvalo hits it. Ringsiders are advised not to wave for the peanut vendor when George Chuvalo is fighting because he will jump out of the ring and bash your hand in with his head. It's his killer instinct.

So George Chuvalo, the Great White Hopeless, is returning to the Garden tonight—come one, come all to see how much punishment the human skull can take.

Jerry Quarry is the heavyweight Chuvalo is testing this time. Quarry's skull is in no danger because Chuvalo can't punch. It's his hands that may be separated from their senses.

The reports out of Canada, where Chuvalo trained, were ominous for Quarry. Two sparring partners broke hands on Chuvalo's jaw.

Quarry, meanwhile, had to adapt to new training methods. "Frazier came at you but he tried to duck a punch once in a while," he said. "This guy never misses. He wears you out." Accordingly Quarry gave his sparring partners iron masks. He knew he was ready when he hit one mask 250 shots in one round. Veteran observers thought that if Chuvalo could step up the pace to 350 he could pull an upset.

An upset is unlikely because it would ruin Chuvalo's drawing power. People come to see him bleed and marvel at his ability to take it. He has disappointed them only twice in major fights. He has crowd-pleasing losses to Floyd Patterson, Oscar Bonavena, Muhammad Ali, Ernie Terrell and even Buster Mathis.

But Chuvalo has won fifty-five of his seventy-two fights, which tells something about how he keeps getting invited to the Garden. After each loss he goes back to the north woods to build up another winning streak. In six months he can beat three lobster fishermen in Nova Scotia, two seal hunters on Hudson Bay and an eskimo in the Yukon.

With frightening reports of a trail of broken hands behind him, Chuvalo is matched with another heavyweight hopeful. Beating him has become one of the requirements of the New York State Athletic Commission for a heavy-weight to renew his license.

His fights follow a pattern. Chuvalo chases his oppo-nent tirelessly, corners him, and takes smashing flurries on the chin. His face becomes swollen, discolored and bloodily triumphant. He has never been knocked off his feet. He should have been a linebacker.

The postfight scene also follows a pattern, starring Chuvalo's manager, Irving Ungerman, who in his other life is the chicken-plucking king of Canada. If Budd Schulberg and Dr. Frankenstein collaborated on the prototype of the fight manager, Irving Ungerman would be the result.

While Mrs. Chuvalo sits in a corner sobbing, and Chuvalo holds an ice bag to one eye and mumbles through puffed lips that he may retire, Ungerman cries like a chicken plucked live. He was robbed. He can't win a deci-sion in New York. He was butted all fight long. We'll kill the guy next time.

You can only hope there are no more next times. George Chuvalo is a very decent fellow. Eventually all punching bags split open and are thrown away.

Swollen, discolored and bleeding, Chuvalo kayoed the hand-weary Quarry in the seventh round.

III.
Bread
and
Butter

Football and basketball, along with baseball, are the bread-and-butter games of the sports page. They present opposite challenges for the sportswriter. In football it is to penetrate the militaristic fog and the face masks. In basketball it is to freeze the eddying tides and emotions that rush past you at courtside.

When I came to New York the Giants had become losers after a decade of success. Fans were sullen. I was tolerantly bemused, on the theory that nobody wins forever and they had earned the time to rebuild. I reported their foibles more earnestly when it became apparent that the front office was wallowing in the past and would never have enough time to rebuild. This closed off some sources on the team and opened others. A player I had never been particularly friendly with volunteered to reveal the inner workings and feelings of the team, provided he would be anonymous. His reports fleshed out my own observations and were reinforced by information I received from secondhand sources who were close to other players. Following are the first two parts of what turned out to be a five-part series over a period of three months.

MARANOIA I

The most recent blowup among the Giants was symptomatic of a very deep problem on the team. The players can't play and the coach can't coach.

Deeper than that is the management problem. Call it Wellington Maranoia.

One of the Giants who can play a little and is frustrated a lot says, "Alex is a super guy but he's no coach. He's just happy to have a job. It's not his fault—he shouldn't be there. But as long as they're making a million dollars a year there's no incentive to make any real changes at the top. They'll never turn the team over to a strong leader. The worst part of it is that I don't see any end in sight.

"The miracle is that we've won two games. We'll win a few more and they'll think we have the nucleus to build a winner. They still don't know how unbelievable it was that we won nine games last year. Without Tarkenton we'd go zero and fourteen."

According to this Giant, practices are disorganized and the situation on the sidelines during games is chaotic. Disorganization and chaos are not exactly new phenomena in football, but the Giants seem to be refining them to an art. In the free-scoring game with the Packers, the Giant said, Webster stood there exclaiming, "Gee, this is a terrific game" instead of trying to get things under control. We may applaud his perspective, but the players think he should find a seat in the stands if he wants to behave like a fan.

Webster is a fan, though. And like any fan would be, he is flattered when the committees that run the Giants tell him what they're up to. There's the front office committee, which is said to have made deals without consulting him. There's the defensive committee, which barely acknowledges his existence. There's the offensive committee, which actually permits him to play with *X*s and *O*s from time to time. The Giants survive this committee system, such as they do, because they have a bright veteran quarterback who is, in effect, the offensive coach, which is the job most head coaches reserve for themselves.

Fran Tarkenton took that role last year after that brouhaha in New Orleans, when the members of the offensive committee kept giving him different suggestions, in stereo, from all sides. Webster cleared up the static by becoming a one-speaker conduit, thus enabling Tarkenton to ignore one silly suggestion instead of many.

This week Webster continued his on-the-job training in the matter of Spider Lockhart, whose feelings were hurt when he was benched by Norb Hecker, chairman of the defensive committee. Webster reminded everyone that he's the boss—only reminding everyone that he isn't.

In addition to Tarkenton and Lockhart, two other Giants have publicly criticized their coaches this week. Willie Young finally made public the unhappiness of offensive linemen who were taught a new blocking system that has now been abandoned. Fred Dryer knocked the defensive committee for not playing Jim Kanicki.

The inmates are not necessarily correct in their views of the people in charge of the asylum, but this wholesale criticism from team leaders reflects a lack of respect, if not affection, for Webster. It also indicates that they wouldn't mind playing elsewhere.

Tarkenton has practically broadcast his feelings. After an exhibition wipe-out, Webster enumerated the positives he saw, while Tarkenton said that anyone who saw positives didn't know what was going on. When Webster said the Giants would use tricky formations to stimulate the offense, Tarkenton noted dryly that people, not formations, win football games. Tarkenton also has made recommendations on trades and last Sunday he actually made the offensive substitutions.

Alex Webster has the title of head coach because of the galloping nostalgia and "Giant family" mystique of Mara. Due to this Maranoia, the Giant informant fears that the independent, strong-willed Tarkenton may be traded. For a thousand yards of tape, no doubt.

MARANOIA II

After Fran Tarkenton scrambled away from the Giants in a salary dispute just before the first exhibition game, Wellington Mara, who leads the league in speechifying, called a team meeting. He ended it with an emotional plea. "This," he said, grabbing the Giant emblem on his shirt, "is all that matters now."

The players listened to Mara in attitudes of solemnity, then played as bad as the law allows, while Mara was telling everyone that Tarkenton had retired, which he had not.

"The guys couldn't believe it," said an informant on the Giants. "Nobody gave a rap about Fran leaving. We thought it was funny. Hell, we knew he'd be back. Can you imagine getting all that worked up before an exhibition game? I had to put my hand over my mouth to keep from giggling, and I wasn't alone."

A month later Wellington Mara exercised his constitutional right to lecture the players again, after the Jets humiliated them. This was the Cross of Gold and Win One for the Gipper speeches rolled into one.

"When he got up there," said the Giant, "you could see everyone saying to himself, 'My God, here it comes again.

We're going to have to meet the challenge. Every time we get up we have to meet the challenge.'

"He had a handful of three-by-five cards with notes on them. He said we looked like such a bunch of bums he was ashamed to bring his kids around. He said we were like bums on the Bowery—our wives and families wouldn't care for us, we had to pick ourselves off the floor. He said anyone who hadn't signed his contract by the start of the season would just have to play out his option. And then he warned us about stealing sweat-suits. Captain Queeg."

The thread that ties all this together runs from the Giant emblem to Wellington Mara's children, the family crest and the family. He has always made much of the team being a family, an extension of his home.

There is something nice and old-fashioned about filial devotion, something amateur in spirit when applied to a professional team. Which is, unfortunately, the problem. You can't run a modern big business like a candy store. And you can't treat today's young adults like ten-year-olds. Wellington Mara and the Giants are victims of future shock. They can't cope with the changes.

Item: When Fran Tarkenton ended his holdout he had a long conversation with Mara about the team, advising him, among other things, that the players felt restricted by his ubiquity. Mara's response was to order Tarkenton and a handful of others to shave off seedling mustaches.

"Sure it bothers us to have him around all the time in that ridiculous jogging suit," the Giant said. "Would you want your boss looking over your shoulder every minute? And his kids hang from the rafters like bats. You can't get away from them."

Item: Bruce Maher, the salty safetyman of a few seasons back, was turned loose by the Giants because he cussed in the dressing room.

Item: The Giants did not pursue Roy Jefferson of the Colts because he was considered too militant or Bob Brown of the Rams because he was considered a troublemaker, after they played out their options. The Redskins and Raiders have found them to be sweethearts, on if not off the field.

Item: Spotting Pete Athas roaming a dormitory hall without any clothes on and then seeing him relax in bed in the same uniform, Alex Webster asked a veteran if the rookie was queer. Athas, you must understand, is Greek, and you know about Greeks.

But Alex Webster, one of the sweetest men on earth, is a symptom rather than a cause of the Giants. He isn't a coach. Except that he is—because he is a member of the Giant family. No other qualifications are necessary. No outside applicants need apply.

"They're living in the past," the Giant said. "All you hear about is how they used to do things. The trainer tells you how Gifford and Rote had their ankles taped. Who gives a crap?"

Watch your language, son. That sound in the background is Wellington Mara clearing his throat for another speech.

Fran Tarkenton and Fred Dryer, the best players on the team, forced the Giants to trade them after the season. Two years later the Giants went outside the family for a coach.

As you get older, the users and abusers of power often become as interesting as the games and the people who play them. Two more owners coming up.

WISMERING

This is how Harry Wismer had to pass through those Pearly Gates.

"Saint Peter! Congratulations. Did you hear that Charles de Gaulle is buying the Philadelphia Eagles? Saw the contract myself. . . . Bill Shakespeare! Congratulations. One of my favorite writers. Got a story for you. Vince Lombardi will be the next police commissioner of New York. . . . Henry Ford! Congratulations. The new Mustang is a beauty. I understand George Romney is going back to American Motors. It's a fact. . . ."

Harry Wismer wismered. Harry Wismer would go through a town like a truck with a loudspeaker on it, just talking, making things up as he went along, anything that might result in a few paragraphs in the newspaper. ("Charles de Gaulle will buy the Philadelphia Eagles, Harry Wismer, owner of the New York Titans, said yesterday.") The stories couldn't be checked for a few hours and would wind up in the *Strawberry Plains* (Tennessee) *Gazette* the next day.

Why did he greet everyone with "Congratulations!"? "It makes people feel good," he said. "Congratulations can mean anything. It rings a note. It's wonderful and it's a great opening line. Congratulations!"

It must be remembered that Harry Wismer was a radio and television phenomenon, so wismering came naturally. He was a product of that tradition, which still lingers, that felt that if the air wasn't filled with footballs it should be filled with talk. The sound and the fury, not the content, was what mattered.

Wismer didn't broadcast football so much as he sold it. His adjectives were like boxes of soap chips: great, super, colossal, fantastic. It's true that he once had a runner speed past the fifty-five-yard line and it's also true that he would concoct new rules to make up for flubs, but the last impression of him was his unflappable enthusiasm.

Of a field goal attempt, he once wismered, "It's a beautiful kick. End-over-end. Terrific. . . . And it's no good."

Of a fumble: "In his own sparkling way, Jones fumbled the ball."

And between play-by-play, Harry Wismer would give you social notes from all over. Mr. and Mrs. Joe Sideline from Vermouth, Michigan, are here. Congratulations! Joe is the new vice-president of the Sideline Water Bucket Company. And I just saw Tom Monster of Monster Sporting Goods. Congratulations to Tom and his wife, Gertrude, for having their fifth little Monster. Congratulations to everyone at this wonderful football game.

Harry Wismer's wismering bluster made him rich and famous enough to get the American Football League going. He got the Huntses and the Adamses and the Hiltons, real money people, interested in the new league, and he helped sell the league as a package to TV, while the NFL still had individual team contracts. The real money people and the TV contract kept the AFL alive during its formative years.

That's a pretty solid accomplishment, but the bluster will outlive it in memory. One other not-so-bad thing about Harry Wismer: he resigned as a director of the Redskins because of what he considered shabby treatment of an injured player, and he openly criticized George Preston Marshall for failing to hire Negroes.

With the Titans, Harry Wismer was something else. "We all get to irritate people unconsciously," said a man who knew him well. "He seemed to do it on purpose." Others couldn't remember anything good to say about him.

Wismer knew what sold. He hired Sammy Baugh as his first head coach because he was Sammy Baugh. "We got eight-column headlines in the *Times*," he wismered, spreading his hands eight columns wide. He tried to sell AFL football with subway ads featuring the pudgy face of himself on the sound but awful theory that he was the best known Titan. Once he asked a writer to substitute his name for Baugh's whenever it was used in a story the coach gave. Wismer said he would sign every top college prospect, throwing around big numbers like adjectives, but he signed few of them. When Baugh said he'd like to see more players and less talk, Wismer fired him. Baugh wouldn't go unless Wismer paid him, so Wismer made him the assistant backfield coach. "I'd rather be assistant backfield coach," Baugh said. "It's a job that wouldn't keep me very busy."

Wismer's attendance figures at the Polo Grounds were said to include the head, eye, ear, leg, arm and finger count. He didn't have the real money, the oil and hotel money, to ride the pioneer years out. The league had to meet his last few payrolls. He lost close to $2 million in three seasons. The last thing he ever sold was a football team.

The other day Harry Wismer died. He was fifty-six. The *Times* didn't give him eight columns, but it did give his obituary a full column, more than most of us will get. You can hear him now: "Congratulations! I got a full column in the *Times.*"

ART ROONEY'S PARTY

Joey Divan is in New Orleans. Joey Divan is the retired heavyweight street-fighting champion of Pittsburgh. The story is told of the time he wiped out half the Pitt team the night before a game with Notre Dame, he being a Notre Dame fan and all. Joey Divan is in charge of security at Steeler workouts. Art Rooney brought him down.

Steve DiNardo is in New Orleans too. They call Steve DiNardo "Dirt" because he is the head grounds keeper at Three Rivers Stadium in Pittsburgh. Art Rooney brought down "Dirt" and the rest of the crew for the Super Bowl too.

Elmer Kirally couldn't make it, bodily. There are only two thing that could keep Elmer Kirally from a Steeler game—a wedding and a birth. His marriage last year was scheduled for the day the Steelers happened to play the Raiders in the play-offs. The ceremony was held at halftime in a church, the pre- and postceremony celebrations taking place in front of a television set in the parish office. Now, as luck would have it, Mrs. Kirally is expecting a baby Sunday. Elmer's car is ready for the dash to the hospital. Should it come during the game, he will take a portable television along.

Pittsburgh, and Art Rooney, have been waiting forever for a championship game. Western Pennsylvania, one of the richest veins of football talent, has never before had a team that played for a professional championship. That means the forty-two-year-old Steelers, and that is why their seventy-three-year-old owner is making it the biggest party a football man ever gave.

"I promised that if we ever made it to the champion-ship, I would invite all my friends," Art Rooney said. "We've got them scattered all over town. I probably will be the first owner to lose money on the Super Bowl. I don't care. It's a great day for all of us."

How many friends does Art Rooney have? Well, a secretary in the Steelers' office is charged with the responsi-bility of checking the obituaries in the local papers for his friends and friends of friends. It is not unusual for him to go to two and even three wakes a day.

That is more than an old ward leader's habit. It is a reflection of one man's unusual love affair with the place he calls home. Rooney, son of a saloon keeper, and his wife have lived in the same house for forty years al-though the neighborhood has changed from predomi-nantly Irish to predominantly black. He would no more leave the neighborhood than he would leave the city with his struggling football team. "My faith, my family, my city and my friends are the most valuable things in my life," he said.

So, in addition to his five sons and many of his thirty-four grandchildren and close friends, Art Rooney has brought to New Orleans 192 stadium and office employees and their families, and thirty more from Philadelphia, where he owns Liberty Bell race track, and fifty from Yon-kers, where he owns the raceway, and "a planeload" from Green Mountain, another track, in Vermont.

And a football team that will play the Vikings for the championship of creation.

"Those forty-two years were filled with frustration," Rooney said. "Sometimes when you lose you duck in and out of alleys. It's great to be a winner. It makes you think you know what it's all about."

What was that again? The Steelers did stumble and bumble interminably, and largely because Art Rooney wasn't as good at operating a football team as he was at betting and running horses. But he has always known what it is all about.

The Super Bowl has a history of promising much and deliver-
ing little. These are some of my contributions to the carny barking.

THE BROTHERS MICHAELS

Walter Michaels left Poland in 1911 at the age of nineteen because he didn't want to be drafted into the army. He
came to America, settled in Swoyersville, Pennsylvania,
went to work digging coal around Wilkes-Barre. He
worked thirty-five years in the mines, where he was a legend for his strength, and he dropped dead at fifty-four.

Walter and Mary Michaels had seven sons and a
daughter. One son was killed at Guadalcanal. Their daughter died. The others got at least a start in college; the two
who had to quit and go down in the mines are retired now,
at fifty-five and fifty-two, with silicosis in their lungs.

The remaining four sons played football and got degrees. Joe Michaels was the first. He was a high-scoring
tailback at Penn in the early forties. The Steelers drafted
him but he ignored them to become a high school science
teacher.

"Our father forbid my older brothers to play football,"
Lou Michaels said. "But Joe sneaked out and beat Kingston
7–6 with a touchdown and an extra point to stop their
sixty-game winning streak. When he saw the headlines in
the paper he said, 'All my sons will play football.'"

Walt Michaels, Jr., went to Washington and Lee and
then on to the Browns and fame as a linebacker. He is the
defensive coach of the Jets.

Lou Michaels, the baby of the family, went to Kentucky, made All-American and is the place kicker for the
Colts.

"Two sons in the Super Bowl," Walt Michaels said
with misty eyes on the day the Colts and Jets won league
championships. "How would you like to be Mrs. Michaels
today?"

Walt Michaels is blocky and handsome at thirty-nine,

handsome the way Lou Michaels described their father. "Not like Frank Gifford. Just handsome, like a man." Lou Michaels is thirty-two and he has thick John L. Lewis eyebrows and the build of a wide vein of anthracite. Lou, who didn't get married for a long time because he was something of a mama's boy, talked about his brother and his father and his mother.

"Walt is the best brother anyone ever had," he said. "He was the only real brother to me. He's my idol. He's the one who put me on this field. When I was a kid he mostly talked to me about right and wrong and he never told me wrong. He's been my guide through life. My father died when I was eleven.

"Walt got me into prep school and college, and he told me to develop something extra, just don't be a player, so I started kicking. When I was drafted by the Rams he told me not to sign my contract until I talked to him. He made himself unavailable, and every time I told that to Pete Rozelle (then the general manager of the Rams) the price went up. Walt said that sometimes you just don't want to be found.

"We played opposite each other just once, in an exhibition. I was an offensive tackle and he was the linebacker. I had to screen him on one play, but if I had to hit him a downfield block I would have fallen down.

"My father was the kind of man who would have gone to Rozelle for this game and demanded that he figure out a way to make it a tie 'because no son of mine is a loser.' He never had a dollar in his pocket. He had a quarter, for two nickle beers and a shot. It took me a year to save twenty-five pennies as a kid and one day he told me to get him a quart of beer with them. I was mad and I stayed mad. Now I'd buy him a brewery.

"My mother knew it all. She used to say something that tickled me to death. People would ask her why her sons were better than others. She'd say because they were bigger and stronger and knew what they were doing."

Mrs. Mary Michaels still lives in Swoyersville. She is

seventy-two and she has twenty-five grandchildren and eight great-grandchildren. The boys are flying her to Miami for the Super Bowl.

"I felt sorry for the boys for what they had to put up with on the field, it was so tough," she said. "Now it's good because all the younger boys are getting good schooling. There'll be some doctors and lawyers."

Edward Michaels, Lou's son, is nineteen months old and weighs thirty-five pounds and he may go on the first round of the draft. Lou calls him "The Animal." Walt calls him "The Beast." "He kicks with his left foot, like his father," said Mrs. Michaels, "and then he puts up his hands and says, 'Good.'"

The brothers Michaels are staying less than a mile apart in Fort Lauderdale, but they are incommunicado.

"I'll talk to him after the game," Walt said, "if he still wants to talk."

"He always beat me more than I beat him," Lou said. "Sunday is my revenge."

"Whatever comes of it," Walt Michaels said, "it's great."

Old newspaper saying: if you have the story, tell it; if you don't, write it. That one just had to be told.

SUPERSCAM

The Louisiana Superdome squats on fifty acres of downtown New Orleans like a half moon. In scale and shape and texture it is so out of synch with the city's old skyline and peeling decay that it could be taken for the tent of an evangelist from outer space. It is the biggest room in the world. It is the new religion. It is tomorrow's heroic ruin.

It also appears to be a superscam.

The Super Bowl was supposed to be played in the Superdome this year, but the interior decorating has barely begun. During construction, second- and third-generation pigeons that have never seen the light of real day have taken up residence in domed condominiums.

Well, the pyramids weren't built in a month either. In time the Superdome will be completed—then what? Will the people of Louisiana find out that they were the pigeons? Or, when the plate is passed to pay for the shrine, will they feel that it fills their spiritual needs?

Nine years ago they overwhelmingly approved a referendum to back the bonds required to build it. The $40 million Astrodome in Houston was a huge public relations success, in no small measure because of the Louisianans who went there to cool off. Promoters convinced them they needed a We're No. 1 showcase of their own.

The promoters insisted that a pleasure dome would cost $45 million, $50 million tops. Skeptics tried to get them to put that in writing on the referendum. It wasn't necessary, the promoters insisted.

The referendum turned out to be a blank check. And when the Saints came marching into town and regularly drew crowds of 70,000 at Tulane Stadium, the numbers on the check escalated by leaps and bonds. The dome became a Superdome, capacity 80,000. And the bill for it now reads $163,313,315, or ten times as much as the whole Louisiana Purchase.

The Astrodome, despite its comparatively modest price, has never shown a profit. Adam Richards, comptroller of the Astrodome, said of the Superdome, "I don't see how they can ever make it pay. If they had an event every day they couldn't do it. It's going to cost someone a heckuva lot of money."

The Astrodome has some 250 events annually. A quarter of them are baseball games. New Orleans doesn't have a baseball team yet.

At this stage there are few quibbles with the Superdome as a facility, although any stadium with 80,000 seats built both for football and baseball is likely to generate a number of quibbles. If the Astrodome was as big as all outdoors, the Superdome is bigger. It has two unique features. Stands can be rearranged to form a 19,000-seat basketball-hockey arena. A six-sided television screen will hang from the apex of the dome. Also the ramps and hallways are tiled and rugged.

Seattle is building a purely functional domed stadium with 60,000 capacity for a reported $50 million or so.

Supporters of the New Orleans project claim its benefits to the community can't be measured by bottom lines. It has inspired a $500 million building boom, they say, including 7,000 hotel rooms for the important tourist industry. (A 4 percent tax on hotel bills is assessed to help pay off the opulent playpen.)

Critics point out that other downtown areas, in Saint Louis and Pittsburgh and Cincinnati, for example, have been revitalized with stadium projects at a fraction of the cost of the Superdome, and with less jarring impact on the senses. It is, they suggest, sacrilege to plop down a fifty-acre electronic instrument on the birthplace of jazz.

"When I grow up I hope they spend my tax dollars on more important things," a precocious ten-year-old said. On what? Last November a referendum to build new schools was defeated in New Orleans.

The ringer I brought in for the last quote was my daughter, Jamie.

TELEVISION SHOW

The first Super Bowl had uncertainty going for it. The third Super Bowl had Joe Namath going for it. The other Super Bowls have been Hackensack in the garbage-burning season.

As Super Bowl sites, Los Angeles had a scent of glamour, New Orleans offered the hurly-burly of the French Quarter, Miami gave us sun. Houston showed us what the Super Bowl is about.

The Super Bowl is a television show, a business convention and a football game. It is a peculiar American blend of cold and hot passion, like a Philadelphia pretzel smothered with mustard.

As symbolized by the Astrodome, with its artificial outdoors, Houston is an ideal television studio for major events. It has been that for championship fights and Billie Jean King–Bobby Riggs.

Fueled by the oil and space industries, downtown Houston has quickly become a forest of grim, no-nonsense skyscrapers. The Regency Hyatt Hotel that was Super Bowl headquarters, unlike its swinging sister in Atlanta, resembles a twenty-first century cellblock. Corporate city for the corporate game.

In part because the game itself has evolved into the anticlimax bowl, the primary impressions run to the feverish foreplay leading up to it.

Item: Ford, which spends $10 million on advertising and promoting pro football, had an allotment of 2,500 tickets.

Item: American Express threw a series of parties for executives of corporate giants. Walter Cronkite, for a reported fee of $5,000, gave a short informal address at one of them. Also present were fifteen NFL players, each paid $500 plus weekend expenses for themselves and their wives, to mingle with guests. Alex Karras got a larger fee for a private pregame analysis of the game.

Item: Bruce Devlin and Billy Talbert were among the golfers and tennis players imported by corporate party givers to play with guests.

Item: National Football League Properties, which merchandises NFL-endorsed products, gave sales seminars in hustling everything from cigarette lighters to cat food.

Item: The NFL spent $75,000 on a hoedown—roast pig, country music, sawdust—in the Astrodome.

Item: In the midst of the energy crisis, the Houston airports were so crowded with private jets that some of them had to park in Beaumont and San Antonio after depositing their corporate cargoes.

Item: Because of a shortage of limousines, a leaser had them shipped in from as far away as Spokane, Washington. They leased for $250 a day.

A few impressions from this orgy of excess.

"The business of America," said Calvin Coolidge, "is business." So is the business of sport.

As our top one-shot circus maximus, the Super Bowl gives us a glimpse of how things work in this big, rich country. One has the feeling of being in the presence of a secret government.

Since the game is held in a neutral city, the passion that championship spectacles usually evoke is absent. The passion goes into the preparation and partying.

In the world of wheeling, dealing and selling, it is the wheeling, dealing and selling themselves that are the real game. The other game, the thing they are wheeling, etc., seems incidental.

WHY HIM?

After the generation gap sixties, in which Joe Namath became a symbol of rebellion in the same white-shoed backfield with Muhammad Ali and Bob Dylan, Terry Bradshaw was seen as a squirt of fresh deodorant. He was going to be a hero to parents as well as children.

Bradshaw was not only a terrific quarterback prospect, but he was modest, well groomed and a Bible reader. Clinching the matter, he wore the same black shoes as his teammates, the Steelers.

But something happened to the scenario. The parents grew up.

Joe Namath was in New Orleans yesterday, taping a pre-Super Bowl television show. As he strolled through the French Quarter with Don Meredith, little old ladies from Dubuque paid homage to him as the prophet of the seventies.

Flower print dress: "How's your pantyhose, Joe?"

Pink pantsuit, brushing him as she held out a $5 bill for him to autograph: "Oh my God, I injured his tackling hand."

Meanwhile, in another part of town, a bearded, cigar-smoking blond god was explaining why he wasn't as dumb as some folks thought. It was Terry Bradshaw.

In his fifth season, Bradshaw and the Steelers charged through the play-offs into their first Super Bowl. "It's been an uphill struggle," he said. "It wasn't a dream come true."

Until the last two weeks Bradshaw had been fitted with a dunce cap instead of a helmet by teammates, opponents and critics. At a time when quarterbacks have been invested with renaissance fantasies of physical, emotional, mental and occult power, Bradshaw didn't measure up.

"I was supposed to be the savior of the team," he said. "It was too much for a twenty-one-year-old."

Compounding it, the team became so good that it frequently was the savior of him, confirming him a remedial student of the game.

"I've been labeled Ozark Ike and Dummy and Country Bumpkin, and I hate it," Bradshaw said. "You don't have to be Einstein or graduate magna cum laude to play quarterback. All you need is common sense. But if you talk slow and have a clean-cut, square face they think you must be stupid. I'm not stupid. I had to learn like everyone else. I've had peaks and valleys and now I've arrived."

So, even gods pay dues. As he has struggled to master his craft, and his own self-doubts, Bradshaw has been through personal changes that have jarred and matured him too. His parents, he said, thought his beard was an act of rebellion or a mask from his woes. He was benched, booed and divorced in 1974.

His response was not what you would expect in 1974. He went back to his Bible and his record player for solace. "They fed my soul," he said.

They feed him humbling pie. Yesterday Bradshaw had a paperback with him entitled *The Late Great Planet Eares,* dealing with Biblical prophecies of doom, and he recited a few lines from his favorite country music. "Why me, Lord? Why do the good things happen to me?" And, "If heartaches were fame in love's cheating game, I'd be a legend in my time."

Is Terry Bradshaw preparing himself for the worst? Should he lose Sunday, as well he may to a brainy minister's son named Fran Tarkenton, he will have to defend his intellect once again.

As one of the resident Joe Namath watchers in New York, I've done more than my share of columns on him. Since I devoted a chapter of a previous book to him, I've elected to go with a fragment in this collection, to illustrate the witting conspiracy between a superstar and the media to exploit a name that sells. Superstars use the media to negotiate and bargain, using inflated numbers (as promoters often do) that seldom bear any relationship to reality. The media goes along with it on the theory that the bigger the number the better the story. A columnist gets caught up in the frenzy of manufactured news and has to say something.

WILL HE OR WON'T HE?

Is he is or is he isn't? Will he or won't he? Why? Why not?

Joe Namath's genius for keeping people guessing about his future is as instinctive as his genius for throwing a football. Like all the great ones, he was born with it. When he spiraled his first rattle out of the crib he gurgled, "These diapers stink. I wanna be a movie star."

On a raw, wet day fit for neither man nor quarterback, Joe Namath's twin genius was in full flower yesterday.

Treating his possible departure from the Jets like alternate sides parking, he said before the game that it is doubtful that he'll be back and after the game that he might be back. Sundays, of course, you can park anywhere. Monday, Wednesday and Friday he's going. Tuesday, Thursday and Saturday he's staying.

Namath's genius bloomed during the game when the Jets beat the Bills on his late touchdown pass. So, if indeed it was a farewell performance, it was the last bottle of a vintage wine and it went down as richly as ever.

But is he is and will he?

By word and deed—the high that the recent winning streak has been for him—Namath indicates he wants to keep playing. He may be merely negotiating for a bigger, better long-term contract. There's one terrific danger if he gets it. Who's going to ask is he is or will he?

Namath carried out the charade for another six months, managing it to a nice crescendo with the fairy tale that a World Football League team was offering him $4,500,000. The last six numbers were in cash, the rest in fantasy futures, and Namath signed with the Jets again. The media swallowed it whole, eagerly, from start to finish.

Talented mavericks like Namath who do battle with football's impersonal system help define the system. Two more coming up.

THE TOUGHEST QUESTION

John Riggins, like Joe Namath, is an enigma wrapped in a bandage. Namath's future with the Jets may be in tedious doubt, but the Jets' future with Riggins is a fire engine of a different color, as Joe Kuharich used to say.

Coach Charley Winner has said in a fit of overstatement that Riggins could be "the greatest fullback ever," which he has modified to, "When he's playing he's the best in the business," which is still pretty good.

When he's playing. The question about Riggins is whether he is capable of giving them a full championship season. That's the toughest question to ask of a football player because it's a tough game that makes hard and perhaps excessive demands of toughness. Implicit in the ethic of putting one's body on the line, or in the backfield, is the willingness to play hurt, providing the player can help the team. Is a professional duty-bound to do so?

Since he has but one body, John Riggins thinks not. He has missed ten games with injuries in three seasons, and in every case the Jets have expressed doubts about his commitment if not his courage.

Team physician James Nicholas identified the issue when he said Riggins was capable of playing after two of the four games he sat out with a shoulder injury this season, but that he himself, as a civilian, would do as Riggins did. Riggins explained that he would hate to wake up in twenty years suffering from an injury he could have avoided by being careful as a player.

That certainly is the intelligent way to look at it—Joe Namath played hurt as a college senior and wrecked his knee for life—but from the Jets' point of view, can they win with careful players? "That attitude in an important player," said one Jet, "can be contagious."

Because Riggins is immensely gifted, the Jets tolerate his instinct for self-preservation in much the same way they tolerate Namath's heroic vulnerability. It's worth putting up with. Said Charley Winner, "Some players can play with injuries and some can't. If a player feels he can't, it's no use playing him because he won't perform. It's like religion or politics—I can't change his feelings. I'm just glad we have him and don't have to play against him."

That is the enlightened way to look at it, as many coaches do today. Few of them still use techniques of fear and humiliation to effect miracles of healing. Although there have been ruthless coaches and unethical doctors who would send players into battle who didn't belong there, injured players with an overdeveloped sense of loyalty or overwhelming fear of losing their jobs have been their own worst enemies far more often.

Riggins learned to trust his instincts after he suffered a knee injury two years ago. He had seen the Jets cut his predecessor at fullback, Matt Snell, commenting then, "When your tank is empty they get rid of you." X-rays of his knee were negative, but he felt something rattling around and he refused to play. Later an operation uncovered a floating piece of cartilage.

There is one element in all this that has been impossible to measure in Riggins. Larry Csonka is celebrated for playing hurt, but he said when the Dolphins played the Jets that he would have rested if they didn't need the win. The Jets haven't played with anything big at stake since Riggins joined them.

That game with the Dolphins proved to be big for the

Jets and Riggins. He decided to suit up that morning and was instrumental in the upset that followed. "I felt tears coming to my eyes after that game," he said. "It was the best feeling I had after a game since I was a kid.

"I wouldn't play for the front office, but if something was at stake I would play for my teammates if I could. I'm not a rock. I have to live with these guys."

WRIGHT AND WRONG

On the final play between the Redskins and the Bears, Curt Knight lined up for a field goal attempt that would decide the outcome. Along the sidelines, as in the stands, there was bedlam. One voice could be heard above the madding crowd.

"Odin, Odin," pleaded Steve Wright of the Bears at the top of his large lungs. "Odin, where are you now that we need you? Odin, blow; Odin, blow."

Odin is the Viking god of weather—bad, mean, blowy weather. It was blowing pretty good at Soldier Field but George Allen swore there was no wind at all until Knight's high, deep and true parabola began to descend. Then a gust faded the ball just off target.

Of course, Steve Wright, as almost any coach will tell you, worships pagan gods. He has been viewed as a heretic by such high priests as Bear Bryant, Vince Lombardi and George Allen. And Wellington Mara. They saw him as Steve Wrong, a football player who laughs.

"Football coaches think I'm undermining them because I see the humor in the game," Steve Wright said. "You know something? They're right."

Now in his eighth year in the NFL, offensive tackle Wright is playing first-string through an entire season for the first time since high school. His troubles began at Bear Bryant U.

"A freshman coach gave me a forearm in the face—split both lips and bloodied my nose," Wright said. "I told him that from then on it was Newton's third law: action and reaction. Bryant's favorite trick was grabbing the nose guard and bringing the helmet down on a player's nose. He tried it on me once and I leaned away, laughing. You know how that went over."

Wright next exasperated Vince Lombardi. Lombardi had a respect for talent that transcended petty grievances and he stuck with Wright for four years. On one occasion he beat on Wright's chest because he didn't seem to be killing himself in practice. On another occasion a toilet flushed while Lombardi was giving his pregame kill-for-the-love-of-God sermon, and out waddled Wright with his pants at half-mast.

"I had great respect for Lombardi," Wright said. "But he was an emotional guy and I wasn't. He interpreted that as not taking my job seriously. My feeling about his pep talks was: get it over with and let's get out of here and play. I don't need that bull. A lot of pros don't."

The Packers traded Wright to the Giants, who suspended him midway through the season. Wright had been caught mocking the bosses. "The word I got on our trips was that Mara sat in the back of the plane to make sure the married guys didn't talk to the stewardesses."

Wright rode the bench for Bill Austin of the Redskins last season. He liked Austin because he left him alone. He gives George Allen high marks but wasn't personally fond of him "because he lied to me and then was mealymouthed when he traded me—I had to say, 'Spit it out, George.'"

Jim Dooley of the Bears is nice too, because he leaves Wright alone. "I had a confrontation with [line coach] Jim Ringo at the start. I told him not to give me any bull. If I do the job play me and if I don't do the job get rid of me, but don't bull me. Not playing is a bummer, but taking bull from a coach to make him feel good is worse. I doubt that I'll be here very long. They've got a guy named W. Clement Stone, a millionaire friend of George Halas, who gives us pep talks. On the road we have a two-hour siesta time Saturday afternoons when we have to be in our rooms. This is ridiculous. We're grown men. Now do you know why I laugh? How can you take that seriously?"

As Abbie Hoffman once said about Jimmy Piersall, "He showed them it was a game so they locked him up."

Today I would also want to explore with Riggins and Wright the sources of their nonconformism.
My attitude about drugs and a famous university's attitude about football aren't exactly conformist.

DIZZYLAND

The charge in the San Diego Chargers—what little there is of it—apparently is still taken orally. There must be a moral here someplace.

The Chargers were exposed as a proving ground for the drug industry and the amphetamine champs of the NFL during a court suit brought by a former lineman, Houston Ridge, who claimed he sustained a disabling injury because he was drugged up.

The Chargers and the league agreed to a $300,000 out-of-court settlement because, it seems, it was team policy to force-feed pills down the players' throats like stuffing Christmas geese.

Sid Gillman instituted this policy. The NFL, which swoons with operatic distress whenever it is suggested that pill popping is a fact of professional football life, promising greater vigilance as soon as it is revived by smelling salts, now permits Sid Gillman to general manage the Houston Oilers.

Well, in the latest bulletin from Dizzyland, a state report following up on the Ridge case tells us that the Chargers are now voluntarily gulping those little baddies like salted peanuts. The report exonerates the organization, but charges: "The situation is worse today. . . . The state has cut off the legal outlets of drugs for these players. Unfortunately, some of the players are self-medicating themselves."

Which is where we came in last week when George

Burman of the Redskins revealed that a third of his team-mates use the stuff.

What should be the proper response of the NFL to these disclosures?

A promotion campaign should be orchestrated around the Chargers. They should be on national television every week for the rest of the season as living proof of what happens to you when you take drugs. Their time-outs should be punctuated by public service commercials like so:

> The San Diego Chargers are the amphetamine champs of the NFL.
> But they aren't the champs of anything else.
> They have won seventeen games in the last four seasons.
> Try amphetamines.
> They really help you perform.
> Don't they?

All over America amphetamines will be flushed down toilets.

The Redskins, being successful, would be a harder sell. The NFL should wait until the play-offs and hit the public with this approach:

> For the third straight year the Washington Redskins are in the play-offs.
> For the third straight year they have lost in the play-offs.
> One third of the Redskins are on drugs.
> Two thirds aren't.
> Maybe the Washington Redskins would win the play-offs if three thirds weren't on drugs.

Some smarty might reply that the Redskins might win it all if three thirds were on drugs, and where do you go from there?

The problem is how do you stop a man from doing what he wants to do to his body? In fact, as long as he isn't hurting anyone else, should you try to stop him?

The league has tried to discourage pill popping through education. Police work is the next step—drug tests, urinalysis. The players are opposed to that. It would be a blow to the NFL's pompous image of high moral purpose to have to resort to that.

Some football players can't handle their fears as well as others, and are less susceptible to other forms of stimulation, so they use drugs for artificial courage. As long as there is no hard evidence that drugs help performance, and as long as players are made aware of the possible harmful side effects, I really don't care what they do. Any more than I cared whether Hemingway drank or Satchmo puffed funny cigarettes.

A FIFTEEN-FOOT KAZOO AT CHICAGO U.

In keeping with its classic academic standards, a typical cheer at the University of Chicago used to go:

Themistocles, Thucydides, Peloponnesian War,
X square, Y square, H_2SO_4.
Who for, what for, who are you going to root for?
Chicago, Chicago, Chicago.

Followed by a demure "rah" and a mock kick by the cheerleaders, all Quiz Kids going-on Susan Sontags.

This was fine in the old days, but now varsity football on a modest basis is back at Chicago, thirty years after Chancellor Robert Hutchins banned it, partly because they couldn't compete in the Big Ten anymore and partly as an overreaction to overemphasis, and it is a very different scene. One of the more popular cheers today goes: "Workers of the world unite—fight!"

Another dandy is: "You've got the points, we've got the joints [marijuana]."

Jay Berwanger, the All-American halfback who was the first pick in the first pro draft in 1936, wouldn't recognize the scene. Neither would Amos Alonzo Stagg, who coached Chicago powerhouses. But it's football and if it seems to be choreographed by Fellini and Abbie Hoffman all the better.

There was the halftime show at the Homecoming game. While Ohio State was crushing Illinois with the best football players free tuition, room and board could buy, accompanied by several hundred marching tooters and bongers, some of America's finest young scholars were having a scrum with the North Central jayvees, and fifty soulful freaks blew on kazoos.

Barbara Yondurf, a junior majoring in urban studies, is the head cheerleader, one of eight bouncing braless activists. She described the festivities.

"We did a parody of Homecoming Days," she said. "The week before we played at Marquette and they had a real Homecoming, with a Homecoming queen. She was flown onto the field in a helicopter and got a ride in a limousine.

Our Homecoming queen was a blue refrigerator, carried onto the field on a stretcher. It represented all the frigid football queens.

"The kazoo band was a motley crew of hippies. They roamed all over the field in circles, chaotically. Instead of claiming we have the largest drum in the world, like most colleges, we had the largest kazoo, about fifteen feet long. Everybody yelled, 'We're No. 1.' Meanwhile the announcer was describing the marches they weren't marching. He'd say, 'That was "The Stars and Stripes Forever" ' or 'the Chorale from Beethoven's Ninth.' Then he said, 'Now they're forming a bust of Mayor Daley. Now they're forming a bust of the bust last Wednesday night.' "

It is an intellectual Mets scene. Fans are encouraged to suggest cheers. Originality is applauded wildly.

"One of our favorites is, 'Get rid of the referee—anarchy, anarchy.' Another is, 'Mutilate, mutilate, mutilate.' And, 'Ho, Ho, Ho Chi Minh, Chicago U. is gonna win.' "

As for the football, Barbara Yondurf said no one was too sure what was going on, largely because there is no scoreboard or clock. But the stands that were built for 500, optimistically, were overflowing, and everybody was having a terrific time. "The coaches are hysterical with joy," she said. "They're supposed to have a good player, but I don't know his name."

The head coach is Walter Hass, who played for Bernie Bierman at Minnesota. He has a squad of thirty, half of whom played high school football. He isn't quite sure what the students are cheering, but he is thrilled with their enthusiasm, as are others. "John Anderson, the oldest C [letter] man, who played in 1906, and other alumni are talking about giving us a dinner, like in the old days," he said.

After the Homecoming game the students tore down the goalposts and, singing "We Shall Overcome," carried them to the university president's home and propped them there.

I don't cover much college football, for professional and personal reasons. It has been completely overshadowed by the pros in the New York area. (Not much of an excuse, admittedly, because small-time college football is a fun spectacle.) The games are played on Saturdays and I have an aversion to covering games on Saturdays when I have to cover games on Sundays. Pros are fairer game for criticism, and are around much longer for inspection than undergraduates.

The next series of columns focuses on coaching and coaching. I find basketball coaches generally easier to get to know than football coaches because they aren't as obsessed by secrecy, and they seem to relate better to people—athletes and sportswriters—as people.

THE POWER OF NEGATIVE THINKING

Dick Bestwick, the offensive line coach at Georgia Tech, has refined the Vince Lombardi technique of building up by tearing down. This is what he tells his boys:

"Let's face it. The reason that you're playing offense is because you aren't good enough to play defense. When you play guard, it's because you aren't smart enough to be a quarterback, not fast enough to be a halfback, not rugged enough to be a fullback, not big enough to be a tackle, and don't have the hands to be an end."

Presumably the power of negative thinking enrages the boys and woe to the other guy. In the pursuit of greater glory, let us build up by tearing down the rest of the squad.

"You tight ends. What are you but glorified tackles. If you had any guts you'd be linebackers. If you had any speed you'd be fullbacks. If you had any brains you'd be dangerous. Schultz, I saw you last night in the Crystal Lounge. You were a tight end all right. Monahan, when was the last time you bought a round? You're the tightest end I ever saw. And God forbid you should have to catch a pass over the middle. Talk about hearing footsteps. You guys hear the grass grow. You're uptight ends.

"Cornerbacks. Wide ends with hands dipped in bear grease. Wilson, are you sure that stickum you use isn't dropum? No wonder you lost your playbook. You couldn't hold on to a pair of gloves if you were wearing them. Barnes, I know you were a great basketball player, but they don't penalize you in this league for tackling. Just stick your head in there. If it gets knocked off you won't miss it. They'll have to look for it like it's a contact lens.

"Running backs. Smith, running to daylight doesn't mean the sidelines. Thomas, faking is the last thing I'd think you'd have trouble with. You've been faking all season. And when's the last time you threw a block? In kindergarten? Borders, you'd be all league if you could memorize the plays. Even numbers to the right, odd numbers to the left. No, stupid, that's your left foot.

"Defensive linemen. The last time any of you tackled a quarterback it was Joe Namath, who has two broken legs, and it was on a Saturday night. Meyer, I read where you had fourteen unassisted tackles last week. They weren't tackles, they were guys running over your face. Brown, must you fall into every trap? When nobody blocks you it isn't because they've forgotten you, it's because they think you have the brains of a water buffalo. If you baboons don't do any better I'll trade the bunch of you for a new set of dummies. At least I don't have to feed them six times a day.

"Wide receivers. Girls, I think you're adorable out there away from the big boys. I'm going to call a meeting to introduce you to your teammates. Brandt, I wouldn't say you're afraid to get a hit on a turnaround, but you're the first end I ever saw who plants his feet solidly in midair.

"Safetymen. You're like left fielders and first basemen. There's no other position to hide you. You're too slow to play cornerback, too small to play anywhere else and too ugly to cut. Stay out of my sight. I'm going to be sick.

"Linebackers. You guys get more glory for doing less than the CIA. With a good line in front of you, you'd have to pay to get into the ball park. Without a secondary to make up for your mistakes, you'd be run out of the ball park. Ratske, are you sure you didn't go to college at the Lighthouse? Anderson, you really stink. They run away from your side of the field so much because you haven't taken a shower since the preseason.

"Quarterbacks. If I had as much money as you, Williams, I wouldn't waste my time studying game plans either. Did your speech writer fix you up for your next luncheon? Has Johnny Carson been calling plays for you? You're the first quarterback I've seen whose IQ can be measured by the distance you can throw a football.

"Now, fellas, all you have to do is believe in yourselves and nobody will lick us."

HOW IT IS

For seven years Tom Nugent filled the University of Maryland football with laughing gas. It spiraled euphorically, end-over-ended giddily, bounced crazily. He thought the game should be fun.

Tom Nugent's idea of fun was to enliven Saturday afternoons with passes and schoolyard plays—cross-country laterals, wild kickoff returns and so on. He was a great showman but he was a sound fundamentals man too. Years earlier his first play at Florida State, famous for its student circus, featured a halfback in motion—doing flips and cartwheels—while the fullback slammed up the middle for fifteen yards.

Maryland football caught on again and the alumni came back to the campus in record numbers, but Nugent had a fatal weakness. He didn't win championships and he didn't go to bowl games. His teams were notorious for beating people they weren't supposed to beat and losing to teams they were supposed to beat. At VMI, where his career began, he beat Georgia Tech and lost to Catawba.

So, despite the revival and the razzle-dazzle, Tom Nugent was jettisoned last year. Maryland's idea of fun was winning them all.

Lou Saban, who had won two straight AFL championships in Buffalo, was recruited to replace Nugent. Saban didn't want to be a professional anymore and Maryland didn't want to be semiprofessional anymore.

Last Saturday Maryland lost its opener to Penn State by a touchdown. Monday Saban fired four seniors, two of them starters. He fired them ceremoniously, in front of the squad. This did wonders for their character.

The four players had not been discipline problems. Saban said they might become morale problems. Their biggest problem was, simply, that they weren't good enough.

"I have nothing against them personally, but as seniors, as boys you expect to be your leaders, they were a tremendous disappointment against Penn State," Saban said.

"We need a new start and a new feeling. Seniors can be bad for the team if they aren't first-string, if they're going to be grumpy and grouchy on the bench. This wasn't an overnight thing. I've watched them. One of them complained when I had him running with the second team. One of them came in twenty pounds overweight. I knew their past history in tough games. It was not a quick action."

Not quick, just harsh and cruel. A Bud Wilkinson might have demoted them, seeing it as his obligation not to stigmatize them with a public dismissal, hoping they might react well to adversity, having the confidence in himself to overcome their disloyalty, real or imagined. A Tom Nugent would have told a few snappy jokes at the next quarterback luncheon, installed a triple reverse punt for Wake Forest this week and left it at that.

A Bear Bryant would have marched the whole team into a pit and scrimmaged them for a few weeks, trusting that the weak and the lame would be intimidated or embarrassed into quitting school, leaving him with extra scholarships to hand out.

Saban's approach wasn't that primitive. It was merely professional.

"Sure it may seem harsh," he said. "Sure feelings were hurt. Sure it's drastic. But what easy way is there? If they're demoted to the third-string, won't everyone know it? The only thing we have done is tell them they're not good enough, they didn't match up to our standards. We told them to become students and get their degrees. They keep their scholarships.

"What was the sense in prolonging the agony? I'm a firm believer that people don't change overnight. The business of breakdowns in crucial spots had to stop. You can't wait until the middle of the season. We had to establish that you have to go all out, that football required spirit. It's going to take two, three years to rebuild and we thought we should start now.

"It's discouraging to the players, it's a shock to them, but they have to be responsible. These are not kids. They are twenty-one and twenty-two. Two of them are married. If they don't do well, they ought to be man enough to take it."

Saban himself was fired from two jobs, at Northwestern and from the Boston Patriots. He knows what the name of the game is.

"When I was at Case Tech [in Cleveland] the purpose was to turn out engineers, not football players. I understand that. But this is big-time college football. The college wants to have a representative team, show progress and put on a good show. I understand this too. I have to be selfish. I have to think of self-preservation. If the coach doesn't win, the coach goes.

"That's how it is. I'm taking a realistic approach. I'm not a hypocrite."

He isn't. The university is.

A LEARNING EXPERIENCE

"I told a kid he was doing everything to make me throw him off the team. I told him we need him, he can help us, but he must decide himself whether he wants to leave because I'm not going to get rid of him. He stayed and helped us win a championship.

"Our star player was very upset because he got some quick fouls. He was getting on the referee from the bench. I told him to keep it up, so he calmed down. He's negatively suggestible.

"One of our best players sauntered into the gym real slow at the tap-off. He changed into his uniform like Superman and was on the bench in one second flat. I say, 'Are you all right?' He says, 'Yeah. I had a problem.' In a few minutes I put him in the game. None of the kids objected.

"Unbeknownst to me, a player was sick. We were doing wind sprints and he wouldn't do them. I said to the team that if one man doesn't do it you all have to do more of them. The next day I apologized to them. What was I proving? Why did I have to punish them all? I tell them I make mistakes too.

"One kid, six feet seven inches—and we don't get many six-foot seven-inch kids—was ambivalent about playing. I told him to be his own man. He quit and wrote a play that was produced at school. I think that's fantastic."

The coach is not Sigmund Freud or John Dewey. He is Ed Kramer of Lehman College, which has won its second straight City University championship. The reason: they are the most disciplined team in the league.

"I have no rules of behavior. Some kids are upset about

that. My methods work, I think, because I let them get the anger out of themselves.

"Coaches are rigid and inflexible because there's a fear of losing control. It never happens here. That doesn't mean we don't have problems. Players have problems, coaches have problems. I don't think you can solve all problems by yelling.

"But I can be authoritative. I surprise myself sometimes what a dictator I am. To coach the game itself you have to be a dictator, preferably a benevolent dictator.

"One kid who came from another school said my practices are the most disorganized he's ever seen, but my team is the most organized. My only rules are play as hard as you can, move, pass the ball to the guy who's free, shoot if you have a shot. I hope all the shots are lay-ups.

"The fun of the game to me is helping each other. They used to be skeptical. One-on-one is the game now. I told them they didn't have to dribble to win. They thought I was crazy. Now they think I invented a new game. They don't know I used to sit in the 50-cent seats in the side balcony at the Garden, watching CCNY. We averaged twenty assists a game. That's unheard of today.

"For kids who can't play, they're beautiful to watch. I've watched Maryland play. You know something? My kids play better, a better brand of basketball."

Ed Kramer makes $18,500 as a physical education instructor. He gets credit for five of the fourteen hours he has to teach for coaching basketball. None of his players have scholarships. His security and their volunteer status—why hasn't somebody thought of this before?—help make the coach-player relationship a teacher-student relationship.

"The key to teaching is to form a relationship quickly to get the student to be willing to change by showing him you can benefit him. I think I have a good relationship with my kids. I would like to think they're getting a wonderful learning experience. I read where Lefty Driesell and John Wooden create men. I don't know that I'm creating men. I'm trying to help them be better.

"They know me and I know them better than anyone

in the world. We've shared good and bad times. They love each other and I think they love me and I love them."

THOSE CHAMPIONSHIP SEASONS

Farrell, Pennsylvania, probably isn't the right place to examine the reality behind Jason Miller's prizewinning play, *That Championship Season,* but it is the one we are stuck with. It is the Pennsylvania State basketball champions of 1952 who cavort and writhe across the stage, politically ambitious and frustrated in their middle years. Farrell won the championship that year.

Trouble is, there is no one "that championship season" in Farrell, as there is in the play. Farrell may have the most remarkable high school record, all things considered, in the country. With an enrollment of 625 students in a town of 11,000, it competes against schools with two to seven times as many students in the cities, and it has won the state championship seven times in twenty-three years.

"We have a good shot at an eighth this year," said Eddie McCluskey.

Eddie McCluskey coaches the Farrell basketball team. He is fifty-six years old. Like the retired coach in the play, he is a martinet with a reputation for teaching smart, aggressive basketball. "They call me the little Vince Lombardi," McCluskey said. "Everyone toes the mark on my teams." Also like the coach in the play, McCluskey is not admired by his adversaries. "Some coaches charge me with being a green-eyed monster," he said.

In the play the coach is a bachelor wed to past triumphs through the game of adult politics. One of his former players is the mayor. Another is a powerful businessman. A third is a junior high school principal. The coach urges them on for the coming election with the win-at-all-costs sentiments and passions of that championship season. (A fourth player is a wry drunk, the fifth, who disapproved of the coach's philosophy, is no longer part of the team.)

Eddie McCluskey, as a guest of the producers, saw the

play a year and a half ago. "The coach and I were a little alike," he said. "Winning was everything to a certain degree. I'd sacrifice most everything to win, but I wouldn't break the rules. Like him, basketball is my life, although I have a family and he didn't.

"But things out here are different than in the play. Like the play, this is a mill town—Sharon Steel—but those fellows stayed in the same town, while my kids have gone on to bigger things. Very few kids stay here if they go on to college. If they stay they work in the mill or at Westinghouse. We don't have many athletes in politics.

"I felt sorry for those players. My guys went on to other fields and were successful. Those players seem to be living in the past. The coach too. I don't live in the past. It seems to me that that championship was the only thing he had and he wanted to hold on to it. Here I am going for another one.

"To me basketball is a means to an end, something that will help kids face the challenges later on. These kids know they'll have a fight on their hands in life and basketball shows them they can cope with almost anything. And it's the only way they can go to college."

How this deeply competitive ethic affects the frightened hearts of men is a question that playwrights and not coaches pose. Eddie McCluskey is satisfied that it works in Farrell, for kids and adults. The 3,000-seat gymnasium is more than half sold out with season tickets.

"Funny thing," McCluskey said, "we had a reunion of the 1952 team, a class reunion, the same year the play opened. They called the team the Mitey Mites. Julius McCoy, at six feet one inch, was the center and our biggest man. He went on to become an All-American at Michigan State. He had a lot of polish for a black kid. I knew he'd do well. He's an aid to Governor Shapp. Anthony DeCello, a little guard, went to Washington and Jefferson, my old school, and is an outstanding attorney in Pittsburgh. Herky Hoffman became a first-string quarterback at Penn State. He's with Firestone Rubber. Nick Dann went to Marietta College. He's in intelligence for the government.

The only one still in Farrell is Si Alli. He's a mailman."

It is the season of championship seasons again all over the country, a familiar season in Farrell, Pennsylvania.

Ideas for columns originate in many ways. That one was suggested by Beano Cook, then a public relations man with the American Broadcasting Company. I think it's the only time a PR person has given me a good idea outside his own professional interest.

PRESS

Press Maravich was one of the great two-handed bombers. Clair Bee knew. Moby Dick knew.

Press Maravich—his name is Pete but Press stuck because he delivered the *Pittsburgh Press* as a boy—came out of West Aliquippa, Pennsylvania, steel country. He worked in mills from midnight to eight o'clock in the morning while going to high school and playing ball. He got a scholarship to little Davis and Elkins college in West Virginia.

Little Davis and Elkins came to Brooklyn to play LIU in 1938. Clair Bee thought so little of little Davis and Elkins that he turned the team over to an assistant and went to the Garden to scout Hank Luisetti and Stanford. At the half little Davis and Elkins was winning and a call went out to Bee. He rushed to the gym and LIU won on a last-minute basket. Press Maravich scored twenty-nine points, a terrific number of points in those days. Bee was so impressed that he gave him a private clinic after the game. "That was Clair Bee," Maravich said.

This was Moby Dick, the Unknown Whale of World War II. Press Maravich was a navy pilot hunting Japanese submarines. He saw this huge shadow in the water and dropped some bombs on it. Oil came to the surface. "We cheered like hell," he said.

It proved to be a whale. And that proved to be the story of Press Maravich's life until Pete Maravich came along. His direct hits produced a lot of blubber and not much else.

He played professionally for four years in the leagues that preceded the NBA. He was one of the top guards and made as much as $4,500 a season. Pete Maravich will make that for combing his hair.

Press Maravich went back to college on the GI Bill and earned his second and third degrees. He took a job in a Pittsburgh high school teaching English and coaching, and working in a steel mill on weekends. After three years of that he returned to little Davis and Elkins as head coach. His salary was $3,200. The first thing he did there was cut down a place in the woods for a new gym, create local interest, collect a few dollars and practically build it himself. The gym seated 8,000. It's still there. In 1956 Maravich hit the big time—Clemson, the Atlantic Coast Conference. He was so excited about the opportunity that he neglected to ask what it paid. "I figured it had to be $8,000. When I saw the first check I couldn't believe it. I was making $5,000."

"At Clemson," said Maravich, "they didn't know a basketball from a turkey bladder." Six years later he took over at North Carolina State, where they knew the difference very well, for $8,500. He won two conference championships in four years and asked for a raise. "We'd been starving. We were always in debt. They turned me down."

Wherever he had been and wherever he went, Maravich had to start all over. "Build, build, build. That's all I know," he said. But what he built best was a son who could do things with a basketball nobody had thought of. "I taught him the tricks to keep him from getting bored with the game."

N.C. State made a costly mistake. Father and son went to LSU. Father got a five-year contract at $15,000. Son did it all. LSU is now building a 15,000-seat arena. Son will sign for $1 million. And father will have to rebuild all over. "I have to recruit in the Midwest," he said. "The kids think Baton Rouge is in South America."

Press Maravich said he wouldn't give up the last three years for anything, but the sum of the scuffling from West Aliquippa to the National Invitation Tournament has taken its toll. His wife, a basketball widow besieged by crank calls when the Maraviches brought their pagan religion to football-mad LSU, has a case of nerves. He is an old fifty years old, graying and stooped, though the open-pit fire still burns on the sideline and his tongue shoots off sparks of hot steel.

"His life ages a man before his time," Pete Maravich said.

"I want to die on a basketball court," Press Maravich said.

THE EIGHTH WONDER

There are certain things you do not expect to see in this sporting life.

You do not expect to see Joe Namath leaning back in an easy chair, kids and dogs yapping around him, the little woman fetching his slippers.

You do not expect to see Muhammad Ali at a loss for words.

You do not expect to see Charley O. Finley act as a mascot for a team of mules.

You do not expect to see Wilt Chamberlain coach.

Look again.

Wilt Chamberlain is a coach.

Wilt Chamberlain is coaching the San Diego Conquistadors. This is like casting James Cagney, George Raft and Edward G. Robinson as the parole board. This is like putting Rose Mary Woods in charge of the tape recordings at Decca.

Even while helping coaches win, Wilt Chamberlain used to send them to early graves or hair transplants. He resisted them, ignored them, criticized them, embarrassed them. As he matured he tolerated them. Sometimes he showed up for practice.

Now Wilt Chamberlain is one of them. He is one of them because, as has been the case since he started to grow out of knee pants, Wilt Chamberlain can scarcely walk down the street without somebody trying to stuff his pockets with money. This time it was a wealthy dentist named Dr. Leonard Bloom, who had grandiose visions.

Prime among them was an arena with 20,000 seats for his Conquistadors—better known in the ABA as the Qs. Dr. Bloom thinks big. The Qs could not even fill their 3,200-seat gym.

What Dr. Bloom did was get a proposition for a 20,000-seat arena onto the ballot in a San Diego suburb. Then he stole Wilt Chamberlain from the Lakers so the referendum would be approved. He gave Chamberlain $600,000 to be a player-coach.

Then the courts ruled Chamberlain was ineligible to play for the Qs this season and the voters rejected the proposition. Dr. Bloom was left with a $600,000 coach who thought coaches making a twentieth of that were stealing. Novocain, nurse.

But Wilt Chamberlain is indeed coaching and apparently not doing a half-bad job. The Qs are playing more respectably than anticipated. And their coach has missed only one practice (when, commuting from his mountain-top castle in Los Angeles to San Diego, fog caused his flight to be rerouted to Phoenix).

Last night, unfortunately, Wilt Chamberlain and the Qs found their way to the Nassau Coliseum in the rain. The Nets beat them 134–108. It wasn't that close.

Wilt Chamberlain, resplendent in about seventy-five yards of brown suit, noticed that too. Occasionally he shouted an instruction—"Wait for a better shot" followed by a heave from Suffolk County—but for the most part he fumed quietly. "You should, as a coach, have a certain amount of dignity," he said. "But I can see the anxieties that build up. They have to be released some way. I get chewy stuff so I can't open my mouth too much. As a player you have natural outlets."

After what he called a "superbad game," Chamberlain opened his mouth for fifteen minutes behind closed doors. He said he was practicing one of the theories he postulated across the seasons. "Giving constructive criticism when the mistakes are fresh in the players' minds," encouraging them to participate in a dialogue with the coach. "They weren't concentrating and I can't help them with that," he said. "I'm a terrible concentrator on the foul line. They tried to help me for sixteen years. You seen what they done."

Now that Wilt Chamberlain is a coach, we seen everything.

If I had my druthers, as we used to say in Oklahoma, I'd druther do more series and follow-ups. That's one of the directions I may move toward. Six years separate these studies of one man's family.

THE WALKS

Albert Walk is a basketball father, Sylvia Walk is a basketball mother, Warren Walk is a basketball brother and Neal Walk is a basketball son. The Walks spent a terrific ten days in New York last night, coming up from Miami to the National Invitation Tournament and opening and closing in one.

Neal Walk was the one on the Garden court, a six-foot ten-inch center for Florida, a second-team All-American, holder of twenty-four Florida scoring records, a senior.

Albert Walk led the cheering section in the side loge. He is a six-foot four-inch advertising executive and holder of every father-son basketball record there is. "I've missed three of his games in four years," he said. "Two were on New Year's Eve." That includes trips to Panama and Venezuela.

The game with Temple last night wasn't a minute old before Sylvia Walk, a handsome woman, moved down a row because Warren Walk, a six-foot seven-inch high school senior, was "making me nervous."

"The college coaches call me about Warren and the pro general managers call about Neal," said Albert Walk, his basketball-father grin as wide as the foul line. "Everybody promotes me and pitches me."

There is no greater ecstasy for a basketball father, but

right now Neal Walk and Florida were having trouble with Temple. Walk was guilty of walking and committed other turnovers. "Come on Neal, play some basketball," Albert Walk said. Walk was charged with three fouls in the first half. Albert Walk looked at Warren Walk with an expression that asked, "What did he do?" Warren Walk said, "He belted him." Albert Walk decided, "We're in trouble now." But Neal Walk was doing good things too, wheeling in the pivot, rebounding tough against two men guarding him in a zone defense. "Beautiful fake, I like that move.... Beauty, baby," Albert Walk enjoyed.

Temple began to pull away in the second half. Sylvia Walk played with her rings nervously. When the score got to be 59–47 Albert Walk announced, "It's all over. This game is history." Sylvia Walk said, "No it's not." Albert Walk was right.

Neal Walk played well after a shaky start, scoring twenty-six points and getting seventeen rebounds. A dozen pro scouts liked what they saw. "I'm impressed with his size and desire," Red Auerbach said. "He's going to be a helluva pro."

He fouled out with a couple minutes left. "That's it, his last college game," his father said. "I don't think he played good. He lost the ball too many times. In two, three years he's going to be a great ballplayer. I gave him a basketball when he was six. In high school he was six feet eight inches and 165 pounds; he'd fall down if you looked at him. He's still only twenty. He'll improve."

Sylvia Walk said, "He'll definitely make the pros because that's what he wants. But I think my husband and I will have to settle down. We're both terribly involved."

For Albert Walk it's only a beginning though. Next season his responsibilities as a basketball father will take him God knows where to see both sons. "If I felt it was a deterrent to them I wouldn't go," he said. "But they seem to enjoy playing for me."

Neal Walk wasn't particularly pleased with the game. His team lost and he thought he was sloppy. "I knew this was my future tonight," he said. "I knew all the scouts

would be here. I hope they noticed the good things I did."
Basketball is his future. "I think a person wants to be
happy, to do what you like. Basketball is what I do best."

As for his basketball father, "He took me to the park
as a kid and said this is where it's at. He's followed me
everywhere. I'll never forget that. I think it's admirable."

There are people in Florida who say it's a toss-up
whether coach Tom Bartlett did a better job handling the
father or the son. Bartlett said of Albert Walk, "He's never
interfered."

"I've got only one thing to say about the father," Red
Auerbach said. "Oy."

SOMETHING HAPPENED

Something happened to Neal Walk.

The Phoenix Suns, for whom he played for five years,
said he didn't seem interested in play anymore. "He lost his
intensity," said general manager Jerry Colangelo.

"Things stranged me out," said Neal Walk.

Two years ago the Neal Walk NBA graph was soaring
to the top of the page. He averaged twenty points and
twelve rebounds. He was walking taller than his peers ever
thought he would. "I wanted to prove I could do that," he
said. "I was giving 175 percent. All I thought about was
basketball."

Goodbye to all that.

"I did it against the best," Neal Walk said. "Now I'm
moving on. Growing up. They say you play like your personality. Maybe my real personality is growing up."

Jerry Colangelo said, "He had a vibrant glow on his
face at twenty-one and twenty-two. It's gone now. The
game has become too much of an effort, a job."

If there's a vibrant glow on Neal Walk's face, it would
be as hard to find as a sheepdog's left eye. There's a lush
beard where the glow used to be. His beard, his vegetarianism, his jeans are the new Neal Walk. "I used to be what

people expected me to be," he said. "I played the role of an athlete. My life was basketball, girls and clothes.

"Then I had some personal problems. But I met some good people, and I started to be my own man. My values are changing. What my father wanted me to be, that's all over."

Neal Walk has a basketball father who used to follow his college team around the country. When Walk was drafted by the Suns, his father moved from Miami to Phoenix.

The rest of Neal Walk's life began at age twenty-five. He split with his wife of nine months. He was traded to New Orleans and then to the Knicks. "It hasn't been a big trauma," he said. "In fact it's been interesting. I wouldn't trade this year for anything. A whole lot of things hit me at once, my senses were open to them, and I'm learning. Life is a stream, and I'm just going with it."

That's a fine image, but can it work for the professional athlete? For an awesomely talented Kareem Abdul-Jabbar, anything works. Short of that, raging rivers usually work best.

"Most scouts were skeptical about Neal in college," Jerry Colangelo said. "He didn't have the God-given talent to run and jump. But I was convinced he'd make it on his fantastic attitude. That attitude made him the player he was, and when he lost it he became a facsimile of what he was. And I think it was a disruptive force on the team.

"I'm not judging what the changes may do for him personally—we were very close, and I wish him well—but you have to perform. I feel if he comes out of it, the New York chemistry can do it for him."

So far Walk has gone with the downhill streak of the Knicks. "Next season I'll be ready," he said. "But I don't look at the season as a crisis, as horrible, as a loss, just part of life. I can see positive things in it. I like the Knicks. I still get pleasure out of the game. I'd like to play more. Sun shines, rain falls."

Rick Barry represented a different kind of change in the athlete.

ALL-AMERICAN BOY

A man once threatened to send a rocket to Nassau County to find out if there was intelligent life there. Yesterday the New York Nets of the ABA and Nassau County made a trade for Rick Barry. The quest for intelligent life there is not ended.

It seems that hardly a day has gone by in the last three years when Rick Barry has not been fast-breaking from one team to another, lawsuits trailing behind him. He is the quintessential modern athlete—gifted, good-looking and corrupted by the business ethic of sports.

After two outstanding seasons, Barry jumped the San Francisco Warriors for Oakland of the newly formed ABA. He did it for the best of reasons: $50,000 more per season on a five-year contract, including stock options. He said yesterday that he wound up losing money on the deal, but that's the way the ball bounces. "I've suffered by moving," he admitted. "But it hasn't been that bad."

So far so good. All-American boy takes All-American leap into the unknown and falls on his All-American face but comes up shooting.

The Oakland franchise failed despite Barry. It was sold to Washington, D.C., interests with Barry, whereupon he signed a five-year contract with the Warriors, giving him the lead in five-year contracts in both leagues, but not endearing him to the new ownership or new fans. A court ruled that Barry had to fulfill the last two years of his ABA contract, but he is appealing.

So far so bad. All-American boy doesn't want to play by the rules.

Despite or because of Barry, the Washington franchise failed too. It was going to Virginia for the coming season, which didn't suit Barry, so, lawyers having failed him, he turned to journalists. He calculated that a few well-timed insults would get Virginians so riled up that he would be able to buy out his contract or force a trade. He informed his new constituency that he intended to be fat and indifferent, that he didn't want his children talking with southern accents, and more of the same.

"I said those things without malice," Barry said. "Maybe it wasn't the nice thing to do, but it was the only thing I could think of. They were up in arms and I can't blame them. If it didn't work out I would have apologized."

It worked. The Nets traded a No. 1 pick and some $200,000 for Barry. "It looks like I'll be playing for the Nets, but I have a legal and moral commitment to the Warriors too," he said.

The corruption of a Rick Barry does not happen overnight or in a vacuum. He was a kid out of New Jersey who was avidly recruited by Miami. He was drafted by the Warriors, which had been a pioneer and prosperous franchise in Philadelphia before it was sold to San Francisco interests. The owners did this kind of business long before any athlete thought of it.

The twenty-six-year-old Barry assumed a sad posture of cynicism that he seemed to believe fashionable for the big city. "It's like having my cake and eating it," he said.

He is eager for big city endorsements to hop into the pockets of his English walking suit. But what would you buy from an elegant basketball bum?

Hell hath no scorn like journalists used and lied to, but Barry's position was no different than that of owners who have seized the main chance regardless of their word or contract. I think I can lay my hands on one of those owners in about eleven paragraphs.

THE LOBBYIST

When John Kennedy announced the appointment of his brother Bobby as attorney general, he was asked what his qualifications were. "He will," said the President, "get on-the-job training." Larry O'Brien, who ran presidential campaigns for both Kennedys and may yet run one for a third, yesterday was named commissioner of the National Basketball Association. He will, of course, get on-the-job training.

Coming from Springfield, Massachusetts, the birthplace of basketball, O'Brien is familiar with the size and shape of the ball. Basically that qualifies him. After all, all he knew about stamps before he was named postmaster general was that they had to be licked. In no time he found out which side.

More important to the owners of professional basketball, and probably to the players and possibly to the fans, Larry O'Brien is familiar with the size and shape of the United States Congress.

More important than that even, as national chairman of the Democratic Party, he was captain of the majority team.

If form holds true, not only will the NBA merge with the ABA but when they play their version of the Super Bowl the NBA will be allowed to use six players to the ABA's four.

Finally, as the man who won a Watergate settlement from the CREEPs (Committee to Re-Elect the President) who bugged his office, O'Brien has a winning streak of one as he inherits lawsuits against the NBA by the ABA and the Players Association.

So, like most commissioners, O'Brien is the right man for the right time for a group of businessmen who want to maximize their economic interests. He is a lobbyist.

There's nothing sinister about that, yet. Nor is he the first politician to hold such office. His predecessor, Walter Kennedy, had been a mayor. The American Football League, needing a popular figurehead, started with a war hero–governor, Joe Foss. Baseball followed Judge Landis with Senator Happy Chandler.

The NBA and the ABA want to merge, but the Players Association effectively opposed them in Congress. The bottom line was that the owners pleaded poverty but refused to open their books to support it.

This season eleven NBA franchises set attendance records while just three had sharp declines. The NBA would have us believe all the teams need food stamps. Consider Seattle, which had the second largest attendance in the league.

Sam Schulman, president of the SuperSonics, is very hot for a merger, now. Player salaries, he weeps, are out of control. But a few years ago, when the Sonics were an expansion team, Schulman thought free enterprise was wonderful. In fact he's the single NBA owner most responsible for all the high salaries, achieving that distinction when he seduced Spencer Heywood and Jim McDaniel into breaking lucrative ABA contracts so he could give them more lucrative NBA contracts. Having reached the play-offs, Sam Schulman doesn't think free enterprise is a good idea anymore.

Nobody will have to give food stamps to the oil shieks in short pants either; the players have proved they can fend for themselves, in salary negotiations, in Congress and in the courts, where they are suing to abolish the reserve clause.

Larry O'Brien denied that he has been told that his principal assignment is to achieve a merger—it is, he said, Hubert Humphrey preserve us, "on the back burner"—but if there's another reason why he got the job he couldn't think of it. He admitted that "long-time relationships in Washington should put me in a comfortable position to communicate" if necessary. And, Democrat though he be, "The rights of the owners must be preserved if the NBA is to flourish."

O'Brien seems as amiable as he is garrulous and evasive, reflecting a politician's instinct to freeze the ball. Someone should brief him that since he left Springfield they've invented the twenty-four-second clock.

Rick Barry and Larry O'Brien were presented at press conferences. Games themselves offer a broader choice of subject matter, which very often is the problem. Sometimes the game speaks for itself. Sometimes the games-within-games are meatier for the columnist. And sometimes, as you will notice, you don't know what to do.

A CORPSE SITS UP

With eight minutes gone in the first period last night the Garden was transformed from a rollicking funhouse with a broken applause meter into a funeral home.

Willis Reed had a great fall and all the king's horses and all the king's men and all the king's doctors with all the king's cortisone seemed incapable of putting the Knicks together again.

They were losing by ten points to the Lakers and their big man was out. Any rational basketball degenerate would, at worst, whisper a curse at the fates or, at best, say too bad gang, it's been a memorable season.

"I was sick inside when I saw Willis," said Dave DeBusschere. He understood. He understood that of the two teams trying to win their first NBA championship the Knicks were now second. "You never give up, but inside you knew our chances were very slim."

And none.

But in one of those inexplicable melodramas that make theaters of ball fields the Knicks got out of the casket and ran the Lakers back to Los Angeles. They won 107–100 to take a three-to-two lead in the play-offs.

"It was," said Walt Frazier, "unreal."

There was no immediate magic to it. No superhuman effort by a divinely struck agent. In fact, for quite a long time not much of anything happened. The game got sloppy, as though something had been drained out of the Lakers too—the desperate need to be at their best when Reed was playing. The Knicks were spastic. The Lakers, faced with an outmanned team, were ordinary. They extended their lead by only three points to thirteen at the half.

"They could have demoralized us and made us pick up," Frazier said. "They blew it."

The Knicks tried a new formula in the third period. DeBusschere, at six feet six inches, was the tallest player in the lineup and he guarded Wilt Chamberlain. They tried to take advantage of Chamberlain's inability to cover whatever quicker forward he would be matched against. On defense the Knicks gambled recklessly to neutralize Chamberlain and forced a lot of turnovers. But they couldn't put much of a dent in the Laker lead, earning only high marks for professionalism and gallantry. "I kept making steals," said Frazier, "but they seemed meaningless."

They weren't. The Knicks whittled the score to 82–75 as the period ended. The fans saw them sit up in the casket and broke through the sound barrier. The Knicks pressed all over the court. The Lakers panicked all over the court.

The Knicks outscored the Lakers 32–18 in the last period. Their forwards had free shots. The defense forced ten turnovers in the period, thirty in the game. They allowed the Lakers just twenty-six shots. Chamberlain took three, Jerry West two.

"This is not," Jerry West has said, "the smartest team I have ever played on."

The Lakers couldn't have passed a test on Sesame Street last night.

"I'm not sure the Knicks could do that again," West said.

They may not have to.

MATCHUP

Bill Russell and Wilt Chamberlain went head-to-head in play-offs like giraffes foraging for the juiciest leaves on a tall tree, pitting quickness against strength.

Dave DeBusschere and Gus Johnson heaved and strained like huskies in a dogsled race.

To this partial zoological study of distinguished NBA matchups must be added Phil Jackson and Mel Counts. They are to the championship series between the Lakers and Knicks what Ma and Pa Kettle were to movie romance.

"We're not what you would call the smoothest ball-players in the world," Mel Counts said. "There's nothing fluid about us."

"We're awkward people," Phil Jackson said. "We must be some sight."

Have an oversized flamingo and a pterodactyl ever thrown elbows at each other while wearing short pants? That's what the sight looks like.

Counts is seven feet tall and weighs 235 pounds and has a prominent beak. He is a one-man endangered species, the only such forward in captivity. What is remarkable about him is that he is as graceful when airborne as he is not when grounded. Apparently he learned how to fly before he could run, and to shoot before either.

"Jackson and I have weaknesses and we try to make the best of it," Counts said. "We're not spectacular, but it seems to me that we get the job done, and we do it very well."

"We're not good ball handlers," Jackson said. "I feel I'm more mobile than him, and I've got sharper elbows."

Counts had the best of Jackson in the opening game, eleven points and nine rebounds to seven and two. Score one for the flamingoes. Counts even tried to impale Jackson with an elbow as the quicker Knick dribbled around him. In retaliation Jackson's elbows played on Counts's ribs like a glockenspiel when he reached toward the ceiling with his soft jump shot.

"There are bonier guys in the league," said Jackson, giving a clinic in comparative anatomy. "Mike Riordan really has hard bones. John Havlicek has points all over him. But they're a different problem for me with their speed. I have to play Counts the way they play me, run him. He's playing the best I've seen him in years, but I'm starting to make things happen on offense too."

At six feet eight inches with the square-shouldered wingspan of a biplane, Jackson is an even stranger looking bird than Counts. Tonight they'll fly out of the aviary for the second game. Don't forget your binoculars, bird watchers.

WHAT HAPPENED?

The Knicks beat the Lakers 99–95 in the second game of the play-offs last night. This much is certain. The series, tied at one game apiece, resumes Sunday. That seems certain too. Everything else is a dark abyss.

What happened?

Jerry West: "You know who hurt us? Earl Monroe."

Where was Gail Goodrich in the second half?

Dean Meminger guarded him. Held him to four points.

Where was Earl Monroe then?

On the bench. Hurt.

Willis Reed stole the ball three times in a few minutes.

Bill Bridges: "Did he steal it from me? I don't remember."

Yes.

From Goodrich too. And Jim McMillian.

But where was Wilt Chamberlain? Did anybody see Wilt?

He missed eight out of nine foul shots. He didn't feel like running.

"I guess Willis thought he could take a few swipes at the ball until Wilt came down," Bill Bradley said.

Willis Reed: "I was taking calculated chances."

Walt Frazier: "He stole 'em in slow motion."

Red Holzman: "They underestimated his wingspan."

Where were you, Wilt?

"When you win, they don't ask where you were."

Bradley: "Wilt got some big hoops."

Wilt got two hoops.

Jerry West: "You know who hurt us? Bill Bradley."

Bradley got ten hoops.

Reed: "We weren't tired in the first game like people thought. It's the difference coming out of one series going into another."

Holzman: "We were living, eating, talking Celtics for two weeks."

"I dreamed I was traded," Jerry West said.

Walt Frazier had one assist in forty-eight minutes.

Where was Dave DeBusschere?

On the bench. Tired.

"Jackson played good," said Holzman, "so DeBusschere sits."

Dean Meminger didn't take a shot in twenty-three minutes. No hoops that way.

Is basketball really the City Game?

Bradley: "I'm from the country. Jackson is from the country. West is from the country."

"In the country you play everything," Willis Reed said. "In the city you play one game."

"It's a country game and a city game," said Bradley. "The American game."

What if they traded Jerry West to Philadelphia?

"They announce my retirement tomorrow."

Why were the fans leaving with three minutes to play and the result still in doubt?

They have to beat the traffic.

"It's not New York," Bill Bridges said.

Maybe they know the Lakers.

But how did the Lakers make it so close?

Holzman: "We thought we had it in the satchel."

Why did you take that dumb shot, Frazier?

"Good question."

Why did you make that dumb foul, DeBusschere?

"I'd do it again."

Jerry West: "You know who hurt us? Jackson."

Bill Bridges should be in movies.

What happened?

The Knicks won.

I wish I could tell you I had a plane to catch. As I recall, since the game was a bore, and since no games-within-games grabbed me, I thought I would experiment with an impressionistic report of a bewildered sportswriter groping for angles and answers and finding athletes who weren't sure of much besides the final score either. I'm glad I tried it, but I guess you had to be there. Where were you Doc Robbins when I needed you?

DOC ROBBINS

It takes a certain unflappability to win in pressure college basketball, to keep your cool while the tubas and the bass drums and the student body blast into your skull. Little Saint Peter's of Jersey City leads the cosmos in unflappability, which explains why they beat mighty Duke so unflappably last night. Saint Peter's is unflappable because it has Doc Robbins on its side.

Jerene Robbins is the Saint Peter's team doctor. She is a lady doctor. She does all the things that men doctors do, and more. She gives physical examinations. She tapes ankles. She ministers to the sick and wounded. She sits on the bench and keeps score. She wanders around the dressing room telling everybody how great they are.

Since dressing rooms are for getting dressed and undressed, the last thing sort of startles some people. The Saint Peter's dressing room leads the cosmos in double takes. Photographers freeze. Reporters blink. The Saint Peter's kids smile, barely.

"They have plenty of poise," Dr. Robbins said. "I imagine I have something to do with it."

The question that always comes up is, well, does it bother the kids. Obviously it doesn't and shouldn't. The question comes up anyway.

"The freshmen hide in the corner the first couple of times," she said. "After that they forget me."

She walked over to three undressed players last night, slapped one of them on the backside and asked for the naked truth. "Do I have any problems with you?" They smiled, barely.

"I don't have any problems with them, they don't have any problems with me," she said with the sweetest of grins.

"I'm so much older than these kids. I'm just a den mother. It shakes the other teams up more than it does them."

Dr. Robbins is forty-nine years old, looks younger with her gray hair fashionably short. She has worn knee-length black socks, a gray skirt, white blouse and dark blazer for Saint Peter's two NIT wins. Unmarried, she might be mistaken for a middle-aged coed.

She was mistaken for something else before Saint Peter's opening game of the season, against East Carolina in Greenville, North Carolina. "I thought the boys might need some help," she said, "so I put on a blonde wig and chiffon minidress. The coach [Don Kennedy] thought I looked too good, but it really shook up East Carolina seeing this blonde dish traipsing around their locker rooms."

Pete O'Dea, senior center, said this was true. "Before the LIU game last year," he said, "Larry Newbold saw her in our dressing room. He backed out the door stammering, "It's a lady . . . a lady.""

And then there was the time Saint Peter's lost a close game and the players were unhappy about the officiating. The two officials started to undress in Saint Peter's dressing room as Dr. Robbins examined a boy who had been injured. "Don't you think," someone said to the officials, who did not see her, "that you ought to wait until this boy's mother leaves before you take off your clothes?" The officials pulled up their pants like firemen hearing an alarm.

In real life Dr. Jerene Robbins is a chest surgeon and the coach of sailing at Saint Peter's. Her father was a half-Indian cowpuncher. She started at the college six years ago accidentally on purpose. "A friend of mine said you'll get old someday and you won't be able to do surgery. Stay young by staying near young people. He suggested I try for this job. I had no interest in basketball, but I went to a game and a kid got a lacerated scalp. I sewed him up and one thing led to another."

Before last night's game she had an abbreviated schedule. She gave a clinic on postoperative chest surgery care at Pollak Hospital in Jersey City, then visited a new admission to Christ Hospital in preparation for surgery today.

"After that I went to my office and told my secretary to tell everyone I had an emergency. I was too nervous about the game."

While taping ankles, Dr. Robbins gives little pep talks to the players, telling them "to die out there" and "don't give up." Occasionally she is more colorful than that. She warned Elnardo Webster before the upset of Marshall last week, "I'll cut a piece out of your hide every time you drop a pass." He scored fifty-one points and emerged unscathed.

As Saint Peter's ran Duke out of the tournament, Dr. Robbins sat on the bench, squeezed between players, keeping score to quiet her nerves. She was unflappable and beautiful.

IV.
A
Non-Fan's
Notes

I've lumped together ice hockey, horse racing and golf for two reasons. The first is I have to put them someplace. The second is that it occurs to me that I feel about them the way other columnists feel about basketball and Frisbee. I don't go out of my way to cover them.

Which is often my loss. Hockey players live close to their emotions and hockey fans are nuts. A major golf tournament tees up a familiar cast of characters in a lush, tense setting. The track provides a colorful prism into the wonders and lunacy of homo sap.

That settles it. I'm going to start covering more ice hockey, golf and horse racing as soon as I clear my desk.

THE LONG ROUGH

This is about John Shippen, a part Negro part Indian who probably was the first American golf pro and who finished fifth in the second U.S. Open in 1896, in his tournament debut at the age of eighteen, and who died recently in Newark at ninety. Most of his cleated tracks have been covered by time.

John Shippen was given $15, for the year, to instruct members of the exclusive Maidstone Club in East Hampton in 1894, along with caddying duties. He had been a caddy at Shinnecock Hills in Southampton, which had twelve holes that had been built by Shinnecock Indians hired from their nearby reservation, where he had grown up as the son of a Presbyterian minister.

To celebrate the opening of Maidstone's nine-hole course (expanded from three) on August 28, 1896, according to the *East Hampton Star*, Shippen played a thirty-six-hole exhibition against the Shinnecock pro, R. B. Wilson, and defeated him three and two by playing a "careful and patient" game.

In an interview five years ago Shippen said, "As far as I know I was the first American-born pro. All the pros came from Scotland and England when I first came around.

"There was a slight objection to my playing in the Open, but Theodore Haverman, president of the USGA (United States Golf Association), said the championship would go on with me. It would be called off if I didn't play."

The *New York Herald* said that Shippen had been "aptly dubbed 'The Little Wonder.'" He was paired the first day with Charles MacDonald, a stockbroker who had won the first U.S. Amateur championship the year before and who was the biggest name in American golf. Shippen won by five strokes, shooting a 78. He drove the last green, an estimated 175 yards, then considered amazing, and was mobbed by his fellow caddies. MacDonald stalked off and quit the tournament.

"Anyone who plays Shippen," wrote the *Chicago Tribune,* "has to forget his boyishness and pay careful attention to his golf, because, all things considered, he is the most remarkable player in the United States."

Shippen shot an 81 the next day for a total of 159, seven strokes behind the winner, James Foulis. Shippen's purse was $10.

Ken Davis, who managed Maidstone for thirty years, caddied for Shippen in 1903 and 1904. He is seventy-six years old. He said that Shippen's claim as the first American pro was "a correct statement."

"He was an excellent driver," Davis said. "He could outdrive anyone playing at that time. I couldn't estimate how far he could drive; those were the days of the small ball and wooden-shafted clubs. Many, many a day young players would bet him a dollar they could outdrive him. In all those years, until he left in 1915, I never saw but one man who outdrove him.

"He was not a big fellow. He was about five feet seven or eight inches, about 150 pounds. He looked more like an Indian than a colored man. He had a very smooth swing. He was very quiet, a bright and understanding individual. He didn't have much education but he learned quickly and I'd say he was above average in meeting people."

Charlie Thom, a Scotsman who was the pro at Shinnecock for fifty-five years, remembered John Shippen too. Thom, eighty-seven, lives in a cottage at Shinnecock.

"He was a very nice fellow and he was quite a good golfer," Thom said. "We played two matches. He beat me in twenty-three holes. I wasn't feeling well. They made a big fuss about it, about nothing. We had a rematch and I beat him. At the rematch here one of the members said, 'Now we'll get some bets.' He asked me if I was going to try hard to beat him. I said, 'Sure.' He said there was $20 in it for me if I won. John and I didn't bet."

Shippen played in four more opens—in Baltimore in 1899, where he finished near the bottom; in Chicago in 1900, where he was in the middle; in Garden City in 1902, where he finished in a fourth-place tie (no Negro has finished as high), and in 1913 in Brookline, Massachusetts, the year of Francis Ouimet's historic victory, where Shippen was out of the money.

When he left Maidstone in 1915, Shippen went to the Shady Rest Country Club in Scotch Plains, New York, then a Negro club. He stayed there until he retired a few years ago. The most money he ever made, Shippen once said, was $4,000 in a year, including lessons, pro shop sales, etc.

Not much could be learned about his personal life. He had a son, William Hughie. Thom said he caddied at Shinnecock and "could have been a heckuva golfer. I gave him a set of clubs but he sold them." He is said to be living in Southampton but could not be located.

Four daughters survived Shippen. One of them, Mrs. Clara Johnson of Washington, D.C., claimed the body. She was the only relative at his funeral. She could not be reached for an interview.

John Shippen died in a nursing home. He was on relief.

Starting with a short obituary in the New York Times, *it took several days of telephone calling to track down that much on John Shippen. Perhaps few readers could appreciate that, or care less, but it gave me great satisfaction.*

The 1974 Open was played just outside New York. I wound up doing one piece on a golfer I had been curious about for years but never pursued, a second column on a superstar I trailed, on and off the course, for two days, and a third on the surprising winner —the course.

COMING TO TRUTH

The difference between George Knudson and the other 149 golfers in the U.S. Open is that he knows the score before the tournament begins. "I'm here to win it," he said, "but I don't have a chance in hell."

George Knudson is in the twilight of a partly sunny career. "I'm thirty-three going on seventy," he said. "My body and my mind can't take it anymore." Win, lose or miss the cut, he bops from town to town and hole to hole with a secret grin on his lips, wearing dark glasses, like a jazz musician on a stoned trip.

"On a beautiful course," George Knudson once said, "you don't need a ball to play."

In the mid-sixties, his peak years, he saw that he wasn't going to write the great American novel, play King Lear or win the Grand Slam. He decided to settle for something less after winning nine tournaments and learning to hate it.

"When I was young I wanted to be the next Ben Hogan," George Knudson said. "That was a good ambition to have, but I would have been disappointed in myself if I maintained it. I found out there's more to life. You get only one swing at life too.

"I won two out of seven tournaments on the West Coast one year and I was playing so well I could have won three others. I went home to Canada and my coach thought I was really on my way. No way, I told him. I found out I couldn't handle winning. I was too wrapped up in golf, twenty-four hours a day, total concentration—and that wasn't me. I said to myself, 'I surrender. If this is what it takes to win, I'm not cut out for it.'

"Maybe you have to be very bright or very dumb to win. I'm in between."

George Knudson had just come off the practice tee at Winged Foot. He spent a long time hitting tracer shots out to the horizon. Golf fans bunched behind him and others, studying techniques. A golfer could stand there naked in an excited condition and golf fans would take notes on his hip action and backswing. But you can't find out much about a golfer at a practice tee. You can't find out whether he can handle the pressure of a major tournament. Most golfers will think they're at Stubbed Toe instead of Winged Foot before the weekend is over. George Knudson wishes the whole thing could be played on a practice tee.

"The game is how many," he said. "And I've never been that way. I enjoy the art of swinging a club, of know-

ing I'm striking the ball well. I never learned how to score.
I would much rather practice than play. I used to like to
play 'call shot'—describe a shot before I hit it, and then hit
it. When I was superkeen and golf was my whole world, I'd
sit down before a tournament and tell myself what I should
do on each hole, exactly how I would play it. At the end of
the day, I didn't care as much about my score as what I
wasted. If you don't waste any shots it's a good day. I've
never had a good day."

A man who worries more about wasting shots than
making shots can make a good living at golf but he won't
be a winner. That's what George Knudson settled for. If
you can't be as strong and as intelligent on the course as
Jack Nicklaus, or as dedicated as Gary Player, he said, you
might as well relax and enjoy it. If you can't beat it, don't
let it beat you. Check the flora and the fauna. Go home to
the kids. Ski.

"I like golf because you can't pass the puck to someone
else. It's you alone. My competitive spirit is within myself," George Knudson said.

"It's like a high-class poker game out here. I'm glad I
was in it. I'd be disappointed in myself if I wasn't. But it's
torture when you're playing lousy.

"I ask myself what I'm doing here. I'm coming to the
truth with myself."

DRIVE, HE SAID

On the eighteenth hole at Stubbed Toe, where they are
playing the U.S. Open, Gary Player came to resemble a
midsummer Christmas ornament.

Player hooked his drive under a big, lush evergreen,
followed cautiously by himself. From the waist up, wearing his familiar black-makes-me-feel-strong polo shirt, he
disappeared from view. His yellow pants hung like giant
socks from the lower branches.

A flash of silver, the sound of twigs making fire, and
the little white ball flies to safety on an adjacent fairway.

Gary Player is laying three on his way to an exciting bogey and a more exciting 70.

"If you had a computer to read everyone's brain coming off eighteen," Gary Player said, "you'd hear things you wouldn't believe."

Maybe the only thing you could believe after the first round was that Gary Player was leading it. The problem was trying to read his brain—to find out what makes this thirty-eight-year-old man drive himself as hard as he drives a golf ball.

It begins with the transformation of Winged Foot into Stubbed Toe for every golfer there but Player. He takes a Calvinistic delight in testing himself against such an obstacle course. "Every hole is a back-breaker," he said with a grin, as though he had just completed an exhilarating ten-day fast.

Those few holes that weren't designed to be back-breakers turned out that way for Player. He dribbled his tee shot 120 yards short of the fairway on the fifteenth. "I'm going to show you the greatest four wood you ever saw," he said to his caddy. He saved par, putting and scrambling like mad, as he did throughout the sun-perfect day. Which, according to Jack Nicklaus and Johnny Miller, the cofavorites with Player, was impossible. On his way to a 75, Nicklaus tapped one putt twenty-five feet past the hole. Both agreed the rough was too rough.

"Life isn't supposed to be a bed of roses," Gary Player said. "It's a struggle, a struggle."

Why a multimillionaire who has won all the game's honors has to struggle, struggle is a thorny curiosity the Player computer isn't programmed to answer. His purposeful stride, long arms swinging ahead of him like scythes cutting a straight path, speaks of goals as well as holes. Suddenly Player, after winning but two of his six major championships in the last nine years, has won the Masters again and is leading the Open, throwing a challenge at Nicklaus.

"I want to be recognized as the greatest golfer in the

world," he said. "I don't think you should judge us in midstream, in the middle of our careers."

Player's zeal for the game, at age thirty-eight, when the enthusiasm of most wealthy athletes wanes, seems more than a drive for excellence. He has to prove himself over and over. If dieting on nuts, raisins and bananas, or standing on his head, or running in hotel corridors would help, as he used to believe, he'd do that.

His handling of the racial dilemma he finds himself in is typical of how he confronts obstacles. Coming from South Africa, he is like a man trying to balance water on both shoulders. A couple of years ago he was demonstrated against because of his country's brutal policy of apartheid. He can't speak out against it, but he is underwriting a U.S. tour by a black South African, and yesterday he gave a round-trip ticket to a black caddy he is taking to the British Open.

Player has traveled 4 million miles in pursuit of his Holy Grail. When a Japanese lady asked him for an autograph yesterday, he signed a greeting in Japanese. When he wanted to make a point about his backswing to a spectator, he demonstrated with a slow-motion baseball pitch.

Asked what makes him run, his wife, Vivian, said, "It's ingrained in him. It's amazing to me. If you saw him with the kids [six of them] and dogs at our farm, you wouldn't believe he'd leave."

"When I leave home I cry like a baby," Gary Player said.

Why leave then?

"That's going too deep," he said.

LET'S HEAR IT FOR THE COURSE

If they used the same logic at Wimbledon as they used at Stubbed Toe this weekend for the U.S. Open, the nets would be raised six inches because "it's a championship test." The Super Bowl would be played on a field 150 yards long. The fences would be moved back for the World Series. The mile run would be at a mile and a sixteenth and let the whippersnappers break four minutes then.

The seventy-fourth Open wasn't a golf tournament as much as an endurance test. For pure ennui it can be matched only by the avant-garde film classic that catches every snore of an eight-hour sleep. Somebody named Hale Irwin won the championship and the $35,000 that goes with it, but we all know who the actual winner was. It was the golf course, old Winged Foot turned Stubbed Toe. Don't sit on your hands, let's hear it for the golf course.

That's more like it. Listen to that round of applause as the golf course approaches the weary golfers on the seventy-second hole. The golfers need smelling salts, but the course is going up to the nineteenth hole to tell the boys how it did it.

Yes fans, Stubbed Toe had quite a tournament. Brought the great Jack Nicklaus to his knees with bogeys on his first four holes. Taught a lesson in humility to Johnny Miller, the defending champion, with a 22 over par. Held out the promise of a Grand Slam to Gary Player, the first-round leader, then humiliated him. Promised Arnold Palmer his youth, then sent him to a convalescent home on the last nine.

Give the course a green sport coat like they do at the Masters. Arrange fat new contracts with the manufacturers of sand traps, roughs and lawn mowers. Make a deal with a housing development. Book the seventh hole on the Johnny Carson Show; what a sense of humor it has. Call Gary Davidson and tell him the golf course is playing out its option and wants to join his Interplanetary Golf League. Reserve a fleet of 747s to fly it, hole by hole, to the British Open. Notify all the publishers that bidding on its autobiography starts at $500,000. Interviews can be set up through Bob Woolf, the agent. Golf course groupies will be entertained from six to seven every evening.

As for Hale Irwin, winning the Open was a dream come true for Stubbed Toe. "I wanted to win it," it said, "since I was a little driving range." Some say it was the greatest tournament a golf course ever had. The lowest score was seven over par.

The idea, as always, was to make the Open more challenging than the pitch-and-putt courses on the tour. This is a good idea that went berserk. Minor changes to penalize bad shots turned them into capital offenses.

As a result, the golf was no fun—to play or watch. It was worth laughs the first day, as though Don Rickles was the grounds keeper, but it quickly palled. The notion that it was entertaining to reduce professionals to duffers because the real duffers would be able to identify with them made as much sense as casting Robert Redford as a prison guard. Rules that make a Reggie Jackson strike out all the time or a John Havlicek miss most of his shots are silly rules. You want to see them have a chance to perform under pressure, not to dare them to perform. Something has gone amiss to say nothing of a amok when all the thrills are par putts.

The golfers, naturally, praised Stubbed Toe lavishly, at the risk of offending the hosts. Although it embarrassed them, they thought it was wonderful, severe but fair, and a whole lot of other lies. On this course, bad lies.

In its autobiography, it has been learned, the course will say the golfers all stank.

Necessity mothered that invention. Having spent three days at the course, not wanting to interrupt a weekend at the beach, I watched the final round on television (which usually is how a final round has to be watched, because crucial things may be going on at several holes at the same time).

The scene is where the action is and that's where your chances are best of coming up with something immediate and alive. I made it early to the track one day, a rarity for me, and got lucky.

BARN 38, STALL 14

If Willie Mays or Bobby Orr or Jim Brown had broken his leg in two places in his sophomore season there could have been no greater outpouring of what-might-have-beens than there was at Aqueduct and Belmont yesterday when a horse named Hoist the Flag pulled up lame. He was, they say, going to be the fastest of the fastest. "You are going to have to wait 100 years for another horse like him," said Jean Cruguet, his jockey.

Thoroughbreds have been bred for speed until they have become such fragile bursts of protoplasm that only their prolific breeding keeps them from becoming an endangered species. Hoist the Flag shattered the anklelike bone above his right hind hoof ("like a hammer shattering an ice cube," said Alfred Vanderbilt, president of the NYRA) and he cracked the long bone above that simply by doing what he was supposed to do. He was running.

He was running five-eighths of a mile on the training track at Belmont in his last workout for the Gotham Stakes at Aqueduct. As he went into a gallop he pulled up, hobbling. Jean Cruguet dismounted and trainer Sid Watters and groom Bob Cook began jogging toward them from a quarter mile up the track. They sensed that their dreams, like the leg, had been shattered. A half hour later Hoist the Flag was vanned to barn 38, stall 14, and Dr. Michael Gerard, his veterinarian, took X rays. The immediate fear was that the horse would have to be destroyed. They shoot humans, don't they?

A drama began to unfold among those in the family, at barn 38, and in racing places all over the country.

Dr. Gerard called Dr. Jacques Jenny of the famed Penn veterinary school and Dr. Donald Delahanty of Cornell. Watters called the owners of the horse, Jane and Stephen Clark, at their farm in Middleburg, Virginia. All of them made arrangements to fly immediately to New York.

In the bowels of Aqueduct, racing men and officials seemed genuinely aggrieved over the injury. Professionally a great three-year-old would make the Triple Crown races extra special and stimulate interest in all racing. Esthetically Hoist the Flag was seen as a four-legged blend of Nureyev and Ryun, a horse that would mark our time as

Man o' War and Citation marked theirs. The respect for
him as the even-money winter book favorite to win the
Kentucky Derby soon was to be measured in the commercial vacuum caused by his absence. The Gotham was expected to draw three or four challengers at most; now it
would draw ten or eleven horses. A big and unwieldy
Derby field was envisioned instead of a small tidy one.
Vans and cargo planes ferrying horses to distant tracks to
avoid Hoist the Flag might already be taking 180-degree
turns.

The Clarks arrived at twelve-thirty. Stephen Clark is
the heir to a textile fortune, tall, cheerful, sixtyish. Jane
Clark, a handsome woman, was wearing a suede sheepskin-
lined coat, and sunglasses as blinkers to mask her emotions.
They bought Hoist the Flag for $37,000 at the Saratoga
yearling sales two years ago. He won $78,000 in his five
victories, losing only on a disqualification. He is insured for
$500,000 and recently an offer of $4 million was made for
him, and rejected. With War Admiral, Ribot and Tom
Rolfe in his bloodlines, his value as a stud might approach
that if he can be saved.

"You wait for a horse like him all your life," Mrs.
Clark said, her voice cracking slightly. "Suddenly, a short
time after we got him, we knew he could do anything. He
was a lovely horse, sensible and intelligent. We were excited about him. We were looking forward with great anticipation."

"He had every break a horse could get," said Sid Watters, bereaved. "We didn't race him much as a two-year-old.
We tried to put him on good tracks every time he ran. It
was a perfect strip today. A horse hadn't been on it. So
many people asked me what happened. I don't know what
happened."

They were talking about Hoist the Flag in the past
tense.

Dr. Jenny arrived at about two-thirty. He had already
seen the X rays during the car ride from the airport.

"He won't make the Derby," he said to Mrs. Clark,
"but don't worry."

"Thank heavens," she said. "But I don't want to do anything that's cruel to him."

"I'm just telling you what I would do if he were my very own," the doctor said. "To save him as a stud we can proceed."

They decided to wait for an opinion from Dr. Delahanty. He arrived at three-thirty and agreed with Dr. Jenny.

Tranquilized, his leg in a splint, Hoist the Flag stood quietly in stall 14, now and then hopping on his left leg to adjust his balance. Bob Cook, the fifty-two-year-old groom, studied him sorrowfully.

"We weren't worried about him getting beaten. Our biggest worry was that something would happen to him," Bob Cook said. "If he had stood no three-year-old could beat him. No telling how good he was going to be, how fast. This horse never been asked for everything. Won six furlongs at Bowie by fifteen lengths. Won the Bay Shore, seven furlongs, in 1:21 flat. He was putting down some fractions. He was coming up to this race Saturday like a champ. That's what I call him, 'Champ.' Like Sugar Ray Robinson, the best fighter that ever lived. He was the Sugar Ray of horses. He'd liable to be the best racehorse the American people ever seen.

"They told me I'd get a percentage of his winnings. Never asked what it would be. Figured I'd pay my mortgage. He'll have a lot of value as a stud, but won't help me none."

They operated on Hoist the Flag for six hours last night, putting the pieces of his leg together with screws. He will be a love machine after his convalescence. This is what thoroughbreds really do best.

SUPERSTAR

The story may or may not be apocryphal, but it definitely is scatological. The story is that a man in the Midwest wanted to market Secretariat's waste, theorizing that a superhorse might manufacture superfertilizer. Anyone who used it, he would undoubtedly claim, could win every prize at the local farm show by the thirty-three lengths Secretariat won the Belmont Stakes.

The scheme never got off the ground, you might say. Standing protectively between Secretariat's gold ore and the public were a groom and Mrs. Penny Tweedy and Steve Pinkus.

Steve Pinkus is an agent with the William Morris Agency. He is the first talent agent a horse ever had. If Pegasus had had an agent he might be bigger than Zeus in Greek mythology.

Pinkus's job is to screen the commercial offers that pour in to capitalize on Secretariat's fame. He picked up a mug, trimmed in twenty-three-karat gold, a likeness of Secretariat on one side, the Triple Crown records on the opposite side. "It was checked for fading in dishwashers and whether it would break off in a child's mouth," Pinkus said. "Before we approve of anything it must be a quality product. Anyone who wants to be connected with a class, quality winner should have a class, quality product. We are not interested in schlock, in cheap merchandise."

Mrs. Tweedy set the priorities for the commercialization of her wonder beastie. "She should be president of the United States," said Pinkus, impressed by anyone who places quality above quantity in this get-rich-quick time. "Her father believed in high quality and she insisted that we keep that standard. She felt that people in racing should capitalize on Secretariat, so whenever something comes up that someone in racing can do, he gets it."

Among the Secretariat products that will hit the market are silver, bronze and gold medals and ingots, a photograph (by a track photographer), a lithograph (by an artist who specializes in racehorses), a picturebook (by a photographer who is a racetrack buff) and a biography.

The William Morris Agency is more accustomed to talking to two-legged talent—Jimmy Durante, Danny Thomas, Mark Spitz—than four-legged talent. "When I first got involved with Secretariat, they looked at me strangely around here," Pinkus said. His ambition is to put Secretariat in the same league with Mickey Mouse, Bugs Bunny and Flipper as a superstar in the animal league. It had its origin when Pinkus was hired by Jack Krumpe of the New York Racing Association to negotiate television contracts. "We need a star," Pinkus decided. Krumpe told him about the promising Secretariat.

"The first time I heard of Secretariat I thought it was the United Nations," Pinkus said. "I met with Mrs. Tweedy and told her that if the horse did win the Triple Crown the action would be fierce and quick because he would be the first Triple Crown winner in twenty-five years, and because of mass communications. A week later he lost the Wood Memorial, but I had a gut feeling he would win the Triple Crown. I didn't know the first thing about racing, but I knew it, damn it, I knew it."

In his last race, at Saratoga, Secretariat was skinned by a front-runner named Onion. Tomorrow he will take on the best older horses, including stablemate Riva Ridge, in the $250,000 Marlboro. It would seem like a good idea for the big horse to win if all those medals, ingots and stuff are to become hit items. Pinkus says it isn't necessarily so, but what else is Pinkus going to say?

"Secretariat is only human," Pinkus said. "He's a superstar, but he could lose. If he wins he deserves to win. If he loses he'll still be a superstar. He's like Joe DiMaggio. He stands for quality and integrity. Superstars are different. Superstars are special. He would be above the title in a motion picture, he'd play the main room in Las Vegas, and he'd have his own television series."

And you can package the stuff he leaves in stalls.

TIMELY REWARD

If there are any two-legged thoroughbreds of the racing establishment involved in the great social issues of the day, it is a well-kept secret. But there is a four-legged thoroughbred so involved.

His name is Timely Reward. He ran in two of the Triple Crown races in 1951, finishing tenth in the Kentucky Derby and fourth in the Preakness. A nice three-year-old.

Today, at age twenty-two, having run with all the beautiful horses at all the fashionable playgrounds, having sowed many wild oats on the farm, Timely Reward is in the streets where the action is. He is in the mounted police of the U.S. Park Service in Washington.

"He is," said officer Denis Ayres, "the best horse I ever threw a leg over."

With potential policemen now being recruited at Ivy League schools, we should not be surprised to find an equine blueblood walking beat. But, of course, we are. Who among us would choose such a fate if we had the choice of romping unclothed in the pasture, making love and wallowing in grass?

"Most horses pull up by the time they're twenty," said Ayres. "They can't take the eight-hour shift. But he just loves it. He works the mall area between the White House and the monuments. He's a real ham. A great police horse."

A big bay, seventeen hands high, Timely Reward sees two kinds of action mainly: catching thieves who rob tourists and keeping the peace during demonstrations. He has caught many a thief, weaving through traffic better than a police car or motorcycle could and running down sneaky fast lawbreakers better than policemen on foot could. He caught one purse snatcher on the steps of the Smithsonian Institution's Natural History Museum and a car looter on the steps of the Supreme Court building.

But the true test of a police horse and his rider these days comes in demonstrations. Will the horse rear up when he is called a pig? Will he savage foul-mouthed militants? Will he ignore the violence of superpatriots beating up on students?

Timely Reward is especially suited to that kind of scene. He was called a bum and a dog many times in his racing career. Names never harmed him. He was nonviolent.

"He's been in every demonstration for the last six years," said Ayres. "Most thoroughbreds are too high-strung for crowd control work. But he goes into a crowd and stands there. He won't back off. All kinds of things have been thrown at me—bricks, cinder blocks, you name it—but he just stands there."

The thirty-seven-year-old Ayres is Timely Reward's only rider. They usually work a five-day week and they have gone for as long as twelve hours a day. Ayres also has made several appearances with him at the famous Devon (Pennsylvania) Horse Show, where they once won a second-place ribbon. Time was when Timely Reward had famous little men on his back and his working day was much shorter and the crowds much bigger, but apparently he doesn't consider this a step down in class.

After finishing second in the Flamingo and Everglades stakes in Florida in 1951, he ran in the Derby. His jockey was Jimmy Stout, who had won the race aboard Johnston in 1939. Stout, now fifty-six, is a steward at River Downs in Cincinnati.

"I don't remember much about him," Stout said. "He could run a little but he was never close. His owners wanted to have a horse in the Derby."

The *Morning Telegraph* chart of the race reported: "Began slowly and could not secure position." He came in tenth in a twenty-horse field, eleven lengths behind the winner, Count Turf. He was fourth in the Preakness, twelve lengths behind the winner, Bold.

His owners were Mr. and Mrs. Wallace Gilroy, who raced horses in New York for many years.

His trainer was George Odom, who is dead. Odom's son trains here now.

Timely Reward ran in eighty-six races until he was seven years old, winning eight and finishing in the money twenty-nine other times. He earned $64,688.

He stood at stud at Whitepost Farms in DePlains, Virginia, until 1963, siring a number of small-track winners and prize hunting horses. He was presented to the Park Service as a gift and used as a tax deduction.

He is for law and order but he gives a damn.
He still sleeps in the nude.

When hockey expanded into the South, a friend told me he heard some fellows at the barber talk about going to see them play hockey ball. Why not?

BIG, IMPORTANT, CRUCIAL, MUST

The urgency of the play-offs puts a terrible strain on the language of urgency. Is it a "big game" or just an "important game" or, heaven help us, a "must game?" Now, where Shakespeare and Noah Webster and Jimmy Cannon would fear to tread, comes a lion-hearted connoisseur of play-offs to explore the unknown.

"The odd game is a crucial game," sayeth Emile Francis, "and the even game is a must game."

The way the Rangers series with the Canadiens has gone, you can see his point, up to a point. The way the Knicks series with the Celtics has gone, further refinements may be needed.

Obviously the first game in Montreal was crucial because the Canadiens had to win to maintain their home ice advantage, while the Rangers had to win because they had to win one game there to win the series. The Rangers won, giving them a crucial advantage.

That made the second game a must for the Canadiens. But—and here's where we begin to peek into a Pandora's box—what was it for the Rangers? Since the very least a play-off game can be is important, and since the Rangers had already achieved their main objective of winning one game in Montreal, let's leave it as important until proved otherwise.

The Canadiens won that must game, bringing the show to the Garden for a crucial third game. The Rangers were now in the unenviable position of having to win a crucial game and the must fourth game back-to-back or else return to Montreal still needing a crucial win there. The

Canadiens enjoyed the option of winning either a crucial or a must game. They won the crucial game and the Rangers won the must game.

The genius of Emile Francis's odd-even theory was borne out last night when the Rangers won the crucial fifth game in overtime. The sixth game is now a must game for both teams, which is almost critical. It is a must game for the Canadiens because if they lose it's all over for them. It is a must game for the Rangers because if they lose they still have to win in Montreal.

A seventh game is by definition crucial. To call it a must game would be redundant. Crucial-must perhaps. Therefore, simply, crucial.

The Knicks are faced with a similar crucial-must series with the Celtics, but they threw it out of whack last night by losing the must game and falling behind 2–0. Is crucial strong enough for a third game when losing would put them down 3–0? The situation is desperate, but you can't say it's a desperate game. It's the Knicks who are desperate.

What is the third game to the Celtics? Crucial is overkill. If the Knicks win, the fourth game can be defined as must for both sides. But what if they lose? The only solution to that problem may be to cancel the fourth game.

A survey last night showed that the subject is far from exhausted.

"If the Knicks went to Boston tied 1–1," said Woody Allen, "the third game would be important. Down 2–0, I'd say it's critical."

There was one other vote for critical, which is more urgent than crucial. "When you lose the must game," said Walt Frazier, "the next one is critical."

Red Auerbach, whose play-off experiences are Biblical, said, "They're all must games, but the first one is only important. It's not that critical. We've lost the first game five or six times. I'd rate the third game in Boston as important."

Tom Heinsohn said, "The third game isn't a must game but for us it's a must game, a big game. If we lose it, winning tonight doesn't mean much."

Red Holzman said, "When you lose the must game, the next one becomes a must game."

Earl Monroe said, "If you lose the must game, the next one is a really must game."

Really must sounds promising, but Danny Whelan, the Knicks' trainer, had a better solution. "When you lose the must game," he said, "it wasn't a must game."

That may edge us closer to truth, if not urgency. For if a must game wasn't a must game, then it's possible that big, important or critical games weren't big, important or critical. They may have been, good grief, just games.

A BLIND COMMUNIST BUM

Back when hockey was policed by two officials instead of the present three, a referee named Mickey Ion said to his colleague, "You've got to remember one thing. There are only two sane guys here—you and me." Whether he was sure about his colleague is not known, but he definitely had a point there.

Last night at the Garden the Rangers beat the Black Hawks in the third game of the play-offs and played well enough for the long-suffering faithful to entertain visions of a Stanley Cup. But hockey fans are not happy unless they can be miserable too. This is the insanity that Mickey Ion was talking about.

So, midway through the third period—as the Rangers skillfully protected their lead—from time to time, and for no apparent reason, a voice would pierce the night like so: "Ashley is a bum."

Also: "Ashley is a Communist."

And: "Ashley is blind."

Why is Ashley a blind Communist bum? Because Ashley is a referee.

His name is John Ashley and he is the senior referee in the National Hockey League. One theory has it that he is a favorite target of fans—favored over others of his ilk—simply because there is such a mellifluous sound to his name when affixed to various terms of disapprobation. Roll them over your tongue: Ashley is a bum, Ashley is a Communist, Ashley is blind. Countertheories have it that Ashley is just one of many referees who is abused from all sides, having the advantage of being around longest. The number on the back of his striped shirt is 1.

Finally, there is Ashley's mien and bearing, which, in the roughhousing hurly-burly of hockey, seem positively imperious, as though he is above the blood and thunder. He carries himself like a Supreme Court justice on skates, tall and judicial. In Boston he is called "Sir John" as well as those other things. "I don't like him," Bobby Orr once said. "He has the air of a snob." Occasionally he will grin forbearingly at a player who pleads innocence or murder. Last night Stan Mikita pleaded murder from a position on his knees and Ashley grinned at him without breaking stride.

In the first period he showed his style when he caught Jim Neilson in a no-no. Two minutes, Ashley decreed. Neilson protested and flipped his stick, barely over his head, in a rare gesture of exasperation. As fabled baseball umpire Bill Klem said to a bat thrower, "If it comes down you're out of here." Ashley sentenced Neilson to ten additional minutes in the penalty box.

The idea of a penalty box smacks of paternalistic justice, of teacher putting student in the corner and father sending son to bed early. It seems proper and fitting then for players to behave like children and referees like referees. Vic Hadfield, after completing his three-goal hat trick, touching off a great air-horn-blowing, toilet-paper-throwing, hot-pants-wriggling celebration, picked up one of about a dozen hats scaled onto the ice and plunked it on his head as he went smiling to the bench. It was a magnificent moment of pure uninhibited glee. Contrast that with the stuffy boarding-school attitude of the NHL: reporters were not permitted to talk to the Black Hawks or officials after the game.

If Ashley seems to have a bemused view of the violence he is supposed to police, probably it is because he once was a violence-prone defenseman in the American Hockey

League. He has a reputation for permissiveness. "Sometimes he calls everything," said Brad Park, "and sometimes you have to split a guy open thirty stitches before he gets you."

Still, Ashley wouldn't walk out of a play-off game, as a referee did many years ago because he was sensitive to the abuse. And his eyesight, despite his critics, appears as good as it has to be. After all, Bill Chadwick refereed for sixteen years and no one knew that he had just one eye. "Everyone yelled 'Chadwick, you're blind,'" he once said. "They didn't know how half right they were."

When the light blinked on for the next column, I asked a writer friend what he thought of my putting J. D. Salinger on ice. His response was so violently anti—"it's the worst idea I ever heard"—that I knew it must be terrific and proceeded.

THE FAT LADY

The gallant Islanders were ready for the solo dash of the Fat Lady last night. They weren't ready for the gang rush of the Flyers.

The Fat Lady is not a gratuitous description of Kate Smith, the good-luck charmer of the defending champion Flyers. The Fat Lady is what she represents to the faithful who filled the Spectrum with anxiety and hope and hallelujahs. The Fat Lady, in J. D. Salinger's short stories, is a metaphor for the God in everyone, however plain he or she may be. Even hockey fans.

"When she goes out there," said Kate Smith's bodyguard, Sal Gelosi, "it's like God came out on the altar."

It is five minutes to eight and Kate Smith, who is sixty-seven years old, has pregame jitters. She has been brought to Philadelphia by popular demand, by an airplane from Palm Beach and a limousine from New York, and by $5,000. In six years management has played her record of "God Bless America," in preference to the national anthem, forty-six times. The Flyers have won on forty-two of those times. She has made two previous personal appearances in moments of truth, and the other guys didn't score a goal in either of them. Now we are coming up to the seventh game of the Stanley Cup semifinals, and if show biz never hurt religion, religion never hurt show biz. Bring in the Fat Lady.

Kate Smith's hands are clasped prayerfully. On her third finger, left hand, is a chunk of ice you could skate on. A green carpet has been rolled out from the runway behind the Islander goal. An organ has been pushed to the edge of the carpet. The carpet and the organ are cheered as though they are Simon and Garfunkel.

Kate Smith crosses herself, clears her throat and rests on Sal Gelosi's broad back. Sal Gelosi, legs braced at a soldierly angle, looks as big as a limousine in his blackjack, under which, as he puts it, "I am packing a rod." She is resplendent in two thin strands of pearls and a number of spools of green silk.

A wisp of a man nearby says, "I'm her caddy. I'm embarrassed to tell her I'm sixty-two years old and my mother used to listen to her on the radio."

This is Father Casey, the Flyers chaplain, but not an ordinary expansion chaplain, he notes, since he chaplained the Black Hawks for many years. "People in my parish say, 'Pray for them, pray for them,'" Father Casey says. "I tell them I won't pray for them, but it's all right if they do. I don't believe in divine intervention. What happens on the ice decides games."

It is eight o'clock and the call comes for Kate Smith. She straightens her shoulders and moves with sure grace toward a spotlight of ice. She raises two hands, then a fist, a forefinger. She blows kisses. The Fat Lady glows in a halo of cheers.

The Islanders are not entirely defenseless against this. They may not have Irving Berlin, who wrote "God Bless America," or the Andrews Sisters, who sang "Bei Mir Bist Du Schön," on their side, but they do have something. Casey Stengel once said of a young team chasing the Yankees, "They want to be great men," and of the Mets whom nobody could catch, "You can't have a miracle every day except you can when you get great pitching." The Islanders have ambition and defense.

Just in case, they also have a bouquet of carnations for Kate Smith. Captain Ed Westfall delivers them. The Islanders further disarm the Philadelphia congregation by filing past her with ecumenical smiles.

"Kate Smith," J. P. Parise would say later. "Bleep her."

Kate Smith belts out her song. After all these years it is a rendition so stirring that two elderly vendors, women, melt like popcorn butter into supplicants of pure adoration. Sal Gelosi says, "I've been to every big affair with her —the White House—but nothing affects her like this. Nothing. Ever. All she could talk about coming here was the game. She's so keyed up she couldn't sign autographs."

Kate Smith strides triumphantly back into the runway. "I don't want to complain," Glenn Resch, the Islander goalie, would say. "But it's not fair. We're pumped up and ready to go and she's out there for fifteen minutes. It's got to be a life for them."

By the time Kate Smith reaches her seat, the game is over. The Flyers went at the Islanders like seagulls diving for sardines. The first goal came at nineteen seconds, the second at two-and-one-half minutes. They won 4–1.

Yet even that score provided a measure of the surprising Islanders' grit. "It was," said a Flyer executive, "the first time she's been scored upon in person."

Kate Smith agreed with my writer friend. A few days later she was quoted in Earl Wilson's column that she couldn't be the fat lady because she had lost ninety pounds.

V.
And
Then
I Wrote

The columnist wears several hats—
reporter, critic, entertainer, to name three.
Major spectator events command most of our
attention as newspapermen, but all bread and
butter would drive any sports gourmet batty.
And give a distorted picture of what the
sporting life is about. Minor sports, offbeat
stories, playful inventions and occasional uses
of the perpendicular pronoun help retain my
sanity. If they bring the unsuspecting Mets fan
into worlds unknown, and also make him
wonder what I'm up to today, that's nice too.

STOOPENDOUS

On the front page of a recent Sunday *Times* appeared the following ad:

WANTED: Stoop; usable for stoopball. Fair Country Club, 100th St. & 57th Ave., Rego Park, Queens, AR 1–1234—Advt.

Murray Greenberg wants three stoops for his city country club on the edge of Lefrak City. Murray Greenberg is building his dream playground.

It's going to be some playground, this city country club. Two pools. Four handball courts. Four painted skelly boxes. A plot of ground for marbles, or as we street urchins used to call them, immies. And places of honor for Johnny-on-the-pony and kick-the-can.

"We've had trouble getting a counselor who knows all the games we played as kids," Murray Greenberg said. "One guy didn't know what ring-a-lievo was. I had to throw him out."

There'll be grass too. Murray Greenberg is crazy for grass. "Lefrak built these terrible twenty-one-story slabs right next to each other," he said. "I'm trying to bring a little sunshine and grass in. I hate concrete with a passion. Robert Moses built playgrounds with concrete and grass, but the grass was only to look at. You had to 'Keep Off the Grass.' We're going to have signs to 'Keep On the Grass.' "

All this is going to be done on three and a half acres of what formerly was a junkyard. Unfortunately there isn't room for the definitive street game, stickball. Greenberg said you couldn't have stickball without parked cars and fire hydrants and sewers. The parked cars wouldn't be a problem: Salvador Dali created a whole piece of surrealistic art out of a parked car. Sewers, or manhole covers, could be obtained by any adult who used to steal brooms for their value as stickball bats. But the fire hydrants were a problem.

"I wanted to put a few in for effect," Greenberg said,

"but the fire department turned me down. I can't imagine why. Can you imagine a swimming pool burning down?" A forty-five-year-old Brooklyn boy of unbending integrity, Greenberg wouldn't hear of mock fire hydrants. "It wouldn't be sincere."

Sincerity is what he's after in stoops. He could have stoops made in a few hours "for $720 with union labor," but he wants the genuine article, the kind of Depression era stoop he grew up on.

For foreigners, stoopball is one of a number of children's games played with a small rubber ball, preferably a spaldeen high-bouncer. Most of the games, like stickball and punchball, are forms of baseball without the baseball, baseballs being too hard or too expensive or too dangerous, requiring open spaces.

The object of stoopball is to carom the ball off the sharp edge of a stoop step with such force that it eludes the fielders. Different areas of the street and architecture are designated singles, doubles, triples, homers.

Greenberg is willing to pay up to $1200 for a "legitimate stoop with a pedigree." He would go higher, he said, if it was a stoop that, say, Sandy Koufax or Whitey Ford or Joe Torre played on.

"I got about 100 responses to the ad," Greenberg said. "One lady said there were two stoops on buildings being demolished in the East Sixties, but she wanted a finder's fee. Of course nobody played stoopball on stoops in the East Sixties.

"One guy said he would sell me the stoop on a house. I said, 'Are you sure it's your house?' He said, 'No, but it's my stoop.' That's all I need, a hot stoop.

"Another man said he had three stoops, but he had to demolish the houses first. That's the kind of tie-in I can do without.

"And several kids called up and asked, 'What are stoops?' See, they don't play stoopball much anymore. That's the idea of the club, to get fathers to show their kids the games they used to play."

Greenberg's nostalgic search for the perfect stoop goes

on. With the dedication of an archeologist, he is looking for an official six-step stoop with pointed, unchipped edges "to reduce hinder balls." "A defective stoop," he said, "would be like a football field with ruts in it."

When the next civilization stumbles on Fair Country Club, with Lefrak City a pile of bricks, Murray Greenberg's stoops may seem as mysterious as the sculpture on Easter Island. But it is a noble thing he is doing.

"A million laughs," he said. "Should wipe me out completely."

PAPER CAPER

The thing they're going to have to decide before anything else on the twelfth floor at 415 Madison Avenue is whether a paper baseball is a missile or an airplane. If it's a missile, the elite body of judges of the *Scientific American* may stand accused of old-fogeyism.

Silly? Whimsical? Of course. That's the idea of the first International Paper Airplane Competition. And the design of the craft that lands on the moon, or merely on the mound at Shea Stadium, may be discovered in the process.

"People like to throw things," Gerard Piel said, "so they might as well throw paper airplanes."

Gerard Piel is the publisher of *Scientific American*, a magazine that features such articles as "The Solvated Electron" and "Controlled Eutectics." During the recent competition between Boeing and Lockheed for the multibillion-dollar contract to build a supersonic transport, Piel and his staff made an amazing discovery: both entries resembled an old-fashioned swept-wing paper airplane, improvised at one time by every six-year-old in the land, if not the world.

This could turn out to be an especially significant discovery for baseball fans. In the late innings of dull games paper airplanes tend to float, dart, dive and swoop out of the upper decks of Yankee and Shea stadiums. A few barely reach the playing area. Most crash ingloriously in the lower boxes. Now, through research, we may find a prototype that can be guided to predetermined destinations, to taunt enemy pitchers, unfriendly umpires and slumping heroes.

Scientific American launched its contest with ads that noted that professional designers could have saved valuable time on the supersonic project had they paid more attention to amateurs, adding: "We can postulate that there is, right now, flying down some hallway or out of some movie balcony in Brooklyn, the aircraft which will make the SST obsolete. No? Consider this: Never since Leonardo da Vinci, the patron saint of paper airplanes, has such a wealth of flight research and experimentation remained untouched by cross-disciplinary study and publication. Paper airplane design has become one of those secret pleasures behind closed doors. Everybody does it, but nobody knows what anyone else has learned."

An artist, Victor Morcoso, was commissioned to create a trophy, known as The Leonardo, to be awarded to winners in four categories: duration aloft, distance flown, aerobatics and origami (the Japanese art of paper folding). The trophy shows a hand about to launch the classic swept-wing paper airplane.

Well, sports fans, the contest took off. The editorial offices of *Scientific American* now resemble one vast paper hangar for paper airplanes.

"The idea," said contest editor William Yokel, "was to show that even in this day and age of organized research, science can be fun."

Yokel has to tiptoe through his personal hangar to avoid crushing some of the 4,000 entries received so far. They have come from all over the country, from Israel and Barbados and Switzerland and Japan, from architects and a Ford executive who said he knew Orville Wright and housewives and a children's psychiatric ward. Yokel said that throwing paper airplanes has become a fad in England, that American Airlines is providing passengers with paper airplane kits.

Some of the entries are simply ingenious, some ingenious in their simplicity. "Here's a lovely one," said Marcia Siegal, who was hired to handle the overflow, as she launched a little blue beauty. "It has a life of its own." They have come in every size, from a bronze-foil flea to the unassembled fourteen-foot monster that arrived yesterday. They are made of every conceivable type of paper, from IBM cards to income tax forms to report cards to Raleigh cigarette coupons and even to dollar bills "because it's the material that goes fastest." One man said that a study indicated that British army toilet paper was best.

But what to do about a paper baseball? Yokel admittedly was disturbed. He had had a telephone conversation with its originator, Columbia student John F. Clauser, and had received in reply a learned paper with bibliography supporting the contention that his baseball-sized ball of paper was indeed an airplane.

"The major hurdle a paper baseball must surmount," an accompanying letter said, "is the traditional view as to how a paper airplane should look. In a contest designed to elicit new ideas it would seem ironical for an entry to be rejected on the grounds that it didn't conform with old ones. Perhaps the greatest hurdle our humble baseball has to acceptance remains the deeply ingrained image that most of us have of the airplane we first launched in some grade school classroom."

Yokel said this was absolutely right as he studied, with furrowed brow, the launching instructions: "Get Willie Mays."

UP THE IRISH WOLFHOUND

Should you come across a large shaggy rug that gets up and lumbers toward you, don't be alarmed. It's an Irish wolfhound.

Matter of fact, a man in Hatboro, Pennsylvania, came across two such critters recently, one living-room size and one area size. They had escaped from their home and spent a cold, snowy night sleeping by his garage. Not knowing whether to call the police or fetch his elephant gun, he froze—fortunately for dogdom.

The larger one was Ch. Breac O'Shawn McDown of Eagle, just plain Shawn to family, Judy and William

Snuffin. Yesterday Shawn was named best of breed—"Elegant in his depth of brisket, a magnificent coat," said the judge—in the Westminster Kennel Club show.

By the way the man did live to tell the tale. As a fellow said at the show ring on the main floor, "Irish wolfhounds are like Lenny in *Of Mice and Men*. They're big and gentle." You're more in danger of getting drowned by their affection than bitten. A dog that is three feet tall and weighs 180 pounds has a tongue like a mop.

The Irish wolfhound, appropriate to its Celtic heritage, has a fascinating history. Pat Sherwood of Stamford said that one of her ambulatory rugs, with a sense of irony, once stole a book from her children's room: *How To Survive in the Wilderness*. The Irish wolfhound did not survive in the wilderness at all.

Until a century ago the Irish wolfhound was extinct. Oliver Cromwell, no friend of the Irish, even had it in for their big dogs. In order to keep the world safe for democracy, or whatever they called it in the seventeenth century, he ordered all Irish wolfhounds done away with. The dog was a marvelous hunter, used in packs to bring down wolf, stag, boar and elk. Previous conquerors had been kinder to the dogs if not their masters. The Greeks and Romans took them home. "All Rome viewed them with wonder," one emperor's pal wrote.

Piecing together descriptions and presumed likenesses from old prints—Saint Patrick himself is supposed to have owned one—a George Graham set out in 1862 to recreate the Irish wolfhound. He crossbred Scottish wolfhounds, Tibetan wolfdogs and a Great Dane or two to get the desired dogs. By 1885 he had it breeding true, a feat not unlike bringing back the pterodactyl by crossing a pelican with a 747.

Since there aren't many elk to hunt in Hatboro, et al., just what does one do with an Irish wolfhound in this day and age? Even if they are big enough to be stabled, they aren't much good as watchdogs. They're too sweet.

"You know what he does?" said Judy Snuffin, mistress

of Ch. Shawn. She nodded toward him, sprawled nonfunc-
tionally under his blue ribbon. "That's what he does."

Other than that, he makes a terrific pillow for her
six-year-old son and his buddies while they watch television. (A poem dedicated to the Irish wolfhound ends with:
"Yet noble descendant/Of fierce fighting sire/ You are
playing tonight/ With my child by the fire.")

"They're lazy and not exceptionally bright," Mrs.
Snuffin said, "but they're very lovable."

And strong. Shawn picked up his 130-pound baby
brother by the back of the neck and flipped him over the
other day, an instinct remembered from his hunting ances-
try.

Sam Ewing, a breeder from West Chester, Pennsylvania, owns the most celebrated American Irish wolfhound, the retired fifteen-time best-of-show winner
Broughshane. He said, "They're intelligent, but not sharp
like a little dog. There was a coursing meet in England
when a rabbit got loose among several breeds. The other
dogs tried to follow its darting movements. The Irish wolfhound watched it for a moment, then took off for where it
was headed and got there first."

Ewing handled Ch. Shawn yesterday. The cuffs of his
green sport jacket were mopped lovingly.

CALIFORNIA EAST

You go out the Long Island Expressway, make a right
turn at the Jones Beach sign, make a left at the obelisk,
make another left at Gilgo Beach, pay $1 for parking—and
you're in Southern California.

Here it is, the Pepsi generation in bikinis and flower-
print jams. Here it is, on the outskirts of Fun City, the
youth of America getting stoked, hot and locked in on
surfing.

Kids in Coney Island and Rockaway used to hurl
themselves in to shore by "catching a big wave" and "rid-

ing it in." Today that's "body surfing," as opposed to surf-boarding, standing on a flat torpedo-shaped board and schussing on the wave of the present.

As a sign of the times an underground film, *The Endless Summer*, has bubbled to the surface. It is a semidocumentary, semitravelog on surfing, the tale of two golden hedonists pursuing the perfect wave in Africa, Australia, Tahiti and Hawaii. While nearly two hours of this wet journey may seem like a surfeit of surf to some, it evokes the carefree, exhilarating mood of the sport. The only trouble with surfers is that they view their thing—as mountain climbers, bird watchers and gourmet chefs do theirs—as Truth. It's just another game.

For those hardened arteries, young and old, who prefer to build sand castles, the instructive message of the movie is that surfing doesn't mean you have to dare mountainous death-wish waves in Hawaii. There is more fun in small (three- to six-foot) well-formed waves. It depends, one supposes, on whether your fantasies are Jayne Mansfield or Brigitte Bardot.

You can get Bardots at Gilgo, the Hamptons and Long Beach, where surfers have established their most secure beachheads in the area. It has taken a half century for the crest to roll from its origins in Hawaii to its boom in California to its discovery on the East Coast.

On a good day at Gilgo the beach is dappled with tanned and tawny young folk, their boards stacked like flocks of Brancusi birds, their music throbbing from a cacophony of transistors. Out on the ocean they bob on their boards, a wide arc of sitting ducks waiting for the next ride.

Bill Schiavo, a senior at Saint John's, gives lessons. He is a hot, stoked surfer. "When you're hot," he explained, "you're better than good. Stoked means psyched up, excited, turned on by surfing. I am definitely stoked."

As with all pastimes, a mystique of cult and jargon has evolved in surfing. The grotesque aspects so well publicized in California are vanishing in these wellsprings of civilization. The motorcycle brigades are being overrun by middle-class hordes.

"We're cleaning it up," Bill Schiavo said. "If we see some hotshot with a bottle of peroxide in his hair we really work him over if he isn't hot. We'll cut him off in the water and cut him up verbally. The idea is to surf for fun, not status. But if the guy is hot, well, it's an individual sport and he can do anything he wants. Individuality is important."

The hole-in-one, grand slam, 100-yard touchdown run of surfing is being locked in, enclosed in the nave of the wave. It has often been described as either a religious or a sexual experience. It is the hottest, most stoked thing that can happen to you.

"It happened to me when the surf was up to twelve feet," Bill Schiavo said. "All I remember is that I was locked in so tight I could just see straight ahead through a slit, and it was completely quiet. They say it's like being in the womb or having an orgasm. When I got to the beach I started screaming and yelling."

Against this sort of happiness, surf broads rank a temporary second. "Girls are always around," he said. "Good surf isn't."

DOWN UNDER

There is a large cartoon tacked to the wall of *Dame Pattie*'s equipment room showing a bare-chested young lady at the bow of a boat holding up a brassiere to catch an extra puff or two of wind. *Dame Pattie* could have used some help off Newport, Rhode Island, yesterday. Twin engines would have been more like it.

After years of research in naval architecture, sail making and other boating magic, and months of training in seamanship, Australia put the result of all that oceanic effort to the test in the first race of the America's Cup challenge—and it did everything wrong but go down under.

Intrepid, the defender, upheld the tradition of ruling the waves of Rhode Island with a lopsided five minute fifty-eight second victory. It was, alas, a mismatch, ruining an otherwise perfect day for a huge and colorful spectator fleet and the spectator of honor, the real Dame Pattie.

Dame Pattie Menzies, wife of the former prime minister of Australia, watched the race with her husband and a party of official yachting muck-a-mucks from the decks of the coast guard cutter *Active.* Helen Hayes must have felt the same way when she sat in the theater named for her the first time.

"I keep turning around, thinking my name has been called out," Dame Pattie said. "But I think of her as a she, not an I." She has been on a sailboat once in her life, Monday on the *Dame Pattie.* "I've learned quite a bit, but I wouldn't want to sit still for an examination. I still don't quite understand how a sailboat can go into a wind."

One could hardly bring oneself to tell her that the *Dame Pattie* hadn't solved the problem either.

The day broke cold and blowy and clear. Narragansett Bay was speckled with whitecaps as the *Active* left with its precious cargo of sportsmen and women. A coast guard band played "Waltzing Matilda." Aristotle Onassis never had it any better.

Dame Pattie, the kind of first lady you could learn to love, was bundled in a light blue sweatsuit.

"It must be warm," said the wife of a general, in a smart tweed suit.

"Yes, I'm glad I brought it."

Coffee and cookies were served in the captain's stateroom. The captain went around memorizing the names of his guests, making each of us feel as though we owned the ship. Which, as taxpayers, we did.

Rhode Island Sound was whipped into a small fury. The seascape included marvelous old ships—schooners and square-riggers that might have been built inside whisky bottles. They stood out like grande dames in a party of nouveaux riches yachts and military craft that surrounded the course.

Intrepid came into view at 11:30 A.M. Seven men in yellow foul-weather gear were visible; five slaves were below deck manning the winches. As the defender, she was seen as one might see a heavyweight champion removing his robe in the ring, powerful, muscular, yet sleek and fast.

Minutes later enter *Dame Pattie,* her twelve-man crew on deck in orange. She looked like a contender all right.

Intrepid and *Dame Pattie* passed each other a few times as they tested the wind, as if shadowboxing to impress each other. They maneuvered for the start as a ten-minute warning gun sounded. *Dame Pattie* crossed the imaginary line ten seconds to the good, but there was no clear-cut margin from the angle we were watching. In minutes it was clear that *Dame Pattie* was going to have trouble. Her mainsail was luffing (fluttering) and she was keeling (sticking out of the water) more than *Intrepid.* She did not like going into wind, a bad sign. She would have to shoot *Intrepid* out of the water to win.

"We're falling behind, I'm afraid," Sir Robert Menzies said to his Dame Pattie at a buffet luncheon in the officers' mess. She smiled, as though not quite understanding the message of gloom. All that work for naught.

"*Intrepid* shot through like a bondi tram," an Australian writer said. "That's a crazy streetcar that used to careen from Sydney to a surfing beach."

Dame Pattie said, "Oh, we'll surprise you yet."

She had read in the newspapers a few days before that she had been dismasted and that she had had her bottom scrubbed and now, good grief, she would read that she was beaten.

NO MORE MR. NICE GUY

To those of us who don't know a bishop's pawn from a knight's indiscretion, the doings in Iceland have taken on a fascinating dimension of psychological upmanship.

As yesterday's round of cold warring closed, Bobby Fischer was saying he's sorry for all the delays he caused

—ho, ho, ho—and Boris Spassky was demanding the forfeiture of the first game in the chess showdown.

The result is predictable: no more Mr. Nice Guy for Bobby Fischer.

So far the American pussycat hasn't complained about the northern lights, the salty herring or the shape of the playing table, but from now on no holds will be barred.

There is a method to Fischer's genius that is not altogether unfamiliar. We see in him flashes of such legendary prima donnas as Ben Hogan, Pancho Gonzales, Ted Williams, Sugar Ray Robinson, Vince Lombardi and Bill Hartack. He has it all: monkish dedication, antisociability, killer instinct, tantrum-throwing volatility. Small wonder he is favored to become No. 1.

Fischer also brings to mind two of his not-so-uptight contemporaries, Muhammad Ali and Joe Namath. Though humorless, unlike them, he has managed to build up the match with Spassky into a cosmic international event by pounding on his chest for years that he is, like Ali, the greatest. "It's nice to be modest, but it's stupid not to tell the truth," he has said. "There is only one immortal player in the world today and it is Fischer." Like Namath at the Super Bowl, he has not let the magnitude of the occasion intimidate him. He has stayed in perfect character as an enfant terrible.

Fischer's antics have focused on an aspect of chess that few people have been aware of. The way he plays it, it is almost a contact, or collision, sport. Budd Schulberg called boxing chess played on bodies instead of boards. For Fischer chess is boxing played on boards instead of bodies. You can hear him now, "Pawn to king four, take that you rat."

Muhammad Ali says his prefight antics are designed "to kill egos." Fischer had the following exchange with Dick Cavett on television:

Cavett: Tell me, Bobby, what is the moment of reward for you? Like when a baseball player hits a home run. The moment when it's all worthwhile.

Fischer: When you break his ego.

Cavett: You mean when he knows he's in trouble.

Fischer: Yeah. When he knows it's all over and you can see him break inside.

Spassky the champion has been broken inside and outside. He once wept after losing an important team match. (With good reason, since he would not be permitted to travel outside Russia for three years.) He comes across as much the more mature and whole man—he has a college degree and, unlike bachelor Fischer, a family—with a decent regard for his challenger. "The world of chess would be very boring without him," Spassky said.

Few Russians are that generous. Fischer is a threat to a domain they have incorporated into Marxist ideology as an essence of Soviet manhood. They see the arrogant, narrow, single-minded Fischer as a chess-playing Frankenstein, born of a computer, fathered by a barbarian. After losing to him, one Russian huffed, "Well, at least I have my music."

Spassky has a team of advisers with him in Iceland, including a chess psychologist. There is no collective effort for Fischer, a lonely ascetic taking on the mandarins after years of preparation. "I intend to teach them," he has said, "a little humility."

So we have another diversion to pass the summer. In this corner, the champion, Boris Spassky. In this corner, the challenger, Bobby Fischer. Do they wear protective cups in chess?

ACROSS THE RIVER, UP THE RIVER

The urban sports strategist could have deposited his decaying flesh and activated his strained eyeballs in any number of likely places this weekend. I found myself in two unlikely places.

At a squash racquets tournament in Brooklyn and a basketball game in Sing Sing.

Squash is a combination of tennis and handball, played with a small strung racket in a four-wall pit. It takes about half as long as tennis and twice as long as handball to work up a good sweat and it is preferred by clubby Ivy types who don't have the time for the former or the proletarian inclination for the latter. You see them walking all over the midtown area with quick strides and straight backs and long narrow luggage, George Plimptons on the way to some heroic demise.

The best players in the world are Pakistanis because a man named Hashim Khan learned the game from British soldiers as a boy and turned out to be the kind of sire for squash players that Nasrullah was for thoroughbreds. It is difficult to make up a game of doubles without a Khan in it. There were four Khans, including the sixty-three-year-old patriarch himself, at the doubles tournament at The Heights Casino in Brooklyn Heights.

The Heights Casino is a clubby joint on Montague Street, formerly famous as the street where Red Barber told you to buy tickets to Dodger games. This comes up because the match I saw Saturday ended with a terrific and perhaps unprecedented rhubarb. It was better than Ebbets Field. Everybody was wrong.

In a fiercely contested overtime between two Pakistanis and the metropolitan champions, Mel Sokolow and Roger Alcaly, there were three appeal calls within a few minutes and the two judges overruled the referee, one Roland Oddy, twice. Before, during and after the last appeal, Sokolow raised his voice to unclubby decibels and Alcaly threw a tantrum in language that starched the Peck & Peck costumes in the crowd of forty. Alcaly accused Oddy of taking out his frustrations at losing earlier in the tournament. Oddy, neck reddening, tone baiting, advised them to play ball or he would disqualify them. Four expletives later, he did.

This was greeted with a burst of applause from the gallery—thumbs down to the heathens—followed by the forehand of wounded outrage and the backhand of officious contempt. The debate moved to the dressing room where it was punctuated with slammed sweatsocks and an attack, by Alcaly, on President Nixon and Vietnam. Oddy, who

could have defused the tension with tact and/or wit, threatened to take the case to a higher squash court to have them
banned for life or something.

Disillusioned though I was by this scandalous scene of
passion and blood, I must admit I enjoyed it. Because there
is absolutely nothing as much fun as watching grown men
behave like boys. Fleeing back to Manhattan, I could have
sworn I heard someone yell "yabumya" while the Brooklyn Sym-phony tooted and bonged again on Montague
Street.

In contrast I was bathed in gentlemanly decorum at
Sing Sing yesterday.

I wish I could tell you that I felt something deeper
than curiosity about my first trip to the big house, as Bogey
used to call it, but I didn't. Cold and foreboding as the
turreted fortress in Ossining was, it was not a threat to me.
I was going to be sprung in two hours.

I was accompanying the Grand Central Y team, a
scurvy group of wheezers that plays there every year. We
were frisked, the iron gate rolled up and we were bused
past the empty death row to the gym.

The gym was cold. Some 200 inmates sat on concrete
steps. There were ten men on the prison team, all black, in
green uniforms. They had no height, while the shortest
player on the Y team was six feet three inches, and all of
them played in college five to twenty years and five to
twenty pounds ago.

Bob Podhurst, a professor of philosophy at Montclair
State, said, "You can feel the difference, the tension." Barry
Eisemann, an engineer, agreed; on his first trip to Sing Sing
he had been shocked to come face-to-face with a kid whom
he had played freshman ball with at City College. Coach
Bob Goldshol of NYU said that the officials, who were
from town, reminded them to keep things moving after a
foul to avoid flare-ups.

The game was a not-bad Y-caliber game. The prisoners
took a lot of crazy jump shots and made a few. The Y, led
by John Anderisse, former captain of Fordham, knew what
it was doing and scored easy baskets. In the second half

a prisoner walked off the court because his teammates weren't feeding him. Another prisoner led a drive that brought Sing Sing from thirteen behind to within two of the wheezers with a minute to go.

The fans were a better show than the game. They were loud, abusive, demonstrative, good natured, and they raised the roof for spectacular plays on either side. When a driving inmate caromed off the Y's Big Bob Sack like a rebound the fans stomped and hand-slapped for thirty seconds. They were betting cigarettes on the outcome.

The Y pulled away and the game ended with handshakes, way-to-goes, pats on the back. "Next year," the prison coach promised, "we'll have some height."

Gimmick columns, as the next three are, have two basic uses, as a change of pace and as devices to comment on a number of disconnected items. I have no recollection of what inspired me to write the doggerel, having never done it before or since. The awards column is my annual year-end wrap-up. When a national craze like streaking erupts, it can be bent to whatever purpose you deem fit, especially if you don't have another column that day.

WITH APOLOGIES

Limericks, doggerel, rhymes, it's a sin
What a man will do at an Ogden Gnash-in.
So gird yourself for verses of adversity
Tossed off in pain, like Johnny U(niversity).

Homer Jones

Homer Jones, Giant, is the split end homeric
Producing big plays like a regular D. Merrick.
Win some, lose some, catch some, drop some,
Broadway and the Bronx, a gruesome twosome.
There are some differences, vital and dramatic:
One goes for bombs, the other for musical static.

Homer's more complex—his personality's split too;
He's unbeatable deep, but over the middle—phew.

Hair

When you're a Jet you're a Jet all the way
Hair on your face, hair in your play.
Hair, hair, the football establishment hates it,
When it's long, not short, they usually equates it
         —with rubble, stubble, double trouble.
Little do they realize it's part of the strategy
To look unkempt, unshaven, shaggy, scraggily.
Mustaches, sideburns, beards, Fu Manchu
Blitzers get tangled, runners can't get through.
It's not a fetish.
Merely Jetish.

Say It Ain't So, Joe

Joe Namath the swinger is shorn,
Smooth-cheeked as a new baby born.
A gay blade sold out to television's Schick.
Sniff-sniff.
At least Samson had that Delilah chick.

Francis

Tarkenton Fran is a go-groovy scrambling man,
But sometimes when he takes off on the lam
I can't decide if he's effective or uncouth,
If he's a short-order cook or Tarkenton Booth.

O. J.

Fly like an Eagle or shuffle off to Buffalo,
That was the choice left O. J. Simpson, oh.
Caught in the pro draft, to himself he could muse,
"God, I'm going to be frozen orange juice."
Picked off a Southern California tree,
Destined geo-meteorologically

For climes zeroish, snowbound, damp and grim.
Grow a navel-thick skin is my advice to him.

Heidi

Who would have thought that the Fearsome Foursome
     would be
Pinocchio, Hansel, Gretel and Heidi?

Paper Lion

Life mimes art, check Plimpton's caper,
The Lions indeed are made of paper.

Otto Graham

The trouble with Otto
Is a voice un-sotto.
Knocking the refs, feuding with Sonny
May be hilariously funny,
But when you forget to win-win-win,
It's better to avoid the din-din-din.

The Packers

Take this letter to Vincent Dear,
Tell him I'm not a bit sorry to hear
That the House of Lombardi he so successfully bossed
To one championship after another finally has lost.
Losing occasionally is good for the soul,
The world isn't packaged in a Super Bowl.

THE FUN AND GAMES AWARDS

The Lockheed Bankruptcy Ledger to heavyweight
champion George Foreman, the sum of whose financial
obligations appears to be greater than the whole, i.e., in
excess of his income.

The Heads-I-Lose, Tails-You-Win Silver Dollar to

Buzzy Bavasi, president of the San Diego Padres, who said, "The good news is that we may stay in San Diego. The bad news, I guess, is the same thing."

The Captain Queeg Steel Balls to Yankee owner George Steinbrenner, who spied a player shaking a hot dog out of his glove and ordered Ralph Houk to get to the bottom of the prank.

The Order of the Crying Towel to Pepper Rodgers, UCLA coach, who said about losing, "I had only one friend, my dog. My wife was mad at me and I told her a man ought to have at least two friends. She agreed—and bought me another dog."

The Bubble Gum Trading Card to Mike Kekich and Fritz Peterson. "It isn't a wife swap," said Kekich after the Yankee pitchers traded families. "It's a life swap."

The Bad Guys Finish Last Scroll to Larry Jones, football coach at Florida State, who was fired after losing all eleven games. Twenty-eight players quit the team last spring, accusing him of conducting barbaric practice sessions.

The Joe Kuharich Nonsequitur to Ehrlichman and Haldeman for putting Joe Namath on the White House Enemies List.

The Watergate Stigma to the All-American Soapbox Derby, won by an illegally souped-up racer.

The Ms. Universe Backhand to Billie Jean King for slicing up Bobby Riggs and his fellow male chauvinist pigs in the battle-of-the-sexes tennis hustle.

The Critics Choice Column to Dick Butkus, who summarized the Chicago Bears like so: "Mirro Roder is going to be the best field goal kicker in the league. Well, so much for our offense."

The Critics Courage Potshot at five-foot five-inch Mack Herron, who stood up in the New England Patriots' huddle to yell, "Shut up, you big obscenity" at Butkus, and immediately ducked out of sight.

The Silver Nostalgia Bat to Pete Rose, who said, "I feel like I know Babe Ruth and Ty Cobb."

The Good Housekeeping Seal of Approval to Norm Van Brocklin, who blamed the collapse of the play-off-bound Falcons on "the bartenders and whores on Peach Street."

The Bang the Drum Loudly Broken Record to ABC's Monday football telecast, which spent more time promoting its wonderful self than telling you what was going on in the games.

The No Fun in Games Red Square to Russian gymnast czars who dumped on Olga Korbut for showboating and creating a cult of personality.

The Hair Today, Gone Yesterday Clippers to John Riggins, the Jet whose hair style ranged from Afro to Indian to bald to crewcut, confirming the confusion beneath his scalp.

The Charley O. Finley Donkey's Tail to Charley O. Finley, for firing Mike Andrews during the World Series.

The Willie Mays Goodbye America Retirement Ceremony to Charlie Krueger, who said of his fifteen years in the NFL, "I don't know if it's to my credit or discredit."

The Flattery Will Get You Nowhere Confession to Whitey Herzog, who said of alleged attempts to steal the Texas Rangers' signs, "Can you imagine a team that has to cheat to beat us?"

STREAKING

LOS ANGELES—Gary Davidson, who started the American Basketball Association, the World Hockey Association, the World Team Tennis League, the World Football League and the International Frisbee Conference, today announced the formation of a new professional organization—the Associated Society of Streakers.

Davidson said that streaking, the college craze of running around the campus nude, is an idea whose time has come. "ASS will feature the first X-rated team sport," Davidson said.

The innovative promoter, responsible for rules changes in many sports, introduced a new concept in professional scheduling.

"ASS will not have a regular season," he said. "People are becoming bored with regular seasons. We will have play-offs only, an eighty-game play-off schedule."

ATLANTA—The Atlanta Bares revealed today that their star streaker, Henry Aaron, will not play in the opening series of the season on the road against the Cincinnati Sins.

Aaron needs two more streaking runs to break the all-time record. "We think Hank owes it to the people of Atlanta to break the record on Peachtree Street," said Bares' president Blaze Starr. "It will mean a great deal to downtown department stores if he does it on a Saturday morning or a Wednesday evening, when they are open to nine o'clock."

KANSAS CITY—The NCAA today put the University of Oklahoma on probation for three years for recruiting violations connected with their top-ranked streakers. According to the NCAA Violations Committee, Oklahoma gave on-campus tryouts to high school prospects.

NEW YORK—Roone Arledge, vice president in charge of sports for ABC, today refused to deny or confirm reports that the network is planning a Super Streaker show for prime time next season.

Sources in the television industry said that the format would combine the popular game of streaking with the Super Stars show. Athletes who perform in the nude will be awarded extra prize money.

Andy Sidaris, the TV director whose specialty is isolating pretty girls during college games, said that he will be alert to the possibility of Saturday afternoon streaking next season, which could boost sagging ratings.

"I can't speak for the network," Sidaris said, "but it would sure put some zing in the Army-Navy game."

CHICAGO—Avery Brundage, retired head of the International Olympic Committee, is bitterly opposed to adding streaking to the games because "it would violate their spirit."

"Without uniforms," Brundage said, "fans wouldn't know what country the streakers represent."

Advocates of streaking claim that nudity would reduce excess nationalism that threatens continuation of the Olympics. They also point out that underdeveloped countries would be able to field streaking teams that could compete against the major powers.

COOPERSTOWN, N.Y.—Baseball's Hall of Fame has officially changed the wording on the plaques of two great stars, Joe DiMaggio and Lou Gehrig. Their famous fifty-six-game hitting and 2,130-game playing streaks are now "skeins."

"We do not want future generations of fans to confuse baseball with streaking," Commissioner Bowie Kuhn said.

Since a column is a statement by the clearly identified writer, the use of the perpendicular pronoun usually is redundant. In special cases it may be necessary, but most often it can be circumvented without seeming affected. In the last few years, however, I have been doing occasional pieces that are personal and that are best told in a personal style. There is even an exception to that rule, as in the first of these columns.

I SPY

The Giants play their biggest game in seven years Sunday against the Rams, a game that could mean as much as $2 million to the players and organization as well as incalculable riches to fans. For a few minutes yesterday the Giants suspected that they might be blowing the whole thing before the kickoff.

There was a man on a roof acting very much like a spy, and the Giants didn't detect him until they had run through all the supersecret stuff they are planning to spring on the Rams.

"Some people," muttered Alex Webster, never suspecting he was being put on, "look for every little edge."

Some people means George Allen, who seems to hire his assistants out of the CIA. The Rams coach has a reputation for what Tex Schramm of the Cowboys once called chicanery. Three years ago, before a big game with the Rams, the Cowboys spotted a fellow in a car outside their practice field. They took the license plate number and traced it to a rental agency and then to a Rams scout. When Schramm complained, Allen took the offensive. He said the Rams had seen a suspicious fellow watching their practices from a eucalyptus tree.

The Lions suspected that Allen struck again last year. They prepared a new goal line offense that they thought had never before been seen on earth. But when they got down to the goal line in the game and deployed into the formation, linebacker Maxie Baughan began to shout, "Here it is! Here it is!"

Sweet innocents that they are, the Giants took no precautionary security measures this week. Trusting souls that they are, they even practiced yesterday at the bleacher end of Yankee Stadium, which is clearly visible from the roofs of 825 and 831 Gerard Avenue.

The only problem the spy had was getting into the buildings. Signs in the vestibule of 825 warn tenants about loiterers and three nice old ladies eyed the spy warily as he studied the names over the buzzers. When he whisked into the lobby after someone opened the door, one of the ladies croaked, "Who you looking for, mister?" But he was into the elevator and gone. "They wouldn't understand," he said, "if I told them I was looking for Fran Tarkenton."

The spy watched Ron Johnson run end runs and Tucker Fredrickson run trap plays for fifteen or twenty minutes. He went unnoticed despite all efforts to be noticed, emboldening him to try 831. From there the view was perfect; voices could even be heard. The spy hovered over the Giants for another fifteen or twenty minutes, still unnoticed, although he became more brazen still. He peered over the ledge through fingers cupped like binoculars. The Giants went about their business industriously.

Finally, after the spy did everything but semaphore, he was sighted by an assistant coach, Jim Katcavage or Joe Walton, who walked to the far sideline and told Wellington Mara and Ken Kavanaugh. They huddled, stealing glances at the rooftop presence. Alex Webster was informed. He walked to the closed end of the field and huddled with grounds keepers.

Now, discovered, the spy became a furtive figure in black, sneaking around the roof, popping up behind this corner and that, calling on remembered eight-year-old devices to taunt the opposition. He focused imaginary lenses and scribbled imaginary information.

Soon the players too were scanning the apartment house. Half a dozen grounds keepers appeared on the near side of the field, searching for the intruder. It seemed to be an organized gesture of warning. Just then the practice broke up.

The spy came down from the roof and out of the cold. Now he slipped into the Giants' dressing room, in the guise of a reporter. Sure enough, the Giants were talking about him.

"He could've had a high-powered rifle," shuddered Tony Longo.

"He had binoculars," said Wellington Mara through clenched teeth, "but he didn't have a camera."

"We'll see Sunday," said Webster.

Webster was properly grim. Coaches spend thousands of retina-ruining hours looking at film and making game plans. For the Giants that may mean stay close until Tarkenton thinks of something, but it is important for the morale of the coaches to feel they have a hand in it.

"You change maybe 15 percent for a game," Webster said. "The guy could see everything: what holes we plan to hit, how we changed our blocking. And there's not a damn thing we can do about it now. It's a shame, but some guys just have to have an edge."

The spy slipped out of the stadium, chortling fiendishly as he trained his binoculars on the rooftops of Gerard Avenue.

Alex Webster appeared so crestfallen that I had to tell him it was I who was the spy before I left his office. Wellington Mara later told people he knew it was a hoax. Sure he did.

THE ONLY REAL FRIEND

I have a difficult time compressing Norm Van Brocklin into a column. My experiences with him are at odds with the experiences of others. I can't forget the former, in which I have an emotional stake, or ignore the latter, in which I have a professional stake.

Lately, as he has become a winner again, the paradoxes, if not the feelings, have begun to sort themselves out. Norm Van Brocklin, now, seems to me to be another happy victim of the win-at-all-cost ethic.

He is one of those successful people who can deal with people only on his terms.

His only real friend is victory.

Athletes say you have to pay the price to win. That's the stiffest price of all.

I knew Van Brocklin in Philadelphia. He went there in 1958 after a brilliant and stormy career with the Rams, whom he led to one championship and innumerable controversies. Recently, before Bob Lee came to his rescue in Atlanta, Van Brocklin was asked what kind of quarterback he was looking for. "A guy who comes in and throws three touchdown passes in the first game," he said. "Like me." But it is unlikely that Van Brocklin the coach would abide a headstrong quarterback like himself—witness his run-ins with Fran Tarkenton—and neither did Sid Gillman. "I wanted to coach the team," Van Brocklin said with the self-mockery of truth, "and Gillman wouldn't let me."

In hindsight it is clear that Van Brocklin got along famously with most people in Philadelphia because he could play quarterback, coach, and do anything else that had to be done to win. The terms were his, and he elevated the Eagles from the outhouse to the penthouse, express, in three years.

Additionally Van Brocklin was a gracious and quick-witted presence who enlivened the start of the pro football boom. He was and is a facile verbal caricaturist. At one time half the players in the NFL got their nicknames from him, including "Big Daddy" Lipscomb. He tossed off delightful lines with the aplomb of a screen pass. Some current examples: of Bob Lee's scrambling touchdown against the Vikings, "It's like getting money from home without writing"; of Harold Carmichael, the six-foot eight-inch Eagles' end, "He can eat apples off a tree without using his hands."

Further, Van Brocklin, who had married his college biology teacher, seemed to be a devoted family man. It did not occur to me until a couple years ago, when he adopted three children after his three daughters had grown up, how much the family meant to him as ballast for the brutalizing business of coaching.

There was nothing not to like about Norm Van Brocklin in Philadelphia. But the Eagles found something. When he announced his retirement after that championship season of 1960, they reneged on a promise to make him head coach.

I wrote some scathing columns about that. The Eagles denied their role, and their president, who was fire commissioner of the city, tried to put heat on me through my editors. Shortly thereafter, at a banquet honoring him, which Eagles management attended, Van Brocklin issued a statement confirming my information.

Several years later I saw, and felt, a side of Van Brocklin that others have seen in Los Angeles, Minnesota and Atlanta. Over drinks we discussed the struggling AFL. I said the new league was signing some good young players and eventually would reach parity with the NFL. He disagreed and, having just lost a few high Viking draft picks to the AFL, reached across the table and began to strangle me with my tie to explain the wisdom of his argument.

Choking off debate that way, I learned across the years, was not uncommon for Van Brocklin.

Across the years too, players traded by him came away with horror stories of his relations with them. His ability to caricature, turned inside out, is an instrument of cruelty. Like Vince Lombardi and Paul Brown, he can reduce a hulking young hero to bitter marmalade with one slashing stroke of his tongue. But unlike Lombardi and Brown, Van Brocklin did not win fast and make the players crave such treatment.

"If you don't discipline them," he said the other day, "they won't know you love them. There's no love on third down and one. You need discipline then."

While the football community continued to regard Van Brocklin as a genius, it was commonly held that his inability to communicate with the modern athlete—his unshakable 1950s values that equated bell-bottom trousers with fat-cattism—doomed him as a coach.

Now he has the Falcons bound for the play-offs. I'm pleased. He needs to win so desperately.

The Falcons lost their last two games and didn't get into the play-offs, and Van Brocklin was fired during the next season. Last I heard he was on his pecan farm, blaming Communists for his troubles.

GUEST SHOT

Seems that I owe a lot of people—a couple dozen, if you're counting—an hour of sleep.

This is to add another five minutes to the debit side of the ledger.

Two weeks ago my name appeared in television listings for the Dick Cavett show. These people informed me the next day that they stayed up until past their bedtimes to see how big a fool I would make of myself, but that I fooled them and did not appear. I could have told them a week before that that would happen, when the show was taped, had I been foolish enough to realize that my nonappearance would get into the listings anyway.

Muhammad Ali and Joe Frazier were the main eventers on the show. I was what we in the newspaper dodge call filler—something to throw in should they have to fill time at the end. Since Ali was carrying on like Ali, I was as unnecessary as a shadow during shadowboxing.

Feeling unnecessary is one of modern man's most terrific feelings. But I must admit that I wished I had the three or four hours back that I had spent making arrangements for my nonappearance.

But today I want to show the kind of guy I am by having Dick Cavett as a guest in my column.

Even in this age of happy hostility, I am not bitter. I sympathize with the imperatives of show biz (one Ali is better than a platoon of Russian jugglers and an army of sportswriters). Dick Cavett, who was a high school wrestler, is always welcome here.

I'll get to him in a moment, after a few words about Denny McLain, Alex Karras and Monte Stickles, who, like Cavett, are former jocks in show biz.

McLain, Karras and Stickles are relevant because they were among the athletes I appeared with on radio and television in recent months while traveling coast to coast and border to border doing a tap dance for my book on pro football and gambling.

The only thing that happened to me that measures up to my nonappearance with Cavett, in fact, was my appearance with McLain. McLain, at twenty-nine, has retired from baseball, having squandered a $1 million pitching career with various escapades, including gambling. Now he is the host of a talk show on a Detroit TV station. The station is located in a suburb. The suburb was buried under a foot and a half of snow on the day I arrived. Taping schedules were discombobulated. And I had to sit around for six hours holding hands with the other guest, Alex Karras. By the time we got on we were both too zonked to care.

Monte Stickles, the former tight end, has a telephone talk show in San Francisco. He's a sharp, funny guy who probably will make it good someday because he also works at it. One irate listener called to say he was a government worker and he took umbrage over our discussion of gambling, an illegal activity. Stickles handled him so coolly that five minutes later the man was asking, "Is it really possible to win if you bet on one game each week?" A second guest on the show was an angry citizen who was starting a sports lobby for fans. "You trying to get a pension for them?" Stickles mused.

Gee, this really is embarrassing. Here I am down to the last inch of my column and I haven't gotten around to Dick Cavett. I apologize to all his followers who stayed awake through this to find out about his wrestling career. I'm sure he'll understand how tough it is for a columnist to squeeze in all his invited guests.

LENNY

Lenny Shecter, who used to occupy this space, died Saturday. He was forty-seven years old. He had leukemia. Having elevated irascibility to an art, in his life and writing, he went out in character. He ordered his wife, Ginny, and the doctors to get the damn tubes out of him and let him go. He was a good friend of mine.

This is how irascible Lenny was. He professed to hate children. What he hated was that we turn them into images of our imperfect selves, that we stifle their creative juices. They would grow up to be more people who lied to themselves, hid under the covers of illusion, became obsessed with dumb batting averages and ballplayers. Recounting the sappiness of homo sap, on paper as well as in person, Lenny sounded like Zero Mostel as the fully realized Rhinoceros. He roared.

Well, I brought my daughter, then two, to the Shecters one afternoon, and somehow she managed to combine the entree with the dessert. She cleaned out a dish of ice cream with a chicken leg. "Any child who can eat ice cream with a chicken leg," he conceded, shaking all over with laughter, "can't be all bad."

This is how irascible Lenny was too. His only sanctuary from the lunacy of the species was a golf course. A heavy man—"Don't call me heavy-set, I'm just fat"—he seemed weightless as a balloon chasing a little white ball around. I never realized how important that small piece of landscaped serenity could be to him until I committed a horrendous breach of etiquette while we were playing in a foursome at Poland Springs, Maryland, headquarters of the second Sonny Liston–Cassius Clay fight. I inadvertently dragged my golf cart across a corner of a green. He roared.

Now it struck me as hypocritical of Lenny Shecter to dress me down for such a minor gaffe. His irreverence toward stuffy tradition was monumental. I told him so. He roared again. We proceeded to agitate each other for the last nine holes, entertaining our partners, Dave Anderson of the *Times* and Stan Isaacs of *Newsday*. Then, after Dave carried me for seventeen holes, I made my only semidecent shot to help us win. Lenny wasn't very competitive, but I recall that he seemed to be grumbling to himself all the way to the clubhouse with the injustice of it all.

Professionally Lenny Shecter is best known as the coauthor of *Ball Four* with Jim Bouton. *Ball Four* was the culmination of his career as a sportswriter, for he was among those of us who believed that the truth was ultimately more rewarding and entertaining than the fiction of pablum we were fed by the establishment. It was a landmark book as well because it demonstrated that he was right to spend as much if not more time with the Jim Boutons as the Mickey Mantles. Mantle gave us his talent. Bouton gave us his smaller talent and his deeper feelings and sensitivities.

Ball Four demonstrated something else about Lenny. It

was a celebration, a funny look at the games and gamesmen we play and watch, on and off the field. The controversial aspects of the book confirmed his reputation as a curmudgeon—later reconfirmed with a magazine profile of Vince Lombardi that probably was the first insight into the dehumanizing demands of big-time football—but much of his best work was wonderfully funny.

Another book, *The Jocks,* was Lenny's farewell to sport as a daily journalist. It was as bitter and sour as he had become toward professional athletics and the part sportswriter-fans played in perpetuating myths and glorifying louts. That was a look at the dark side of the moon, overdrawn but much needed as ballast for the innocents who saw only the light side.

But there was a celebration even among those cynical pages. A celebration of an obscure marathon runner who symbolized to Lenny the purity of sport, a celebration of Casey Stengel, who symbolized what all sport should be about—trying and laughing.

Lenny had been, in my judgment, one of the very best baseball writers there ever was. He covered Roger Maris's pursuit of Babe Ruth with a novelist's eye, piecing together in an unheard-of thirty straight daily stories a drama that was heroic in its humanity more than its history.

And then the Mets. With a few others, Lenny set the tone for the acceptance of their lovable ineptitudes, recognizing the flavor that Stengel and the fans added. It was Lenny, I believe, who transformed a clod of a first baseman into the legend of Marvelous Marv Throneberry.

Beneath Lenny's irascible crust there was an irascible interior, but beneath that there was a bellylaugh that was on the side of the angels.

CLASS REUNION

We were sixteen, seventeen, eighteen, still better with our bodies than our heads, just starting to find out about the possibilities in ourselves. We made the discoveries, and burned energy like firewood, playing games, endlessly, tirelessly. We went to Lafayette High School in Brooklyn. Saturday, after more than a quarter century for some of us, the boys of autumn had their first reunion. A few of the girls, cheerleaders, came too.

There had been many promising athletes in our neighborhoods, poor and middle-class kids whose horizons never stretched beyond the streets, schoolyards, playgrounds and empty lots. Harry Ostro stretched us further. He was a football coach who gave his heart to the game and pulled us along with him. Saturday was for him and us. Mostly us.

We came from California and Maine and Florida and Mississippi and Michigan and Washington, D.C., and local outposts to see what had become of us. We stayed to see who we had been.

What had become of us was best put by my brother Richie, who said, "Down in Washington we wonder who the grass roots are. I found out. They're my teammates."

I was the fullback on the first of many unbeaten teams at Lafayette, Harry Ostro's first team, in 1947. My brother was a guard and captain on the second unbeaten team, in 1951. The 1952 and 1953 teams also were unbeaten. I was the backfield coach in 1951 and 1952, which I mention because I was acquainted with the athletes of that entire era.

One of them, a basketball player named Sandy Koufax, is in the Hall of Fame. Ken Aspromonte is a major league manager. Al Goldstein was a first-team All-American. George Brancato is a head coach in Canada. Sam DeLuca graduated from the Jets to the television booth.

The 1951 and 1952 teams were remarkable teams, perhaps the best in the city's history. Roger Kahn covered one of our games for the *Herald Tribune* and wrote that any college that wanted to improve its record should give scholarships to the team en masse. Saturday those teams seemed even more remarkable to me.

Art Metrano was a sophomore in 1952. He is a character actor and comedian today, praised in the *New Yorker* as one of the funniest new talents around.

John Sprizzo played behind DeLuca. He is better known as the attorney who with his partner successfully defended John Mitchell in his recent trial.

My brother is the chief of staff of the Joint Congressional Committee on Economics under Senator Proxmire. He has been named one of the top ten aides in Congress. He is the single person most responsible for uncovering cost-overrun scandals in the Pentagon. He is writing a second book about related matters.

The reunion was an extraordinary emotional experience, like walking through a time machine with a heart for a motor. A group of men in the prime of life, only a few of them flaccid with the years, hugged and kissed and laughed and fought back tears. I loved them all, even the sour former teammate, now a lawyer, who said he hated my column and, unsolicited, insisted that Richard Nixon was the greatest American who ever lived.

Sandy Koufax, who rejects all entreaties to appear in old-timer games, came down from the Maine woods. He seems as painfully withdrawn in crowds as he did when he came to my house once to see my brother and waited for him in the shadows of a foyer. John Sprizzo was a strong, awkward kid who tried like hell. His teammates called Sam DeLuca "Sanitary Sam" because he insisted on wearing clean underthings at practice. Art Metrano, known as Harpo because of his curly hair, was a tumler and a clown with superability as a tackle. Fortunately for him he decided to concentrate on the tumling and clowning. "A lot of people in Hollywood have been refining their skills since they were kids," he said. "Football doesn't help me now, but it's like I had another life, and they didn't."

That is what it is for most of us. We flashback to those pure, uncomplicated championship seasons of growing up, remembering the plays we made, the rituals we followed, all a rite of passage that insinuated itself into our marrow. Going unbeaten seems like a piece of immortality, like the heroes of our childhood.

For some of us, football opened doors to better possibilities in ourselves. I never felt it did that for me. It was a good experience, but I wonder whether it limited my horizons.

I wonder too about some of us who weren't at the reunion, and some of us who have never outgrown that time. Where is the brainy quarterback who disappeared years ago and calls his parents periodically to let them know he's all right and then hangs up? And I want the fellows who didn't come because they haven't amounted to much professionally to know that wouldn't have mattered.

AFTERWORD

Where is sportswriting headed, besides Super Bowl MLX, Kuala Lumpur and every appeals court in the land?

After the last decade, things will never be quite the same. It is established now that we have to deal with all the theaters of life that are connected to the theater of games. It is established too that we have to deal with the athlete as a many-sided person rather than as a one-dimensional sporticus.

While we sing the music and muse over the madness of the sporting life, we must, as they say, keep our eye on the ball: people. For me the fun of games is the opportunity to observe the splendor and the absurdity of people as they truly are, revealed in their unconscious actions and utterances. We must use whatever is available to us—the writer's research, insight, humor and style; the social scientists' findings on individual and group behavior—to go to the heart of sport.

H. L. Mencken once said, "I know of no subject, save perhaps baseball, on which the average American newspaper discourses with unfailing sense and understanding." In a society hooked into and on television, superior reporting and editing are required to tell the story better than TV can show it. The journalism schools are turning out the talent to do that. Publishers whose standards of sports journalism are as low as the salaries they pay must not turn away the talent by neglect.

They must be convinced that, just as participation soars in such pastimes as tennis, skiing and sailing, the toy department, as Jimmy Cannon called it, now sells adult games.

LM

ABOUT THE AUTHOR

Larry Merchant has worked for the *Stars & Stripes* in Europe, the *Wilmington* (N. C.) *News*, the Associated Press, the *Philadelphia Daily News*, the *New York Post* and the *London Observer*. He has written two previous books, *And Every Day You Take Another Bite* and *The National Football Lottery*. A native and resident of New York, he is forty-five years old. He has a daughter, Jamie, twelve.